Traveller Storytelling in Scotland

To Lindsay

Traveller Storytelling in Scotland

Folklore, Ideology, Cultural Identity

Robert Fell

EDINBURGH
University Press

Edinburgh University Press is one of the leading university presses in the UK. We publish academic books and journals in our selected subject areas across the humanities and social sciences, combining cutting-edge scholarship with high editorial and production values to produce academic works of lasting importance. For more information visit our website: edinburghuniversitypress.com

© Robert Fell, 2024

Edinburgh University Press Ltd
13 Infirmary Street
Edinburgh EH1 1LT

Typeset in 10.5/13pt Sabon by
IDSUK (DataConnection) Ltd,
and printed and bound in Great Britain

A CIP record for this book is available from the British Library

ISBN 978 1 3995 2634 0 (hardback)
ISBN 978 1 3995 2636 4 (webready PDF)
ISBN 978 1 3995 2637 1 (epub)

The right of Robert Fell to be identified as the author of this work has been asserted in accordance with the Copyright, Designs and Patents Act 1988, and the Copyright and Related Rights Regulations 2003 (SI No. 2498).

Contents

Acknowledgements	vi
Abbreviations	viii
Introduction: Ethnicity and Otherness	1
Part I	
1 The Travellers in Scotland	17
2 How do Stories Mean?	38
3 Cultural Identity and Storytelling	57
Part II	
4 Negotiating Cultural Identity	77
5 International Tales and Traveller Ecotypes	99
6 The Burkers and Ideological Resistance	121
7 Storytelling and the Supernatural	146
8 Magical Places, Magical Money	167
Conclusion: Storytelling as Cultural Continuity	188
Bibliography	196
Index	216

Acknowledgements

My wholehearted thanks go to William Lamb and Neill Martin, the supervisors of the doctoral thesis on which this book is based. Their enthusiasm, outstanding feedback and unfailing support made my doctoral project a pleasurable and rewarding experience. Thanks to Anja Gunderloch and Bairbre Ní Fhloinn, my examiners, for their meticulous appraisal of my work and the inspired feedback that made the final product that much better. My research was made feasible by funding from the Arts and Humanities Research Council to whom I express my sincerest gratitude. Thanks also to the staff at the Scottish Graduate School for Arts and Humanities, Dee Heddon, Claire Squires and Lindsay Wilson, whose support throughout my doctoral project was second to none. My thanks to the editorial staff at Edinburgh University Press, Ersev Ervoy, Isobel Birks, Sarah Foyle, Grace Balfour-Harle and Tom Dark, whose careful reading and constructive feedback have been very much appreciated.

My sincerest thanks go to Cathie Laing, Shamus McPhee and Davie Donaldson whose generosity in sharing their culture made many of the insights presented in this book possible. For your openness and generosity, Jimmy Williamson and Linda Williamson, and Jess Smith BEM, thank you. Sincerest gratitude to John Slavin, whose unparalleled visualisations of stories inspire me daily. To Alastair Laing for his excellent hospitality and patience, along with our many cheerful refreshments, thank you. To Tony Mullan, for his patience, intuition and support throughout the realisation of this work – slàinte mhath, Tony. Valerie Goodman, Anja Tröger, Erden Göktepe, Étienne 'HT' Sharp, Steven Forbes and Ian Anderson – profound thanks to you all for your uncompromising faith and friendship, from start to finish. To Moonbeam, for your confidence, support and love – thank you, this work stands as testament to our success.

ACKNOWLEDGEMENTS

The material from Donald Braid's *Scottish Traveller Tales: Lives Shaped through Stories* (2002) is reprinted with the kind permission of University Press of Mississippi. Likewise, the material from John Niles' *Homo Narrans: The Poetics and Anthropology of Oral Literature* (1999) is reprinted with the kind permission of the University of Pennsylvania Press. Some of the material presented in Chapter 1 – regarding *The Statistical Accounts of Scotland* (1791–1845) and testimonies from the School of Scottish Studies Archives – appears in an article by the author, published in the journal *Scottish Archives* Volume 28 (2022). Similarly, some of the documentary sources, and Davie Donaldson's Burker narrative, in Chapter 6 appear in an article by the author, published in *Contemporary Legend* Series 4, Vol. 2 (2024).

Abbreviations

ACSTP	Advisory Committee on Scotland's Travelling People
AHD	Authorised Heritage Discourse
ATU	Aarne-Thompson-Uther Tale-Type Taxonomy
DSL	The Dictionary of the Scots Language
GRTHM	Gypsy, Roma, Traveller History Month
ICH	Intangible Cultural Heritage
MECOPP	Minority Ethnic Carers of People Project
MWGGT	Ministerial Working Group on Gypsy/Travellers (Scottish Government)
NRS	National Records of Scotland
OED	The Oxford English Dictionary
SSS	School of Scottish Studies
TAD	Tobar an Dualchais
TAD ID	Tobar an Dualchais Person Identification
TMC	The Man in the Cassock
TSAS	The Statistical Accounts of Scotland
UNESCO	United Nations Educational, Scientific and Cultural Organisation

Introduction: Ethnicity and Otherness

THIS BOOK FOCUSES ON one of Britain's most marginalised and underrepresented ethnic minorities, Scotland's Traveller communities. The term 'Travellers' describes a series of interlinked social and familial communities that have existed in Scotland as distinct from mainstream society since at least the twelfth century (Kenrick and Clark 1999: 51). Recently, writers interested in these communities raised the issue of the underrepresentation of Gypsy, Roma and Traveller history in current scholarship: '"what field?"', they ask, noting that 'Gypsy and Traveller history remains something of a backwater, seemingly cut off from this same flow of historical attention' that is given to other minority ethnic populations (Taylor and Hinks 2021: 629). The same might be said of Scotland's Travellers' cultural heritage and this book therefore examines the unique storytelling traditions of these communities. It also reveals how stories make meaning within the communities that share them and showcases their enduring relevance to contemporary Scottish culture, and beyond.

As of 2011, Travellers have been officially recognised by the Scottish Government in the form of a separate ethnic category. The 2011 census carried out by the National Records of Scotland (NRS) included a separate response category to allow people to specifically identify themselves as 'White – Gypsy/Traveller' (NRS 2014: 2). According to the Scottish Government, the 2011 census results reported around 4,000 individuals as belonging to the 'White – Gypsy/Traveller' category ('A Comprehensive Analysis of the 2011 Census' 2015: 5). The same governmental report also states that it 'should be noted that some organisations working with Gypsy/Travellers in Scotland estimate that the population figure is much higher' (ibid.: 6). It must be noted from the outset that although, from a political perspective, Scotland's Traveller communities are defined as one homogeneous entity, they are comprised of diverse groups spread throughout

Scotland. Moreover, the disparity between population estimates cited above may well be down to the fact that the category itself, or at least the way it is presented by the NRS, is a misnomer. The compound term 'Gypsy/Traveller' is an official one used by governments and local authorities to recognise, and refer to, members of Scottish society; these groups share a certain set of characteristics that set them apart from Scotland's mainstream populations. However, Lynne Tammi points out that 'it is important to note that the term [Gypsy/Traveller] is a contested one [. . .] and consequently is not accepted by all families' (2020: 63). Willie Reid makes this point more firmly:

> [A]s a Gypsy/Traveller myself I am made painfully aware that we have always been defined by outsiders. Countless names and descriptions have been foisted upon us. The language used to describe Gypsies/Travellers is constantly changing and has more to do with government policy than ethnic identity [. . .] society has an incurable urge to label us so that they can painfully squeeze us into a corner
>
> (1997: 32).

Despite Reid's point, some members of the communities use self-defining terms when referring to the communities. Speaking in the 1950s, Traveller Jeannie Robertson informs us that 'the only word that ever I heard them called wis Nachins' (TAD 10285).[1] Stanley Robertson – a prominent Traveller storyteller we engage with throughout this book – uses the term 'Nyakim' to refer to the communities and to which he attaches the meaning 'Old Traveller' (1989: 7). More recently, Kenrick and Clark note that 'in their own language of Cant they call themselves *Nachins* (or *Nawkens*)' (1999: 52). Clark and Greenfields also use the term, commenting that Scotland's Traveller communities are sometimes referred to as 'Nawkins' or 'Nachins' (2006: 16). Author and activist Shamus McPhee, who we will engage with in subsequent chapters, self-identifies using the spelling 'Nacken' (2021b: 180). Davie Donaldson, another tradition-bearer who appears later in this book, self-identifies as 'Nawken', commenting that 'we are called "Travellers" because that's what settled [mainstream] communities wanted to call us, we didn't get to choose' (Online: 'Home').[2] This book recognises that naming conventions are contested, and some detail concerning political definitions of the communities is provided below. Therefore, at this early stage, it is vital to register the way that the term 'Traveller' is being deployed. The term is used advisedly to identify individuals and communities so that it is clear to the reader that reference is being made to a person from within the heterogeneous ethnic group on which this book focuses.[3] Similarly, phrases such as 'Traveller storytelling', 'Traveller tradition-bearer', 'Traveller culture' and 'Traveller worldview' are used to differentiate the concepts under discussion from their mainstream counterparts.

The ethnic and cultural identities of Scotland's Travellers are key concepts throughout this book – concepts that can be interpreted from many different perspectives – so it is important to define how the terms are being used. This is because Scotland's diverse Traveller communities – when viewed as discrete ethnic groups in their proper context – have a distinct sense of their own cultural identities that stand in contradistinction to mainstream Scottish society. Our definition of an 'ethnic group' follows Steve Fenton, where the group members share an acknowledged idea of descent or ancestry and culture (2010: 12). From a legal perspective, the concept of ethnicity was given definitive consideration in the 1983 *Mandla* v. *Dowell Lee* case heard in the House of Lords. During this case, Lord Fraser of Tullybelton recognised an ethnic group as a distinct community by virtue of certain characteristics, namely:

> The conditions which appear to me to be essential are these: (1) a long-shared history, of which the group is conscious as distinguishing it from other groups, and the memory of which it keeps alive (2) a cultural tradition of its own, including family and social customs and manners, often but not necessarily associated with religious observance. In addition to those two essential characteristics the following characteristics are, in my opinion, relevant: (3) either a common geographical origin, or descent from a small number of common ancestors (4) a common language, not necessarily peculiar to the group (5) a common literature peculiar to the group (6) a common religion different from that of neighbouring groups or from the general community surrounding it (7) being a minority or being an oppressed or a dominant group within a larger community.

(1983: HL/PO/JU/18/243)

Scotland's Traveller communities certainly satisfy Lord Fraser's essential characteristics and many of the relevant characteristics that follow. Moreover, the Travellers' cultural identity as an ethnic group has been shaped and influenced by the ever-changing social, political and economic landscape in which they have found themselves over the centuries. Or as Tullybelton sees it, a 'long-shared history, of which the group is conscious'.

It cannot be said that other individuals or communities within Scotland did not experience the same ever-changing landscape, but what can be said is that Scotland's Travellers' choice of lifestyle and their values mean that they have experienced these changes differently. The view from Lord Fraser of Tullybelton is therefore a key consideration. His judgment represents the official recognition of the ethnic distinctiveness of Traveller communities in the United Kingdom. The legality of the Scottish Travellers' ethnic status was subsequently cemented in Scotland during an industrial tribunal in 2008. Drawing on Lord Fraser's ethnic characteristics cited above, Judge Hosie ruled that the complainant had been unfairly dismissed based on their stance on behalf of Gypsy/Travellers. The unanimous judgment of the tribunal – chaired by Judge Hosie – resulted in protection for the communities under the Race Relations Act 1976, amended 2000, and then replaced by the Equality Act 2010.

However, both Lord Fraser's and Judge Hosie's legal judgments fall short of capturing what this distinctiveness resembles in the communities themselves, a distinctiveness that this study illuminates. The remainder of this introductory chapter provides the reader with a brief historical overview of the communities under discussion, then goes on to set out the interests and priorities of this book more specifically. By linking storytelling, folklore and ideology as interpretative frameworks, the reader is furnished with the basic principles that underpin the rest of the discussions. Chapter 1 begins by describing how the conflation between Gypsies, Travellers and other itinerant groups came about and how it continues to cause misunderstandings. Insider perspectives from the communities are then presented, with attention being given to the role that storytelling plays in the cultural continuity of the communities. Chapter 2 offers the reader a critical framework through which we can view traditional storytelling practices and considers the ways that stories function when we share them. Chapter 3 then marries these frameworks with cultural identity to show how ideologies can manifest themselves through traditional storytelling. Chapters 4 and 5 see these critical perspectives brought to bear on examples of storytelling from within the Traveller communities themselves; these chapters also think about the relationships between Traveller storytelling and other well-known stories from across the globe. Chapter 6 takes a fresh look at the legacy of the infamous murderers Burke and Hare, a prominent genre within the Travellers' traditions. Chapters 7 and 8 consider the role of the supernatural in folklore and interrogate examples of 'supernatural' happenings in a variety of contexts. The book concludes with a drawing together of threads, showcasing the cultural continuity of the communities and its links to storytelling and ideology.

This book is, above all, a celebratory look at the storytelling traditions of Scotland's diverse Traveller communities. Its overarching principle is that the social, economic and cultural experiences of the communities are intrinsically linked to their storytelling practices, where stories manifest these experiences in culturally significant ways (Braid 2002). The purpose of this book is not to present the reader with purely objective analysis of the stories, but rather to think about the ways that traditional narratives can be interpreted. Subjectivity is an important consideration then, not only for the storytellers being examined but for the position of the interpreter. Unlike a taxonomical exercise, pure objectivity is neither an aim nor a desire. Instead, highly contextualised and detailed close readings of Traveller storytelling are used to reveal plausible explanations of what the stories mean. To do this, the book describes a series of complementary analytical techniques that are rarely used during the study of the Travellers' cultural heritage, or folklore more broadly. This book is therefore divided into two parts: the first part details the research context using underutilised documentary evidence and then lays out the critical foundations that are subsequently used to uncover meanings within the stories; the second part delivers a variety of case studies from the Travellers' traditions to showcase the efficacy of the methods described in part one.

The perspectives offered within this study are akin to the type of criticism that is usually associated with printed literature. It is demonstrated throughout this book that the same richness and meaning found in printed literature can be also found in oral storytelling. We find that the Travellers' storytelling traditions are especially fertile ground in this respect because the communities share a unique culture and heritage. This book shows that the Travellers' traditions represent a distinctive folk idiom that belongs not only to Scottish folkloric traditions but negotiates perennial themes that resonate on an international level. It is also important to remember here that Scotland's Traveller communities are by no means homogeneous. The purpose of this study is not to describe a 'unified field' of Traveller culture and heritage, or to deliver a comprehensive overview of Traveller storytelling. The Travellers' storytelling traditions share characteristics with wider European traditions – including Irish and Scandinavian cultural spheres – and what this study showcases are connections that give an insight into what sets the Travellers' traditions apart.

Additionally, towards the conclusion of this book, we see how the contested nomenclature described above manifests in stories and how contemporary Travellers choose to define themselves. During this conclusion, the term 'Nackian narratives' is coined to reflect the self-defining prerogative of the individuals involved because some of the storytellers who feature place significant store in self-defining as 'Nacken' or 'Nawken'. The term Nacken (or Nawken) is expanded upon below to introduce its use within the communities and in the literature surrounding Travellers. Perhaps more significantly, Scotland's nomadic or semi-nomadic ethnic groups have, throughout the centuries, continually been defined from the outside. Their otherness has acquired many different epithets, leading to a persistent legacy of misunderstanding. Moreover, the inclusion of the suffix *-ian* serves to differentiate their cultural expressions from comparable folkloric expressions from wider Scottish and European traditions. It is demonstrated how the term 'Nackian narrative' is not only a meaningful way to describe the characteristics of the stories under examination, but a step towards elevating the underrepresented voices of the storytellers from within the communities.

WHO ARE THE TRAVELLERS?

Like many cultures that have existed in orality for much of their history, this is a notoriously difficult question to answer in any objective and definitive way. After spending many years engaging with Scotland's diverse groups of Travellers, the distinguished poet, political activist and song collector Hamish Henderson remarked that it is vain to speak with any certainty about the ultimate origins of these people. However, Henderson suggests that the communities are likely to be descended from an ancient caste of itinerant metalworkers whose status in earlier modes of society was probably very high (2004: 229). Timothy Neat casts the origin of the Travellers in the Highlands further back in time speculating that 'they are the descendants of the Palaeolithic hunter-gatherers' (1996: 223) who were forced out of Northern Europe as the Neolithic agriculturalists began to dominate the landscape. The purpose here is not to attempt to uncover the origins of the Travellers, or to validate their ethnic status in terms of their longevity in Scotland's history. As A. and F. Rehfisch have pointed out, 'literally gallons of ink have been utilized developing theories as to the origin of these people' (1975: 272) without any definitive success. Despite this, Travellers throughout Scotland have expressed having a shared sense of cultural identity that is borne out through a long history of persecution and misunderstanding from much of the Scottish population (Clark 2006: 53, 55). It is argued throughout this study that these social and economic experiences have become embedded, in sophisticated ways, in the stories and songs that the communities share to this day. From this perspective, it is possible to portray the more modern communities' sense of self-awareness and the distinctiveness of their cultural identities.

Discussing Irish Travellers, Bairbre Ní Fhloinn makes an analogous suggestion. The analysis of folklore presents 'another dimension to the already established profile of the Traveller as the quintessential Other in Irish society, and should hopefully serve to enhance our understanding of that ambivalent status' (2015: 156). Further contemporary debate around Traveller representation comes from Mícheál Ó hAodha:

> It can be argued that the institutionalisation of representation, image or stereotype in relation to marginalised and "outsider" minorities such as Travellers has become so engrained within the Western cultural heritage that it has become reified and irrefutably "fixed" within the public imaginary.
>
> (2011: 4)

Although Ní Fhloinn and Ó hAodha focus on Irish Travellers, their insights are pertinent here because the interests and priorities of this book examine conditions where representations of Scotland's Travellers are based on the same institutionalised perspectives. 'The Irish Other is a conception which should be celebrated', concludes Ó hAodha, 'and engaged with on a reciprocal level' (ibid.: 202). A respectful dialogue with members of the communities, both from those living and through archived recordings, is therefore a key impetus of the present study. What becomes clear is that, despite the Travellers comprising many diverse families and social groups, there is an overarching sense that they share certain traditions and folklore that reflect the image of a collective cultural identity. As John Niles has pointed out, 'in any folk culture, the individual and the community are connected inseparably, and yet certain individuals stand out for their mastery of particular expressive forms' (1999: 176). Consequentially, what lies at the heart of this book are the individual Travellers and their own expressions regarding their distinctive cultural identities. This book examines Traveller storytelling traditions to offer insights into the Travellers' individually and collectively unique culture and heritage. Put another way, it demonstrates how individual artistic expressions ventriloquise the ideological makeup of the communities, showcasing their distinctive *Nackian* narratives. To do this, a wide variety of secondary sources are utilised to contextualise the primary source material that is made up of the stories and testimonies of Travellers themselves.

By viewing storytelling at both the individual and the community levels, analysis of storytelling traditions can enhance our understanding of the Travellers as communities with rich, inherently valuable artistic traditions. This analysis is an important endeavour because it is apparent that stereotypical, negative depictions of Travellers, Gypsies and Roma persist in the mainstream media well into the twenty first century (for example, Amnesty International, *Caught in the Headlines* 2012: 1-12; Okely 2014: 65-85; *Ministerial Working Group on Gypsy/Travellers*

(MWGGT) 2018: Scottish Government; *Article 12 in Scotland* 2018: 11; Clark 2018: 113). These misunderstandings are also apparent in the political establishment. Nawken activist Davie Donaldson cites derogatory comments from political figures such as the Conservative MP, Gary Streeter, who claimed that 'most of them [Travellers] are as ethnic as I am' (2017) and Conservative MP Douglas Ross' desire for 'tougher enforcement against Gypsy/Travellers' (ibid.). Coming to the same conclusion as Clark above, Donaldson explains that 'this rhetoric can encourage discrimination' (ibid.). These comments from Clark and Donaldson, not to mention the MPs, highlight the urgency for a more informed engagement with Travellers in modern Scotland. The Scottish Parliament's *Equalities and Human Rights Committee*'s meeting agenda on 7 December 2017 consisted of marking 'Human Rights Day 2017 by taking evidence on human rights and the Gypsy Traveller Community in Scotland' (2017). Within the same agenda, Chris Oswald – head of the Policy, Equalities and Human Rights Commission – stated that limited gains have been forthcoming in terms of the Equality Act 2010 and compelled the *Committee* to focus on Travellers' 'ability to participate economically, socially and civically, [as] a far more compelling approach' (ibid.). In the political sphere, then, the tide appears to be turning on the palpable underrepresentation of Scotland's Traveller communities.

STORYTELLING AND WORLDVIEW

The storytelling traditions of Scotland's Travellers have been attracting the attention of collectors and scholars alike for generations. The nineteenth-century folklorist James Francis Campbell included several Traveller tales in his collection *Popular Tales of the West Highlands*, first published in 1860-62. These tales include a long story from 'Old Macdonald, travelling tinker [Traveller]', that Campbell tells us represented 'an incantation more vividly to me than anything I have ever read or heard' (1860–62 vol. I: xcv). It must be noted here that in present day Scotland, the term 'Tinker' is widely considered pejorative, and an outright racist slur by many Travellers (Donaldson 2018). However, the term is deployed carefully throughout this book, strictly within the context of an objective discussion of its historical usage. At the beginning of the twentieth century, Andrew McCormick questions why Scotland's Travellers have been treated with such contempt over the centuries, applauding them as a 'most intensely interesting class' (1907: 4). Elsewhere, Henderson recognises the prowess of Traveller storytellers when referring to the School of Scottish Studies (SSS) fieldwork activities, which began in the early 1950s (2004: 159). More recently, Timothy Neat highlights the Travellers' uniqueness when he asks why the 'psychological and cultural characteristics of these "outsiders" have provided a strange new fulcrum to Scottish national tradition' (1996: ix).

Given the Traveller communities' cultural distinctiveness from wider Scottish society, the central purpose of the present study addresses two interrelated themes. Firstly, how does traditional storytelling – when transmitted orally and in print through generations of storytellers and listeners alike – condition and represent the distinctive values and worldviews of tradition-bearers and their communities? Secondly, what does the Travellers' traditional storytelling culture actually resemble, and what does it mean? Although much has been said about Travellers' distinctive 'culture', more attention needs to be given to the details. The interests of this study therefore operate in tandem to complement one another; the first analyses how narratives function within the communities, and the second provides detailed descriptions of what the narratives themselves contain. It argues that the stories Travellers share embody a set of unique cultural identities that are based on sophisticated negotiations of Traveller values and worldviews. The overarching premise is that Travellers' stories function as ciphers and the central purpose rests in decoding these ciphers. As Sara Reith points out, 'perhaps the most striking way in which Traveller traditions are used [. . .] is for their implicit symbolic and metaphoric undercurrents' (2008a: 80). Donald Braid goes further, asserting that 'Travellers are creative human beings fully engaged in the modern world and perfectly capable of participating in a dialogue on issues of cultural identity' (1997: 44). Using a variety of diagnostic techniques, the analyses of the forthcoming chapters engage with these undercurrents and dialogues to uncover meanings encoded within the Travellers' storytelling traditions. We uncover that Travellers' worldviews are predominantly defined by oral traditions that negotiate mainstream ideological positions. Throughout this book, the term 'worldview' is understood, following Linda Dégh, as

> [t]he sum total of subjective interpretations of perceived and experienced reality of individuals [. . .] It contains beliefs, opinions, philosophies, conducts, behavioural patterns, social relationships, and practices of humans, related to life on this earth and beyond in the supernatural realm.
>
> (1995: 132)

With these diverse attributes in mind, 'worldview' is a useful term to describe the breadth of experiences on which this book focuses because it allows for the subjectivity of the speaker. Reith's insight into the function of Traveller worldview is also useful to note at this point. The received content of oral traditions, says Reith, engender 'worldviews that provide the foundations for confident creativity and individualism' (2008a: 79). Not only are Scottish Travellers' worldviews distinctive, but their articulation within their storytelling practices also provides individuals from diverse Traveller communities with a sense of confidence in their own cultural legitimacy. Subjectivity is therefore inherent in these expressions because they are based on personal experience. That is, the stories the tellers choose to tell are in themselves telling. At the same time, they can represent the subjective experience of the communities in which the stories circulate because their existence within the traditions indicates that they have culturally significant meanings.

The sophisticated stories are designed so that the listeners can, Reith continues, 'understand and embody the characters, dramatic proportions and locations of traditional texts' (ibid.). The present study goes further and argues that their function, via intergenerational transmission, is an undisguised desire to communicate specific values and beliefs so that cultural legitimacy is sustained. In terms of these values and beliefs, our analytical net can be cast wider than just intergenerational transmission. As one member of the communities recently suggested, 'our history is all around you, you just need to know where to look' (Maggie McPhee, *Gypsy, Roma, Traveller History Month 2021*). The sense that the Travellers' histories can also be found spread out across the country can be viewed as a wider context for the Travellers' storytelling traditions and is something that is captured in subsequent analytical chapters. Furthermore, drawing on a wide variety of sources, we see that storytelling and ideology are intrinsically linked within Travellers' oral traditions. Although much has been written about Travellers and their status in Scottish society (A. and F. Rehfisch 1975: 272), the present study's approach differs because the material drawn upon takes the position of the members of the communities, linking this position to theoretical understandings of storytelling and tradition. This approach is important because the analyses and interpretations of the latter chapters are predicated on close attention to the lived experiences, and socio-economic contexts, of the storytellers and their communities.

There is a distinct lack of scholarship linking Traveller storytelling to critical techniques that foreground the experience of the tellers. Consequentially, this book addresses two lacunae in the study of oral narrative and tradition. First, the context and critical underpinnings present new ways of thinking about how we can critically analyse traditional storytelling. In terms of the contextualisation, Clifford Geertz describes this approach as 'thick description'; Geertz explains that with thick description, the 'aim is to draw large conclusions from small, but very densely textured facts; to support broad assertions about the role of culture in the construction of collective life by engaging them exactly with complex specifics' (1973: 28). Such 'complex specifics' therefore pepper this book to support the broad assertions and conclusions of the associated analyses and interpretations. In the second lacuna, applying contemporary critical techniques to Traveller storytelling, a clearer picture of what Traveller 'culture' does in fact resemble is rendered. By looking at a multitude of examples in some detail in later chapters, this study shows how these techniques can open traditional storytelling up to new avenues of research. Accounts and testimonies from both Travellers and non-Travellers are drawn together to shed new light on the roots of the 'otherness' associated with Travellers, both in the past and in the present day. Diverse examples from a variety of historical and contemporary sources are included, presenting the reader with a nuanced picture of the Travellers' documented history in Scotland. Close engagement with contemporary debates around tradition – and how 'traditional' materials are used – follows to demonstrate how traditions within communities operate as a dynamic cultural resource.

STORYTELLING AND IDEOLOGY

To complement the detail and explanation provided in the preceding sections, the following outlines a central argument of this book. That is, that the Travellers' storytelling traditions and oral histories are far from ideologically neutral, and this ideological differentiation lies at the heart of much of their traditions. When it comes to storytelling, the primary source material of this study, traditional storytelling has been cited as a core constituent of Traveller identity already. Niles posits that Travellers' narratives function by 'articulating the wisdom that has long been accepted in their community' (1999: 193). Elsewhere, in one of the few detailed studies of Traveller storytelling, Braid notes that Traveller storytelling functions to 'contrast Traveller and settled beliefs [. . .] as a way of negotiating identity and difference with outsiders [and] will continue to change in response to the changing world and changing opportunities' (2002: 46, 292). In a 1979 interview – now held in in the SSS Archives, and available to listen to via the *Tobar an Dualchais* (TAD) online resource – the renowned Traveller singer and storyteller Stanley Robertson explains that 'I could take ony ay my family weans [children], and they would tell ye a story, fi auldest tae youngest [. . .] you should preserve cultures' (TAD 65165). What Niles, Braid and Robertson allude to are threads of meaning and cultural identity embedded within the Travellers' storytelling traditions. In the forthcoming analytical chapters, the present study expands on Braid's conceptualisation of negotiating difference with outsiders, draws out some of the 'wisdom' recognised by Niles, and shows what Robertson means when he refers to culture in a Traveller context. What all these conceptualisations of storytelling have in common is that they speak to certain ideological information being transmitted within the stories.

The principle that social and cultural zeitgeists, or anxieties, manifest themselves in storytelling was already observed by Stith Thompson (1946: 13) and appears somewhat obvious to modern conceptualisations of what stories are for. Geertz also argues that artistic expressions, such as traditional narratives, can be viewed as part of a cultural system that can have a social function, and represent localised 'patterns of feeling' (2000: 95). These localised patterns of feeling can be understood as reflections of a consensus, or worldview, within specific communities – and as a recognisable and distinctive ideology. The term ideology is being deployed here, following Raymond Williams' broad definition, as denoting a 'system of beliefs characteristic of a particular class or group' (1994: 175). John Gerring points out ideology's semantic promiscuity when it comes to definitions and regards it as a 'highly flexible conceptual tool' (1997: 957) within the social sciences. Gerring goes on to list a series of definitions, from systems of belief that justify the exercise of power, to Geertz's 'matrices for the creation of collective conscience' (cited in ibid.: 958). For our purposes, worldview and ideology are not interchangeable *per se*, but both terms are understood as denoting observable characteristics within a group of social actors. Where worldviews are subjective interpretations of experienced reality (cf. Dégh, cited above), ideologies are the ideas that are formulated and enacted by these interpretations. As was noted above, Travellers' worldviews are closely connected to their storytelling traditions and can be understood as an inherited resource that functions to inform and sustain the worldview of individuals within the communities. In short, the ideological makeup of the tellers is demonstrable in the themes, plots and characters that are represented explicitly in their stories. The concept of ideology, then, is an effective framework for interrogating the complexities of the stories. It is in the stories that social realities are confronted and ideology is enacted.

To get at ideologies in this way, it is useful to describe how narrative as a mode of communication is being used. The ordering of connected events into written or spoken accounts, narrative, is a foundational part of human societies (Barthes 1975: 237). If narrative is ever-present, narratology, as a science or theory of narrative, can help to facilitate the analysis of narrative as 'expressive culture'. Culture being understood here as bodies of artistic and intellectual work that can reflect the values, customs, beliefs and symbolic practices by which we live (cf. Eagleton 2016: 1). Under these conditions, the form and nature of the society in which a person learns what this understanding means is, of course, fundamental. The culture of the Travellers that concerns us here is multilayered; Traveller culture is at once Scottish, international in terms of the diverse tale-types we find, and at its core, reflects socio-cultural experiences that are distinctly *Traveller*. For our purposes, the phrase 'expressive culture' is used to describe intentional folkloric performances that communicate values and beliefs, the ideologies described above. Narratology is a useful tool in examining such narratives and can be defined simply as an empirical approach to the contents, themes and structure of stories. Narratology, as a discipline, amounts to the organisation of these elements to make narratives accessible for research into their inner workings and meanings (Bal 2009: 3-4). The organisation of narratives in this way is designed to facilitate interpretations; these interpretations are then used to highlight how the narrative is functioning in specific contexts. Moreover, these interpretations involve the study of narrative which 'negotiates and incorporates the insights of many other critical discourses that involve narrative forms' (Onega and Landa 1996: 1). These other critical discourses are discussed in Chapters 2 and 3, where the critical foundations of this study are brought together.

Meantime, through the lens of narratology, we are interested here in what narratives *do* in societies and communities. For Arthur Frank, socio-narratology 'expands the study of literary narratives – narratology – to consider the fullest range of storytelling, from folklore to everyday conversation' (2010: 12). The inclusion of the prefix 'socio' in narratological discourse refers to the relationships that individuals, and groups of individuals, have with one another. In this sense, socio-narratology helps to get at worldview and ideology because the social element of narratological discourse is concerned with the societal conditions in which the narrative is produced and communicated. There are three key tenets of socio-narratology that are key to the critical vocabulary of this book, these are: narratological competence, social location and dialogical analysis. In socio-narratology, narratological competence refers to an individual's access to a collective social or cultural resource. The individual with access to this resource can manipulate and disseminate it using narrative-based communication; stories thereby become one of the foundations around which collective social and cultural resources are based. Through narrative-based communication with one another, human societies compile narrative resources based on shared experiences, expectations, circumstances and anxieties. This is what Frank refers to as an individual's 'social location' within their milieu. An individual's access to the cultural resource mentioned above depends on 'what stories are told where they live and work, which stories do they take seriously or not, and especially what stories they exchange as tokens of membership' (2010: 13). The use of stories in this way becomes dialogical when it seeks to offer interpretations of stories based on a variety of points of view. These points of view include contextual details, such as the Travellers' negatively-charged status in society, the subjectivity of the researcher, and comparisons with other versions of the narratives in question. Within this framework, stories become a major constituent in the way that societies and communities organise themselves. To gain a better understanding of the ideological makeup of Scotland's Travellers, Chapter 1 gives an overview of the recent socio-historical context in which the more modern Traveller communities have developed and then thinks about the ways that the communities use their stories.

Notes

1. All references beginning 'TAD' refer to the track ID on *Tobar an Dualchais* (TAD), a digital archive which contains material from the School of Scottish Studies, The Canna Collection and BBC Radio nan Gàidheal. The recorded material can be accessed via the TAD website by searching the numerical track ID using the 'Search' function – https://www.tobarandualchais.co.uk/
2. More information about the term Nawken can be found on the website http://www.nawken.com/ and by searching Pauline Cairns Speitel's online dictionary at https://travellers.scot/
3. Some members of the communities identify as Indigenous Highland Travellers (IHT) and speak a minority language called Beurla Reagaird [speech of the smiths/artisans]. For more information visit the Travellers Times website and article at https://www.travellerstimes.org.uk/news/2020/10/we-are-minority-within-minority-indigenous-highland-travellers-call-out-recognition [accessed 18 March 2024].

Part I

1

The Travellers in Scotland

THE OTHER, THE 'TINKER' AND THE TRAVELLER

THE GROUPS REFERRED TO by policy makers today as 'Gypsy/Travellers' have been known by a variety of appellations in the past. The most common of these historical names for the Travellers in Scotland was 'Tinker', a term which, as noted above, is considered by many modern Travellers as derogatory and unacceptable. The wider pan-European perspective of Travellers as 'Other' is useful to consider before going into detail about the connotations of the term 'Tinker' and how its meaning became loaded with derision. The works of Heinrich Grellmann (1787), John Hoyland (1816), Walter Simson (1865) and David Macritchie (1894) are evidence of a fascination with the Other in elite European society during the late-eighteenth century, and throughout the nineteenth century. The editor's introduction to Simson's volume from 1865 captures the somewhat patronising interests precisely; 'the discovery and history of barbarous races of men, besides affording exquisite gratification to the general mind of civilised society, have always been looked upon as important' (James Simson 1865: 27). Grellmann's earlier account, *Historischer Versuch über die Zigeuner* [*Dissertation on the Gipsies*] (1787), began an association in the literature between native itinerant groups and immigrants from the Orient by consolidating various stereotypes. Grellmann's negative, stereotypical images of heathen wanderers who 'like locusts, have over-run most European countries' (1787: 2) homogenised all itinerant peoples who shared similar nomadic lifestyles. Hoyland's *A Historical Survey of the Customs, Habits & Present State of The Gypsies* (1816) cites Grellmann often, and the stereotypical imagery of the latter's dissertation is replicated. The first Gypsies in Europe 'appeared ragged and miserable', says Hoyland, and 'in like manner their descendants have continued for hundreds of years, and still remain' (1816: 37).

However, Hoyland's subtitle betrays another interest with these 'miserable' wanderers when he explains that his survey aims 'to promote the amelioration of their [Gypsies] condition' (1816, title page). Hoyland's terminology reveals a paternalistic and patronising attitude, traits which can also be found in Grellmann's work. In his introduction, Grellmann speaks of the need to 'humanise a people [Gypsies] who, for centuries, have wandered in error and neglect' (1787: ix). Simson's *History of the Gipsies: With Specimens of the Gipsy Language* published in 1865 continues in a similar vein to Grellmann and Hoyland. The derivation is clear from the outset when, in Simson's opening chapter, he states that he is 'indebted for my information on the early history of the continental Gipsies, chiefly to the works of Grellmann [and] Hoyland' (1865: 69). In her discussion of the cultural history of nomadic groups in northern Europe, Mary Burke assigns this fascination to the post-Enlightenment Orientalism that was gripping the European intelligentsia, intimated by Grellmann's dissertation noted above (2009: 30). The 'Oriental Other' was initially conceptualised in the form of groups of Gypsies immigrating west across the continent. During the nineteenth century in Scotland, the term 'Gypsy' became synonymous with any group practising a nomadic or semi-nomadic lifestyle. For instance, Simson speaks of 'our Scottish Gipsies' (1865: 340), referring to the communities we know today as Travellers.

Simson's editor, James Simson, explains that 'tinkler [Tinker] is the name generally applied to the Scottish Gipsies. The wandering, tented class prefer it to the term Gipsy' (1865: 7). Within the body of the text proper, Simson also identifies a group who 'call themselves *Nawkens* [. . .] a word to which they attach the meaning of a *wanderer*, or *traveller* – one who can do any sort of work for himself that may be required in the world' (1865: 340). The reader will recall the self-defining term 'Nawken' from the Introduction above and it is in Simson that we first encounter the term in the literature surrounding Scotland's Traveller communities. Returning to the term 'Tinkler', it is recorded in Scotland's twelfth-century Farandman laws, where the groups had legal protection under which to ply their trade as itinerant metalworkers (Kenrick and Clark 1999: 51). In terms of etymology, according to *The Dictionary of the Scots Language* (DSL), the word 'tinker' – variously spelled tynklare, tynclare, tynekler, tinklair, tinclar, tinkard – first appears in Scotland as a surname around 1175 (DSL). Although the DSL notes that the origin of the word is uncertain, it represents 'a worker in metal, a craftsman who makes or repairs metal artefacts, a tinker' (ibid.). *The Oxford English Dictionary* (OED) offers a similar definition, including the element of itinerancy, also noting that the origin of the word 'tinker' is uncertain (OED). As an appellation for Travellers, the term Tinker persisted into the nineteenth century, where, as we will see below, its use became pejorative in the extreme. It is Macritchie's *Scottish Gypsies Under the Stewarts* (1894) that finally recognises Scottish Travellers as a distinct and separate group from Gypsies. 'The word "tinker" or "tinkler", although often applied to genuine Gypsies', Macritchie concludes, 'cannot be regarded as actually synonymous with "Gypsy"' (1894: 13). Following on from Macritchie's contention a decade or so later, Andrew McCormick suggests that 'there were in Scotland, prior to the wave of Romani-speaking Gypsies of 1505, so called Gypsies, or, to put it more specifically, Tinklers' (1907: 393). Burke notes that Grellmann's dissertation inspired the 'Scottish intelligentsia to take notice of indigenous nomadic groups' (2009: 50), and this much is true, based on the Scotland-based writers presented above. Burke goes on to suggest that these nomadic groups were 'subsequently stripped of their locally generated Hiberno-Scottish identity and reconstituted as wanderers of Oriental descent' (ibid.). However, there were people writing in Scotland before Macritchie and McCormick who recognised the difference between native nomadic Scots and the immigrant Gypsies.[1]

In his contribution to *The Statistical Accounts of Scotland* (TSAS), The Reverend John Baird explains that in his parish of Yetholm, he is 'far from regarding the "muggers and tinkers" of Kirk Yetholm as the pure unmingled gipsy race' (1845: 166). Baird goes on to explain that the term 'muggers' refers to the group we know today as Travellers (ibid.).[2] We know Baird was familiar with both Grellmann's and Hoyland's work, however, as he cites both authors in his account of his parish (ibid.). Although intermarriage between immigrant Gypsies and native Scots Travellers took place, it must be noted that they began as different, identifiable groups (Henderson 2004: 174). This view is implicit in Baird's account of his parish when he notes that the Gypsies in Scotland were 'much less distinguishable as a peculiar race than they appear to have been formerly' (1845: 166). The key point is that Travellers in Scotland have been recognised as a distinctive group since at least the twelfth century, but their status, and indeed *acceptance*, within Scottish society has been determined by the ideological priorities of the dominant social groups.

The confusion around their origins, coupled with their alternative lifestyles and associations with other itinerant groups, makes representations of Travellers in historical records bleak reading. In TSAS for Auchterderran in Fife, The Reverend Andrew Murray includes a description of 'a few persons, called *tinkers* and *horners*, half-resident, and half-itinerant, who are feared and suspected by the community' (1791: 458). Elsewhere in TSAS, Reverend Alexander Dobie tells us that the parish of Eaglesham 'is oppressed with gangs of gypsies, commonly called tinkers, or randy-beggars' (1792: 124). More evidence of the demonisation of Travellers comes from the parish of Kinnettles, where The Reverend David Ferney informs TSAS that there are 'bands of sturdy beggars, male and female, or, as they are usually called, tinkers; whose insolence, idleness, and dishonesty, are an affront to the police of our country' (1793: 201). The Reverend Duncan M'Ara reports that Fortingall is also plagued by 'swarms of tinkers' (1792: 455). The animosity displayed by the clergy towards Travellers continues into the nineteenth century in the same pejorative tone. The Reverend William Duff of Grange complains that the parish 'has long been infested by cairds, tinkers, and sturdy beggars' (1845: 219). In Monteith, The Reverend Alexander Gray records that 'vagrants, tinkers, and gipsies from various quarters were numerous; but, by the vigilance of the local police, they have been suppressed' (1845: 1281). In Knockando, The Reverend George Gordon explains that the parish of is 'much infested by sturdy beggars, and tinkers, especially during the summer season, who drain away a great deal of what might otherwise be given to the home-poor' (1845: 81). Writing in *The Friend; a Religious and Literary Journal (1827-1906)*, the anonymous author of an article entitled 'Savages in Scotland' explains that the 'tinkers of Caithness [. . .] herd like cattle [. . .] and the entire social condition of the tinker tribe is of the most degraded character' (1869: 102). The evidence presented here corroborates the conclusion that Travellers in Scotland have existed, and survived, in a hostile environment for many centuries (Rehfisch 1975: 283). However, it must be noted that these disparaging accounts are the opinions of an elite class – embodied by the clergy and the published intelligentsia – and that they are only one side of the story.

It can be taken for granted that the men composing these narratives would not have consulted what were deemed undesirable members of their communities – the Travellers themselves – when collating the information included in their accounts of their parishes. It is not difficult to imagine the Travellers' *persona non grata* status during the nineteenth century in the communities mentioned above. The question presents itself: how did Traveller communities throughout Scotland attract this kind of hostility during this period? One clue comes from an article titled the 'State of Crime in Scotland' published in *The Scotsman* in 1838. According to the author, 'wandering tinkers have earned so bad a reputation in Scotland, that their name is now almost synonymous with thief' (1838: 2). These associations can be lethal, as one broadside from 1719 affirms: 'The Last Speech and Dying Words of James Thomson Tincklar' (Thomson 1719: National Library of Scotland) recounts an act of repentance before being executed for murder, where Thomson explains that he was born of honest parents, but was raised by 'one John Bell a Tincklar, who learned me to Pike [rob] and Steal [. . .] and all manner of debauchery' (ibid.). *The Scotsman's* anonymous author goes on to suggest that this is unsurprising, given that 'one reason of persons quitting one place of abode after another, being that they have committed offences and fallen under suspicion' (1838: 2). Such statements are indicative of sedentarist ideological imperatives that stand in opposition to the lifestyles favoured by itinerant communities. The Travellers' lifestyles in the past simply did not fit with the sedentarist ideology of mainstream Scottish society. This ideological differentiation, and how it is negotiated within Traveller storytelling traditions, becomes a central thread in Part II of this book.

Despite the hostility evidenced above, alternative evidence of the Travellers' renown in Scotland comes from Duncan Campbell. In his *Reminiscences and Reflections of an Octogenarian Highlander*, published in 1910, Campbell believes that Scotland's Travellers antedate immigrant Gypsy groups and laments their decline. 'It seems to me', writes Campbell, 'that the tinkers had been a feature of the Highlands long before any "Lord of Little Egypt" [Gypsy] with his followers came to Scotland and imposed on James V. and his Parliament' (1910: 24). Campbell aligns the native Scots, and probably Gaelic-speaking, Travellers with an earlier mercantile order and laments the loss of their craftwork, 'specimens of which', recalls Campbell, 'were to be found in many households as long as the old social order lasted' (ibid.: 25). When demand diminished for the 'neatly finished and artistically designed ornaments the tinkers had been making for untold generations', Campbell concludes, 'the art was soon lost' (ibid.). Campbell's reminiscences not only capture a sense of nostalgia for a perhaps simpler past, but also hint towards a shift in the relationship between Travellers and wider society. Where once Travellers' ancestors were viewed as artists, it appears fashions changed and the market for such goods disappeared.

This view of Travellers as the descendants of a group of skilled, itinerant artisans is shared by Henderson who suggests that they 'were part – and an important part – of tribal society [. . .] travelling their own territories centuries before the arrival of the Romany gypsies in North-West Europe' (2004: 174). Campbell's account can be read as the Travellers' fate in microcosm; these once renowned and valued artists, free to roam wide territories, fell to mending domestic items. Eventually, as we have seen from historical accounts such as TSAS, Scotland's Travellers are ostracised to the point that they are considered parasitical.[3] Even earlier evidence suggests that the maligned 'tinkers' were once a valued and trusted sub-section of Scotland's urban social milieu. *The Records of Elgin: 1234-1800* from March 1658, tell us that 'John Cowie, tincler [tinker], burges [citizen]' has been tasked with the upkeep of the town clock during his lifetime (Cramond 1902: 307).[4] Elsewhere, the *Historical Notices of Scottish Affairs (1683–1688)* from 1684 details an act 'forbidding any tinkers to go through the town [Edinburgh], but only one to serve the whole town, with his servants' (Fountainhall 1848: 541). It seems that Travellers were certainly deemed useful in terms of the services they could render, but unpalatable in large numbers.

Despite the conflicting accounts of Travellers outlined above, the communities being discussed in these sources were valued members of Scottish society. What these early examples also highlight is a tangible shift in attitudes towards Travellers as Scotland moved towards industrialisation. As one historian asserts, during the industrial revolution '[the Scottish Highlands'] entire economic structure was dislocated [and] much of the old economy of the region and most of its inhabitants, were rendered redundant' (Richards 1993: 216, 220). Thomas Devine agrees, remarking that during the 1760s and 1770s, 'traditional society was destroyed in this period and a new order based on quite different values, principles and relationships emerged to take its place' (1994: 32). Travellers in the Scottish Highlands must have been affected by such societal shifts given the nature of their trades as metallurgists and hawkers of artisanal domestic items. No doubt this redundancy continued into the nineteenth century and beyond, as the Travellers' functions in the everyday economy became less and less tenable (Taylor 2014: 115).

Writing in 1836, one columnist for the *Penny Magazine of the Society for the Diffusion of Useful Knowledge* captures the fate of the Travellers in the public's consciousness neatly; 'the change in circumstances of social life has lessened, if not destroyed, the value of their services', the columnist explains, 'while their vagabond propensities render them a pest to the country' ('The Tinkers of Scotland' 1836: 502). From this perspective, it appears that the change in attitudes towards Travellers was initially linked to the rapid industrialisation that Scotland experienced during the eighteenth and nineteenth centuries. This was not a fate peculiar to Scotland's Travellers. Jim MacLaughlin notes that Ireland's Travellers were similarly maligned as outcasts in the post-Enlightenment atmosphere of 'social Darwinism' (1995: 23). Across European philosophy, the concept of 'stages of civilisation' – stages based on successively more regimented modes of subsistence – of humankind placed nomadic groups such as the Travellers in the 'barbarous' category (Meek 1976: 5; MacLaughlin 1995: 23; James 2023: 110). In this way, the transition to urban, sedentary and industrialised societies coupled with the racialisation of nomadic groups during the post-Enlightenment period has had a major and long-lasting effect on our understanding of nomadic communities throughout Europe.

INSIDER PERSPECTIVES

Colin Clark observes that over the centuries Traveller communities have 'developed a clear sense of [their] distinct social and cultural identity, an identity that was, and still is, held together by overt prejudice and discrimination from the settled community' (2006: 53). However, despite Clark's observations of prejudice and discrimination towards Travellers, many do not view themselves as social pariahs. On the contrary, the SSS Archives provide evidence that Travellers are aware of their distinctiveness from the 'settled or mainstream' population and are somewhat party to their peripheral status in Scottish society. In her autobiography, *The Yellow on the Broom*, Betsy Whyte recalls 'cruel and sarcastic' treatment during her childhood, where her Traveller ethnicity was a routine source of hostility (1979a: 55–56). However, when questioned during an interview in the late 1970s on her views of non-Travellers' perceptions of Travellers, Whyte explains that she 'didnae really feel that I wisnae good enough, I didnae really feel that inside o' me, but I knew that they thought that, so I was having nothing tae dae wi' them' (TAD 64239). Similarly, speaking in 1978, John Stewart explains that Travellers' 'way of thinking, our deep concern inside, our jealousies and oor hatreds, our loves and our likes, are far different from yours [. . .] we would look at a thing different fi you altogether' (TAD 56424). Stewart also expresses a sense of inherent self-esteem when he remarks that 'if you're Traveller brained, and you had the education, you're jumps ahead of the country folk [mainstream population]' (TAD 65889). Through her work with contemporary Traveller children, Geetha Marcus has shown that this sense of otherness persists within the most recent generation of Travellers in Scotland (2015: 60–61). Marcus suggests that young Travellers' reluctance to associate in any meaningful way with members of the mainstream population exacerbates misunderstandings between the two groups (ibid.).[5] What these examples demonstrate is that Travellers, both past and present, overtly distinguish themselves from the 'settled' or 'mainstream' population of Scotland.

Elsewhere in the SSS Archives, speaking in 1979, Stanley Robertson laments the decline of Travellers' shared cultural identity. Robertson describes himself as 'a thoroughbred Traveller, on all sides, and I enjoy being part of that great and wonderful culture' (TAD 85439). Despite this, 'there has been many changes in the traditions of the Travelling people', says Robertson, 'due to that fact that the scaldie [non-Traveller] influence has came upon them [. . .] they're ashamed of their heritages' (TAD 67492). What is at stake here, then, is not only social and political differentiation based on ethnicity, but a tangible sense that Travellers' unique cultural identities are being eroded. The cultural legitimacy of Travellers is something that is expressed by members of the communities themselves. According to John Niles, the traditions and way of life of Scotland's Traveller communities have undergone a metamorphosis in recent decades (2022: 20). Although social conditions have changed since the advent of the SSS in 1951 and its interest in Scotland's non-elite cultural identities, semi-nomadic Traveller identities continue to resist assimilation to the present day (ibid.). Nawken activist Davie Donaldson affirms that certain anxieties persist, explaining that contemporary Travellers are 'often forced to hide our ethnicity for fear of prejudice' (*The Ferret* 2017). During her interviews with contemporary Travellers, Marcus reports similar fears of identifying as a Traveller in modern Scotland; when questioned about coping with racism and harassment, one interviewee said that she tries to 'avoid everything [. . .] and hide in the shadows' (2019: 163). A separate interviewee from Marcus' study recalls, 'I can remember I wouldnae say I was a Traveller because I was terrified and my mum used to always put it in my head that. . . don't speak about it because you're making it worse for yourself *just act normal*' (ibid.: 173, my italics).

More evidence of this prejudice comes from an article published by Donaldson entitled 'The government is at "war with our lifestyle", claim Scotland's Travellers' (*The Ferret* 2017). In his article, Donaldson remarks that modern Travellers 'are struggling to retain our traditional lifestyle while often forced to hide our ethnicity for fear of prejudice' (ibid.). It is apparent that Scotland's Travellers are still subject to discrimination in modern Scotland. One Traveller interviewed by Donaldson believes that 'Travellers are unfairly characterised by the media' (ibid.), and such representations in the media may go some way to explaining the ongoing misunderstanding of Travellers and their culture. Donaldson and his interviewee are not alone. Clark observes that Travellers' voices rarely appear in print media in Scotland, and that this conspicuous underrepresentation in the press reinforces pre-existing misunderstandings of Traveller life and culture (2018: 113). Not only this, but the representations of Travellers are often negative stereotypes. The negative and stereotypical portrayals of Travellers in the media are often the only exposure that the mainstream population give to Traveller communities (The Equality and Human Rights Commission 2013: 4). However, as Taylor and Hinks point out, several 'historians have turned to oral history as a means of generating new evidence and constructing Traveller and Romani-centred histories' (2021: 639). The same impetus applies to the present study when it utilises the SSS Archives at the University of Edinburgh, an archive which houses copious narratives and oral histories from Travellers throughout Scotland. This source of data is important as a diachronic record of Travellers' experiences but, thus far, has been underutilised. This book utilises the SSS Archives throughout to analyse and interpret narratives and testimonies from across the Travellers' traditions.

As noted above, reports in the mass media and the observations of privileged members of society are informative, in the sense that they highlight a resounding ideological differentiation. On the other end of this ideological spectrum, we have what an author in *The Scotsman* referred to as the 'much-neglected' individuals and communities presently under discussion, the Travellers themselves. The SSS Archives contain a wealth of testimony from Travellers describing their experiences of living in Scotland in the latter half of the twentieth century. Speaking in 1988, Stanley Robertson, introduced above, describes his childhood experience as being tainted by a 'great, strong prejudice against us', exclaiming that he does not 'understand what makes people grow up with prejudices' (TAD 85439). Robertson recalls that when he was a boy, he would have stones thrown at him, be called names and be excluded from regular activities at school. Rationalising this prejudice, Robertson sees the Second World War as a fulcrum over which attitudes towards Travellers changed. Robertson explains that 'during the war, the people all united, and the Travelling people became part of the society' (ibid.). After the war ended, however, Robertson feels that people 'looked for something to hold their aggressions against [. . .] so the Travelling people were one of the small groups that got picked upon' (ibid.).

A similar sentiment regarding her early childhood and schooling is expressed by Betsy Whyte. Reflecting in an interview in 1985, Whyte explains that despite the teachers at her first school treating her very well, 'if any damage was done to the school, a window broken, or anything like that. . . "they damn tinks"' (TAD 82053) would get the blame. Like Robertson's conception of the Travellers as universal scapegoats, Whyte describes how, if there was any trouble, people would take 'anybody's word against the Travellers', no matter what was done' (ibid.). However, outside of the educational system, Whyte portrays an idyllic lifestyle where 'everybody went to the fields [. . .] fi the youngest to the oldest' (ibid.). Whyte fondly remembers how the children would 'play aboot in the fields, the mothers would go and feed their bairns when they wanted to. [At] dinnertime they would make a big fire and cook something, and boil tea, tea, all the time' (ibid.). The Travellers undertook what Whyte calls 'piecework', which is a system of payment where the labourers are paid for work done, rather than how long it takes them to do it. In this way, Whyte explains, a measure of freedom was achieved; because the work was not compulsory, as with perhaps a salaried position, the Travellers could say '"come on boys, we'll all go to the burn, leave it for the day", it was just a matter of being able tae be free, I think' (ibid.).

At the same time, this piecework system also suits the farmer, as Whyte explains, 'when you were working in piecework, you never wanted to go [leave employment], but when it was compulsory tae be there, ye jist didnae want to be there' (ibid.). From this perspective, Travellers as seasonal workers would have been an integral part of the agricultural economy, and rural economy more generally, during the early twentieth century, and even more so further into the past. Whyte recounts how Travellers would trade various domestic items with their settled neighbours, and exchange labour with gamekeepers for raw materials, such as various animal horns (ibid.). There is no sense of antagonism between Travellers and the settled population in some of Whyte's testimony. On the contrary, Whyte tells us that 'where we lived, there was no vans [mobile shops] or nae shops, or anything' (ibid.). This meant that their settled neighbours 'were glad to see a Traveller comin', even to get news sometimes' (ibid.). This sort of evidence of the relationship between Travellers and the settled population paints a somewhat ambiguous picture. On one hand, Travellers are scapegoats for society's ills, whereas on the other they are valued seasonal workers and societally engaged in many ways on account of their itinerancy.[6]

As Aoife Bhreatnach has pointed out in the case of Irish Travellers, constructing an accurate account of Travellers' experiences using 'historical' sources is problematic (2007: 34). Bhreatnach recognises that the bias and stereotypical accounts created by elite members of society do little to uncover the true nature of Travellers' experiences in the past. Moreover, Bhreatnach argues that 'believing that Traveller culture only has historical validity if it is ancient is a disturbing beginning for a scholarly or political argument' (ibid.). Although we cannot, at present, construct a conclusive 'origin story' for the Travellers in Scotland, their own conceptualisations of their history are an important part of the discourse. The historical period covered here – from the late-eighteenth century documentary evidence to the twentieth-century testimony in TAD – is significant. However, the evidence presented becomes ever more pertinent because the relationships highlighted are demonstrably negotiated within Traveller storytelling. Chapter 3 brings the reader up to date with the more modern interactions Traveller communities have had, and continue to have, with the central government and policy-makers. Contemporary policy-makers in Scotland, such as the *Ministerial Working Group on Gypsy/Travellers* (MWGGT), have begun to understand that the Travellers' deeply-rooted culture cannot simply be dispelled and replaced by a more 'settled' lifestyle.[7]

TRADITION AND THE ROLE OF TRADITION-BEARERS

When it comes to the social element of narratives, one useful approach has been suggested by Michael McGuire. Like Frank, whose socio-narratology asks what a story does in society, McGuire considers 'the potential of narrative to influence social-political attitudes' (1990: 219). In approaching this question, McGuire envisions various forms of narrative as performing a rhetorical function. This rhetorical function can be viewed as a narrative's ability to persuade and inform. It is inevitable that different narratives function to inform and persuade in different ways – an historical narrative may draw comparisons with previous events, to expose how things might be in the present or in the future. A literary narrative may have a didactic function for children, represent a social or philosophical commentary, or indeed serve purely as entertainment for adults. The relevance of this rhetorical element for the present work involves the ability of a narrative to communicate a certain set of values or beliefs. McGuire concludes that narratives can 'expand or add to a stock of knowledge, or they may interpret new information for incorporation into a body of knowledge' (ibid.: 234). This body of knowledge resonates with the concept of a collective cultural resource discussed in the Introduction to this book. Moreover, McGuire goes on to suggest that a sociological study of narrative has the potential to reveal how narratives are collected and distributed within specific social groups (ibid.: 224). For our purposes, the 'distributors' McGuire alludes to can also be described as 'tradition-bearers', and 'the body of knowledge' as a cultural resource.[8] By viewing storytelling as a form of cultural resource, we can build a nuanced critical approach to understanding what 'tradition' does.

Folklore, or intangible cultural heritage (ICH) – viewed within the context of wider Scottish and European society – forms the primary source material of this study. To briefly recapitulate, we are concerned with what the Travellers' storytelling traditions resemble and how they condition and represent the unique values and beliefs of the communities. Given the central role of ICH, and to describe our point of departure, it is important to state the overarching principles that this book relies on. Firstly, a useful definition of ICH and its functions comes from the United Nations Educational, Scientific and Cultural Organisation (UNESCO):

> The 'Intangible Cultural Heritage' means the practices, representations, expressions, knowledge, skills – as well as the instruments, objects, artefacts and cultural spaces associated therewith – that communities, groups and, in some cases, individuals recognize as part of their cultural heritage. This intangible cultural heritage, transmitted from generation to generation, is constantly recreated by communities and groups in response to their environment, their interaction with nature and their history, and provides them with a sense of identity and continuity, thus promoting respect for cultural diversity and human creativity [manifested in] oral traditions and expressions, including language as a vehicle of the intangible cultural heritage; (b) performing arts; (c) social practices, rituals and festive events; (d) knowledge and practices concerning nature and the universe; (e) traditional craftsmanship.
>
> (2022: 5)

UNESCO's 2003 'Convention for the Safeguarding of the Intangible Cultural Heritage' goes on to broaden the scope of ICH and elevate its potential. For UNESCO, ICH must also be protected to 'promote the peace-building potential of safeguarding efforts that involve intercultural dialogue and respect for cultural diversity' (ibid.: 95). From this perspective, sharing and engaging with the ICH of communities places the researcher in an inclusive, reciprocal dialogue with the individuals and groups who they study. This approach is pertinent as we go on to engage with the rich variety of ICH among Scotland's Travellers. Adopting such approaches can assuage misunderstandings, and the associated conflicts, between the settled, or mainstream, population and Scotland's diverse Traveller communities.

Furthermore, ICH – particularly that of ethnic minorities – represents an inimitable resource for developing better understandings of the communities who share it.[9] By aligning our overarching principles with UNESCO's inclusive ethos around engagement with ICH, this book effectively collaborates with Travellers and their storytelling traditions. Ullrich Kockel and Mairi McFadyen have argued that, in terms of the study of

ICH, 'instead of rigid epistemologies, ethnologists should creatively combine empathetic ethnography with critically-aware theory' (2019: 197). The concept of rigid epistemologies echoes Laurajane Smith's earlier conceptualisation of authorised heritage discourses (AHDs). For Smith, such discourse is reliant on the 'claims of technical and aesthetic experts' and 'privileges monumentality and grand scale [...] it is a self-referential discourse' (2006: 11). The problem that Smith recognised with such discourses is that they tend to exclude non-expert perspectives on the nature of 'heritage' itself. The result is that AHDs continually validate the experiences and worldviews of dominant narratives about nation, culture and ethnicity (ibid.: 299). To resist such constrictive discourses, we must be willing to step outside of AHDs and allow people's cultural expressions to speak from themselves. What is being advocated here is an approach to ICH that has a stereoscopic lens: on one hand, we must resist imposing any meaning or purpose on the Travellers' stories that is based on hegemonic epistemologies; at the same time, we must approach our source material with a critical awareness of theoretical frameworks that become relevant to the cultural expressions that we are working with.

We must also recognise that these two perspectives are not incompatible, allowing for the creative combination of both approaches during our analysis and interpretations. Cultural materialism may help us to understand the impact that economic and technological factors have had on certain narratives; on the other hand, such a perspective would partially neglect, if not wholly, the latent psychological aspects of the same narrative. This form of interpretation, then, utilises both emic and etic discourses. In the folkloristic context, Alan Dundes offers a concise summary of how the etic-emic terms are understood: the etic approach is classificatory, with the analyst creating constructs that are not inherent in the material and where the data *in its context* is not considered; in contrast, the emic approach *does* consider the context and aims to describe the pattern of a culture with respect to how various constituents are related to the whole (1964: 56). Consequently, an emic approach *reveals* patterns, whereas an etic approach *creates* them. However, as Kockel and McFadyen go on to warn, 'what matters most is that we seek to ground our theorising in the lived *emic* experience of the people we are studying, rather than in some fashionable *etic* discourse' (2019: 197, italics in original). The analyses of the present study strike a balance between insider perspectives (emic) and outsider perspectives (etic), deploying an integrative methodology that facilitates a clearer understanding of the narratives under examination. The advantages of this methodological approach are understood and advocated by tradition-bearers within Traveller communities. For instance, Stanley Robertson recalls his great aunt,

Maggie Stewart, teaching him similar principles during his upbringing; 'ye will learn mair in ten seconds inside a thing', Maggie explained, 'than ye wid looking and observing frae the outside' (cited in Reith 2008a: 83). The synergy of these two perspectives maximises the stability of the approach in the sense that 'emic and etic approaches are partly able to counteract one another's theoretical weaknesses in describing culture' (Morris et al 1999: 789). The forthcoming analytical chapters demonstrate how etic systems – such as the Aarne-Thompson-Uther (ATU) tale taxonomy or Thompson's *Motif-Index of Folk Literature* (1955) – can be complemented by emic techniques that reconceptualise the narratives to deliver original insights into their meanings.

At this point, it is appropriate to expand on conceptualisations 'the folk' and ICH to include the narrative element. Licia Masoni explains that folk narrative is 'storytelling in everyday life, a form of communication whose manifestations are prompted by life events and situations' (2013: 430). This conceptualisation of folk narrative aligns well with socio-narratology discussed above; both terms focus on the lived lives of the storytellers, and as Frank puts it, they consider the 'fullest range of storytelling, from folklore to everyday conversation' (2010: 12). Moreover, the adaptability of folk narrative becomes its defining feature – as opposed to a static text – and it is this dynamic faculty that is of interest here. Masoni suggests that folk narrative must be differentiated from static texts, such as printed literature, as folk narratives exist in many versions that do not necessarily conform to one authorised version (2013: 431). This dynamism or adaptability is an essential function of folk narrative. To allow the narratives to reflect the lived lives and identities of the storytellers, they must be able to change. In terms of the function of folk narratives in general, Masoni concludes that 'telling and adapting stories allow individuals and communities to redefine their identity in light of social changes' (ibid.: 469). Despite the practicality of Masoni's conclusion, we find that the Travellers' identities as expressed within narratives are largely *resistant* to social changes and that adaptations within their storytelling traditions function in different ways. As Kockel pointed out while discussing the function of such traditions, 'they are never exactly the same and yet they remain recognisable over time. Change is primarily generated from within' (2008: 12). It is these functions and how they change that is of interest here, functions that this study identifies and interprets.

If the above conceptions of folklore, narrative, and ICH reveal dynamic and ever-adapting forms of cultural expression, where does the 'tradition' come in? Indeed, what is the definition of 'tradition' in the folkloristic context? For some, the notion of tradition connotes some object, practice or ritual that is static in essence, yet mobile through time. At the end of the nineteenth century, Edwin Hartland described tradition as an 'entire circle of thought [. . .] delivered by word of mouth and by example from generation to generation through unremembered ages' (1891: 34). More recently, Simon Bronner has pointed out that 'most linguistic as well as philosophical considerations of tradition begin with a singular source citing the Latin root *tradere*, "to hand over or deliver" and adapting it to the popular idea that tradition is "handed down" from generation to generation' (2017: 39). There is an implication of stasis in this conceptualisation of tradition in that the thing being handed down – the *traditum* – is valuable and should remain intact and unchanged. Eric Hobsbawm's argument that tradition is defined by invariance – because its reference to the past imposes the repetition of inflexible practices – reflects this static element during transmission (1983: 2). Elsewhere, Dan Ben-Amos asserts that '*tradition* does not defy definition, but simply does not need one. Its meaning appears lucid beyond clarification, perspicuous beyond explanation' (1984: 97, italics in original). It is tempting to follow Ben-Amos and assume that tradition does not require a definition. However, Bronner has warned that we can no longer take definitions of tradition for granted in twenty-first century folkloristics (2000: 100). From the perspective of stasis and repetition, the conception of folk narrative described above appears incongruous with the 'traditional', as it resists mere repetition and relies on variation to remain relevant in ever-changing social and cultural environments. For the purposes of our argument, therefore, a more concrete definition of tradition is required to describe its relationship with folk narrative.

Ray Cashman, Tom Mould, and Pravina Shukla have highlighted the 'problematic notion that any alteration in the [traditional] object during or after the transfer amounts to tradition-breaking apostasy' (2011: 3). The authors go on to suggest that 'tradition is both a resource used by the individual and a process enacted by the individual' (ibid.: 4).[10] From this perspective, tradition can be viewed as a process by which contemporary individuals voluntarily acquire, modify and sustain an inherited pool of cultural resources. It is useful here to consider Henry Glassie's conception of an individual's use of tradition as volitional and temporal; the very action of an individual accessing an inherited resource means that they are formulating the future based on the past (1995: 409). Similarly, intergenerational transmission of tradition can be seen as filiation, which entails not only the passing on of values and beliefs, but also the reception that these values and beliefs receive in subsequent generations

(Shils 1971: 127). For filiation to function, the receivers must have a strong conviction in the veracity of the information that is being transmitted. Perhaps the reason Travelling communities have such a strong oral tradition is based on this very concept, that of strong and extended familial bonds, and a high esteem for their ancestors.

For example, the celebrated Traveller storyteller Duncan Williamson tells us of his ancestors: 'I can go back 250 year, to my mother's grandfather. I can tell you where he was born, I can show the spot where he was born, I know his date of birth' (TAD 65494). A more specific example of how filiation works in practice comes from what Braid refers to as an 'interpretive frame' (2002: 155). During a recording session, Duncan Williamson tells a story about a clever fox and an easily flattered crow. The fox, representative of Travellers, is weary of persecution and hungry. The Traveller-Fox comes across a crow, 'sitting up the tree, oh well out of reach, with this lump of cheese' (in Braid 1999: 306). The Traveller-Fox outwits the crow, appealing to its vanity to make it sing and drop the cheese from its beak, exclaiming, '"I'm the fly [clever] fox", he said, "I got your cheese"' (ibid.: 307). Braid sees this story as a metaphorical commentary on Traveller identity, the fox, and non-Traveller identity, the crow: 'the story emphasises the crucial importance', Braid reflects, 'of wit and creativity in Travellers' struggle to survive in an unfriendly world' (ibid.). The story then inspires his son Jimmy Williamson to sing a song. Jimmy's chorus is composed of the lines 'Daddy is a storyteller / Daddy is a singer of songs / and each one has a message / that he wants to pass along' (Braid 2002: 155). For Braid, these two performances function to create an interpretive frame between father and son; because Jimmy's memories of his father's story are meaningful to him, Braid concludes that 'Jimmy has invested creative energy in composing this song and has chosen to perform it for his father [. . .] thereby publicly acknowledging the meaning of this connection to his father' (ibid.: 155–156).

The inherently adaptable folk narrative becomes the ideal conduit through which individuals can voice the contents of their traditional inherited resources. Or, as Bronner so succinctly puts it, '[folklore] presents tradition as meaningful, purposeful activity that is an instrument of knowing and navigating through social life' (2012: 92). Even more precisely, David McKean proposes that Travellers use 'tradition to mediate their relationship with mainstream society' (2015: 208). Furthermore, folkloric expressions can be seen not only to reflect the contents of the resource, but to actively modify and contribute to it. This condition of constant flux and renewal may explain Hobsbawm's pejorative conception of 'invented' traditions (1983: 1), while simultaneously undermining the idea that tradition must be static. Lauri Honko captures this concept well, stating that 'tradition [. . .] would denote the cultural potential or resource, not the actual culture of the group' (1988: 10). The relationship between what is deemed 'traditional', and the above conceptualisation of folk narrative, is key; as Ben-Amos concludes, '*tradition* has survived criticism and remained a symbol of and for folklore' (1984: 124). As early as the 1890s, Hartland realised that variation and folk narrative are intrinsically linked. Like Masoni's dynamic folk narrative, Hartland acknowledges that 'involuntary changes are only such as are natural and unavoidable if the story is to continue its existence in the midst of the ever-shifting social organism of humanity' (1891: 21). This dynamism and how it operates in practice is useful to examine in more detail and to consider the roles of passive and active tradition-bearers.

For Richard Bauman, 'tradition [can be] conceived of as a superorganic temporal continuum; the folk are "tradition bearers", that is, they carry the folklore traditions on through time and space' (1971: 33). Cashman also perceives a profound link between the individual 'tradition-bearer' and tradition: 'we cannot appreciate either the individual or tradition without fully grasping their interdependence' (2011: 319). As an example of how the above conceptualisations of narrative and tradition can be applied in practice, a useful account has been published by John Niles. During his study of oral narrative, Niles spent time in Scotland conducting fieldwork with Travellers (1999: 173–193). He recognised that stories and songs have a significant importance to Travellers and that their uses have specific functions. That is not to say that these perceived functions are unique to Scotland's Travellers, only that these functions are specifically applicable to oral traditions, as opposed to narratives that are printed. Niles notes that 'these forms of expression make sense to them [Travellers] and communicate their values and beliefs' (ibid.: 165). In terms of the functions of oral narratives in Traveller communities, he sees instances of storytelling and song as focal points that serve as platforms for the verbal negotiation of these values and beliefs. These functions resonate well with conceptualisations of folk narrative in general. Storytelling and song for Travellers, says Niles, 'serve as parts of a general intellectual modelling system that helps the members of a group respond appropriately and wisely to the stress of unforeseen events' (ibid.: 171). These unforeseen events become the lived lives of the storytellers, but they can also be extended to wider social and economic changes that have influenced the inherited cultural resource over multiple generations.

The above discussions serve to frame the central contention of this book that traditional material is deliberately acquired, modified and then sustained as a collective resource. From this perspective, and to demonstrate Niles' insights more clearly, it is useful to consider the distinction he makes between active and passive tradition-bearers. A passive tradition-bearer can be described as a member of the community who is aware of certain oral traditions, can name individual stories and songs, but who does not actively change the material. The passive tradition-bearer will not generally perform to specifically organised groups of peers or strangers but may be able to recite elements of the material and will almost certainly be aware of the repertoire of active tradition-bearers. Niles does point out that there is no clear divide between the passive and the active tradition-bearer, although it is rare that the former will make a performance (ibid.: 177). The active tradition-bearer is the individual who does the deliberate acquisition and cultivation of the oral material; an extension to this activity comes in the form of the strong tradition-bearer.

Strong tradition-bearers, Niles explains, are 'unusually competent in their knowledge of a body of oral lore [and] have an exceptional desire for performance' (ibid.: 178). The idea of competence in oral lore is reminiscent of Franks' conception of narratological competence which was described above as an individual having access to collective cultural resources in the form of stories. The strong tradition-bearer is an individual who not only has access to this resource of stories, but also has the power to directly influence the content of the resource. To achieve this, Niles posits that the strong tradition-bearer would be in possession of five key traits: '(1) *engagement*, (2) *retentiveness*, (3) *acquisitiveness*, (4) a high degree of *critical consciousness*, and (5) [. . .] *showmanship*' (ibid.: 180, italics in original). As discussed above, an individual's volition in acquiring the raw materials that constitute an oral traditional resource is key. During the ongoing process of tradition-bearing, the strong tradition-bearer sustains the resource through their retentiveness and can modify the material through a critical engagement with it. This critical engagement with narratives could be viewed as the differentiating factor between the strong and the active tradition-bearer, although there are no definite lines in this hierarchical structure of tradition-bearers.

Folk narrative and variation are intrinsically linked, and Niles recognises that in oral performance, the 'deep structure is subject to surface variation that, over the course of time, can affect the deep structure itself, as societies adapt to pervasive changes in the social or natural environment' (ibid.: 121). The 'deep structure' in this context is the main theme of the story, or the 'tale-type'. A tale-type is a traditional narrative that can be understood independently of any other story (Thompson 1946:

415). Within these narratives exists specific incidents, characters or items known as motifs. These motifs can be used in combination and altered to change the complexion of the story. What Niles is suggesting is that over time, in response to social or environmental changes, these combinations and alterations can accumulate to change the very essence of the story, or its type. Tale-type taxonomy, as an exercise designed to enable cross-cultural comparisons, is contested within modern folkloristics. For Donald Hasse, tale-type taxonomies 'simultaneously make it simple to strip tales of their cultural specificity' and reduce them to 'universal types referred to by alphanumeric codes and brief descriptive labels' (2010: 27). Hasse sees the taxonomy of tale-types as an act of 'translation', where the cultural identity of individual narratives is removed (ibid.: 28). The result is that culturally specific 'variations' of tale-types become secondary considerations and the 'universal' type is essentially more significant (ibid.). Again, what such contestations promote is that variation is inherent in folk narrative, even at the structural level. In this sense, local variations should not be relegated to mere translations of more significant universal stories but understood as culturally specific expressions of cultural identity. Several examples of this culturally specific variation within Travellers' traditions are presented in forthcoming chapters.

The relevance of folk narrative as expression of identity is where the passive tradition-bearers come in. The narratives cannot exist in isolation or be the sole product of an individual. As we heard from Masoni above, folk narratives must be differentiated from static texts such as printed novels because they are rarely, if indeed ever, the work of one identifiable individual. Moreover – whilst discussing the Traveller storyteller Duncan Williamson – Niles observes that 'active tradition-bearers can only flourish as members of a community of like-minded individuals' (1999: 128). The like-minded individuals are the passive members of such communities, and the folk narratives function as nexuses 'of understandings that constitute their knowledge of the past and of the world around them, their social structure, and their moral action' (ibid.: 129). However, dissimilar to like-minded consumers of comic books or Nordic noir, here, the passive tradition-bearer can relate to the stories on an intellectual level *as well as* on the level of community cohesion. For example, Traveller Betsy Whyte has explained that 'Jack Tales' represent a morality lesson, teaching that 'if you kept yersel good, and being kind and nice a' the time as far as was possible, then in the end things will turn oot good fir ye' (TAD 82457).

Elsewhere, Stanley Robertson tells us that 'the men gave ye a very practical training wi' their story' (TAD 50189). While it is true that such lessons could be drawn from Superman's benevolence, or detailed accounts of Danish police procedures, the difference for our purposes lies in the communal nature of the expressions themselves. From both a didactic and practical perspective, active and passive tradition-bearers can condition worldviews; the former in articulating the material in the traditional resource through narrative performance, with the latter giving insights into what the story *does* in the community. A central concept of the forthcoming chapters is an understanding of how storytelling, ideology and tradition-bearers collaborate within storytelling landscapes to shape the cultural identity of the communities. We will also hear from strong tradition-bearers – such as Stanley Robertson and Duncan Williamson – who ventriloquise the cultural and ideological priorities of their communities.

Notes

1. For fuller discussion around the history and perceptions of Gypsies in the British Isles, see Judith Okely's 1983 *The Traveller-Gypsies* (Cambridge: Cambridge University Press) and Angus Bancroft's 2005 *Roma and Gypsy-Travellers in Europe* (Aldershot: Ashgate Publishing).
2. Further evidence of 'muggers' being used as an appellation for Travellers in Southern Scotland can be found in The Reverend Alexander Cuthbertson's TSAS account of Edrom, in Berwickshire (1845: 278).
3. It is important to note here that romanticised conceptualisations of the Travellers' lives in the past are often erroneous; an itinerant lifestyle came with its own complications and hardships, not least because of the Travellers' subaltern status in society and their preference to participate in more informal economies (see Okely 1983: 54–55, and Niles 2022: 19–20).
4. The translations of 'tincler' and 'burges' are from *The Dictionary of the Scots Language* http://www.dsl.ac.uk/
5. Further evidence of persistent misunderstandings can be found in Davie Donaldson's useful online resource, 'Gypsy/Traveller Intersectionality: Strengthening the Role of Social Work' (2021) https://content.iriss.org.uk/gypsy-traveller-intersectionality/index.html [accessed 18 March 2024].
6. Further evidence of social and economic engagement during the twentieth century, from the perspective of the settled population, can be found in the SSS Archives: Adam Lamb TAD 3135; Agnes MacKenzie TAD 51886; Annie Forbes TAD 24874; Hector Kennedy TAD 50181. Unlike the feared and despised individuals that populate TSAS, these perceptions of Travellers from the settled population reveal a more understanding and respectful relationship.
7. Alas, at the time of writing in June 2024, the MWGGT is no longer active. Engagement with the communities is now conducted under the auspices of the Scottish Government's Equality, Inclusion and Human Rights Directorate.

8. The concept of tradition as a resource is by no means unique to the Travellers' traditions, oral narrative or to folklore more generally. For instance, David Lowenthal's *The Past is a Foreign Country* (1985) offers both detailed and eclectic instances of the confrontation between imitation and innovation when it comes to our cultural expressions. See Lowenthal's chapters 'Benefits and Burdens of the Past' and 'Ancients vs. Moderns'.
9. A useful example of what this means in practice can be found in the storytelling traditions of the Hezhen Yimakan in the Heilongjiang Province of north-eastern China. See UNESCO's 2011 *List of Intangible Cultural Heritage in Need of Urgent Safeguarding* (2011: 6.COM 8.6).
10. Henry Glassie gives an analogous definition of tradition at the collective level of culture; 'As resource and process, as wish for stability, progress, or revitalisation, tradition – or something like it with another name – is the inbuilt motive force of culture' (1995: 409).

2

How do Stories Mean?

THE 'ORAL TEXT' – CRITICISM AND INTERPRETATION

Because analysis and interpretation are key components of this book, it is crucial that the primary source material be made as transparent and accessible as possible. To achieve this, this study approaches oral storytelling in the same way that a literary critic would approach printed literature. Niles advocates this approach, citing the 'often irrelevant oppositions of orality versus literacy' (1999: 200) when trying to understand the narrative expressions of any given culture or society. By dissolving differentiations between oral and printed media, oral narratives become open to the same formal textual analysis that amounts to close readings of any given 'text'. These close readings are then used in tandem with contextual factors – such as the cultural identity of the narrator, and/or any metanarrative provided by them – to infer meanings from the narrative. Additionally, close readings can be augmented through the consideration of other contextual factors. These include, but are not limited to: intertextuality, both with printed literature and other recognised narratives, such as *Märchen* [fairy tales] and international tales; local legends; biographical and autobiographical details; and historical incidents that are woven into the narrative and are verifiable by independent corroborative evidence.

This critical approach to oral narrative has been effectively summarised by Richard Bauman, who is:

> Centrally concerned with understanding oral literature *as* literature, that is, as verbal art. This enterprise sets itself against some old and deeply entrenched concepts of the nature and qualities of oral literature. These notions, strongly colored by ethnocentric and elitist biases that privilege the classics of Western written literature over oral and vernacular literature and by nineteenth-century conceptions of "folk" society, have established an image of oral literature as

simple, formless, lacking in artistic quality and complexity, the collective expression of unsophisticated peasants and primitives constrained by tradition and the weight of social norms against individual creativity of expression.

(1986: 7)

The present study concurs with Bauman and rejects these old and deeply entrenched concepts, viewing oral narratives as sophisticated artistic expressions. The storytelling traditions at the heart of this book are thereby opened for analysis and interpretation as art forms. As opposed to a dismissive and somewhat pejorative conceptualisation of oral narratives as the products of an unimaginative subaltern class, oral narrative is viewed as a window onto the creative core of its narrators. More importantly, oral narrative is not limited to 'poetic' or 'epic' narrative alone; other forms of oral narrative are also viewed as being steeped in meaning and produced artfully. In terms of 'vernacular literature' – and more particularly 'the weight of social norms' allegedly restricting the narrator's creativity – Bauman anticipates the extension of 'verbal art' to more quotidian oral narratives. Oral narratives created and communicated in the vernacular abound in the SSS Archives, some of which are considered in detail in forthcoming chapters. Furthermore, the narrators' social awareness is often a central theme and should not be viewed as detrimental to creative expression. On the contrary, social awareness is often at the very core of the creative impulse and gives rise to the narrative expressions themselves.

As an early example of the kind of stories we are discussing here, Traveller Duncan Williamson tells a story about a group of 'old Tinker [Traveller] folk' (TAD 36850) who are turned away from a hotel by its owner, as he finds them 'filthy, dirty folk [who] bring disgrace here to me' (ibid.). An American tourist, who is staying at the hotel, witnesses the refusal and pleads with the hotelier that the Travellers are 'still human beings' (ibid.). As demonstrated in the previous chapter using the evidence in TSAS – where Travellers were often regarded as parasitical – this type of social exclusion based on preconceptions around cleanliness has been affecting Travellers' lives for centuries. Williamson's story, recorded in 1976, is not only an example of his social awareness as a Traveller, but is also an indication that negative attitudes towards Travellers have persisted since TSAS were published in the 1790s and 1845. The abhorrent opinions of one contributor to *The Scotsman* as late as 1958 beggar belief: 'The generally accepted belief is that the tinkers are an immigrant race representing a stage of human development different from that current in the society into which they intruded', accuses Robin S. Crearie, 'it will take one or two generations to eradicate what is a sore problem in

Scotland' ('Integration of the Tinker in Society' 1958: 12). In contemporary Scotland, Sarah Cemlyn and Colin Clark suggest that negative attitudes can stem from service providers, and sometimes the general public, viewing Travellers as social 'drop-outs' that actively renounce the norms of a sedentary lifestyle (2005: 148). The negatively charged ideological 'otherness' of Travellers from the perspective of the settled population, that we have witnessed from the outset of this book, presents itself once more. Moreover, the theme of social exclusion is prevalent in the stories we hear from Travellers. This shows not only that Travellers are acutely aware of their social exclusion, but that its implications are manifested and negotiated within their narratives. At the conclusion of Williamson's story featuring the American tourist, the Travellers who were turned away from the hotel ultimately win the day. The American tourist pays £5000 to rent every room in the hotel, then travels around the country 'and every old Tinker he sees [. . .] he tells them, "come to my hotel", he says, "and enjoy yersel"' (TAD 36850).

Of course, when multitudes of Travellers begin to arrive at the hotel, the owner is incensed and offers the American £10,000 to 'get rid' of the Travellers. The American accepts the money, then he 'went round every old Tinker that was in the place, and give them a good pay, he give them a good feast and a good drink, now he says "on yer way"' (ibid.). Williamson's story negotiates the lived experience of the social exclusion of Travellers using an ordinary social setting that results in an extraordinary outcome. The Travellers' being refused a basic service based on their ethnicity is ridiculed along with the prejudices of the hotel owner. Instead of profiting from the Travellers' business as guests at his hotel, the hotelier is, ironically, punished financially for his ignorance and racism. The protagonist of Williamson's story is the American, with his antagonist appearing in the form of the hotelier. The characterisations in Williamson's narrative represent a dichotomy, a common feature of oral narrative which Axel Olrik describes as 'The Law of Contrast' (1992: 50). The essence of Olrik's law of contrast is that oral narratives such as Williamson's can personify the distinction between perceptions of 'good and evil'. In this sense, the American represents an *ideal*, an embodiment of the values and rectitude that stand in opposition to the ignorance and prejudice of the antagonistic hotelier. Moreover, the humanitarian values of the American that intimate the narrative are ultimately aligned with that of the Travellers when they share in the spoils of the exploit by feasting and drinking. Once the story is over, Williamson is asked if the story is true, and he replies, 'that's supposed to be true aye [. . .] that happened many, many many years ago' (TAD 36850). The veracity of the events in the story are irrelevant because the truth of the narrative is self-evident. Through this hyperbolic narrative, we are furnished with Williamson's view of a world where virtue and empathy are rewarded, and where ignorance and inhumanity are punished. For our purposes, the status of everyday storytelling – such as the example from Williamson discussed above – is being elevated to allow its narratives to be analysed and interpreted.

The suggestion here is not that performances of more elaborate Gaelic romances or hero tales – such as Duncan MacDonald's 'The Man of the Habit' (see Lamb 2012) – are on an equal footing with the everyday stories being told at familial and social gatherings. What is being suggested is that both the quotidian and the 'poetic' forms of oral narrative confer meaning, only in different ways. Lexical analysis of examples of traditional Gaelic narratives compares orally collected versions of the same story, 'The Man of the Habit', also known as 'The Man in the Cassock' (TMC). William Lamb's analysis involves the 'statistical measure of lexical consistency', to address 'questions of variation and authorship in traditional Gaelic narrative' (2012: 112). His points open up the possibility of using similar quantitative techniques to enhance our understandings of the linguistic relationships between oral and manuscript versions of Gaelic romances (ibid.). On the other hand, an alternative analysis of the same story might focus on thematic elements such as the nature of the protagonist, with his ambiguous Gaelic epithet of *Feamanach Fabhsach* [Guileful Tailed One].[1] Alan Bruford and Donald MacDonald offer a different translation of *Feamanach Fabhsach*, suggesting that the protagonist's name means '"false hypocrite", because he is not all he seems' (2003: 454). Given the title of the narrative – a 'habit' being a clerical uniform – both translations give the protagonist a duplicitous and nefarious aspect. In any case, Bruford and MacDonald assert that the protagonist in TMC must be a supernatural character, noting that the narrative represents a visit to the otherworld (ibid.: 435–454). Under these circumstances, favouring a qualitative approach to the narrative, the nature of the protagonist seems to be a central theme.

While discussing Gaelic romances – of which TMC is one – Bruford tells us that 'clerics do occasionally appear', and that they are 'rather sinister characters, enchanters [. . .] or supernatural beings in disguise' (1969: 25–26). Bruford goes on to suggest that the Irish pagan deity Manannán is the most likely candidate for the supernatural being in the case of TMC (ibid.: 26). In Gaelic romances and folktales, Manannán often appears as a peasant-like character, and one who often misunderstands accepted courtly behaviour. This is certainly true in Duncan MacDonald's version of TMC. When we are introduced to the eponymous man in the cassock, he is collecting firewood in the forest and implores Murchadh mac Brian not to 'think ill of me because I'm going to carry this load, for it would have been easy enough for me to have got man after man and woman after woman to come here to fetch this bundle' (MacDonald 2003: 154). Despite the menial task being performed, the man implies that he has many servants at his beck and call. Again, ambivalence seems to be a defining feature of the man in the cassock. Moreover, the man's uncourtly behaviour is evident when he makes a series of *faux pas*; firstly, by entering his castle side by side with Murchadh, then by offering Murchadh the inferior chair in his court, and finally by refusing to drink from the vessel offered to him by Murchadh (Bruford 1969: 139). On one hand, MacDonald's protagonist is a powerful hero who rescues his damsel in distress, through 'trials such as no one of my people ever suffered before' (MacDonald 2003: 157). On the other, he is a lonely sorcerer who compels Murchadh to 'keep [him] in conversation' (ibid.: 155), before luring Murchadh to his castle to spin a blarney in-tale about his heroic exploits. From this perspective, the protagonist of TMC is everything Murchadh is not and Olrik's law of contrast is at work. His clerical garb, churlishness and tall tale conspire to represent an ambivalent relationship with Christianity, and an affront to Murchadh's heroic career. The point here is that meaningful critical analyses can be performed on any given narrative, whether it be a complex Gaelic romance, or a narrativised quotidian experience. The difference being that Lamb's purpose of uncovering variation and authorship diverges from the purpose of the present study, which, as we will see, reveals what the narratives stand for.

An instructive approach to the interpretation of oral texts has been outlined by Bengt Holbek during his study the *Interpretation of Fairy Tales* (1987). Although Holbek's study is primarily focused on fairy tales, he offers a robust theoretical framework in which we can view items of folklore, as oral texts, in general. The dilemma that confronts Holbek from the outset is 'what do these tales *mean*?' (1987: 17). As expressed in the introduction to this chapter, we too are primarily concerned with what Travellers' stories mean. Holbek's theoretical approach, his ideas and methods, can therefore be critically appropriated in the context of Travellers' storytelling. Following Morris Weitz's (1966) survey of literary criticism on Shakespeare's *Hamlet*, Holbek proposes a theoretical framework divided into three categories: description, explanation and evaluation (1987: 188–189). In the first category, description, the critical aim is to present to the reader with verifiable facts and data. For the present study, these descriptions will consist of combinations of such facts and data.

For instance, who the narrator is, including elements of their upbringing, their kin, their religious views, their working life and so on. Additionally, these descriptions will include details that are intrinsic to the narratives themselves: the names of the protagonists/antagonists; the sequence of the events being narrated; the actions of the characters; any specific objects, locations or events; and any metanarrative framing that the narrator may include. Descriptions of narratives are useful in and of themselves, especially to researchers involved in comparative exercises. It is also important that the description of the narratives is as accurate as possible. This description also extends to an identification of the narrative where possible. 'Identification' here refers to cross-examining the narrative under scrutiny with other known tale-types; subsequent chapters demonstrate this technique in practice while remaining cognisant of Dundes' warning that 'naive analyses can result from inadequate or inaccurate identification' (2007b: 70). However, as Holbek goes on to assert, 'no amount of description can eliminate the need for interpretation' (1987: 190).

The second category, explanation, is therefore the key concept. For Holbek, 'explanation is concerned with meaning. The interpreter aims at true clarification, at a hypothesis describing *what* observable facts signify, *how* they relate to each other and *why* they have been put together as they have' (ibid.: 189). With this concise description of the 'explanation' category, Holbek gets to the very kernel of the act of interpretation. The central aim is to hypothesise on the meaning of Travellers' narratives based on their context – both in terms of Travellers as minority communities, and the wider socio-political and cultural context – and then to validate these hypotheses using evidence drawn from the narratives. Of course, explanation under these conditions is problematic, most notably so because of the glaring element of the subjectivity of the interpreter. However, Holbek anticipates the element of the subjectivity of the interpreter, noting that 'the best one may hope for is a more or less adequate interpretation of some of the describable data', and he then goes on to state that during our interpretations we must aim for an 'explanation that does not contradict known facts but accounts for as many of them as possible in a manner that can be shown to possess a high degree of plausibility' (ibid.). The describable data, from this perspective, would be the details that are intrinsic to the narratives, as noted above. In terms of contradiction and accounting for known facts, the interpretations offered are based on contextualisation, also as noted above. In this way, through the combination of description and explanation, interpretations of the Travellers' narratives will be germane, and possess the plausibility advocated by Holbek. Ultimately, the *meaning* of the Travellers' narratives will be elucidated as the corollary of the application of the above-described method.

The final category, evaluation, is outwith the remit of this book because evaluation, in the present context, amounts to value judgements. It is not the intention here to create a canon of Traveller narratives based on subjective value judgements, but to approach the diverse modes of narrative on an equal footing. Extant themes from our primary source material include conflict, family, storytelling itself, food, religion, marriage, lifestyle, and the supernatural. Several of these themes will be explored in forthcoming chapters, with the individual narratives being considered in detail. Additionally, Holbek suggests that in deploying this method involving description and explanation, we must be able to test it, ideally in the field (ibid.: 190). To this end, this study draws upon narratives and insights from contemporary members of Scotland's Traveller and Nawken/Nacken communities who have kindly contributed to the production of this study.[2]

FUNCTIONS AND MEANINGS IN FOLKLORE

In terms of the ideological interest of the present study, the term 'folk narrative' and its connotations are pertinent. The social status of the storytellers and their communities is significant because their status directly affects the stories that they share. Before elucidating what is meant by folk narrative, it is useful to consider the individuals and communities that make up the 'folk', and how the 'lore' of the folk comes to be represented in their narratives. What constituted notions of 'the folk' during the nineteenth century can be neatly summarised with a quotation; for Andrew Lang, the folk consist 'of the people, of the classes which have been least altered by education, which have shared least in progress' (1885: 11; cf. Dundes 1980: 3). Essentially, European intellectuals such as Lang were referring to the 'peasantry' – individuals and communities who were deemed 'uncivilised' on account of their lack of exposure to formal scholastic education. The folk were conceived of in terms of binaries such as rural/urban, illiterate/literate and pre-modern/modern. The point is that 'the folk' were not considered as independent, autonomous social groups. For the ethnocentric European intellectuals of the nineteenth century, the folk had to exist in opposition to the dominant socio-cultural class. The folk, therefore, represented the opposite of civilised society, and conversely embodied traits that were considered vestigial to the 'modern', civilised, educated world.[3]

In the modern sense of the term, Dundes defines the folk as any group of individuals that share a common factor, with common factors ranging from occupation to religious or spiritual beliefs (1980: 6-7). Additionally, the folk in the group will share specific traditions, customs and beliefs – 'cultural markers' – that are linked to their sense of identity and their ideological makeup. As we heard from Clark above, Travellers in Scotland have 'developed a clear sense of [their] distinct social and cultural identity' (2006: 16) and this distinctiveness aligns Traveller communities with Dundes' definition of a 'folk group'. Despite the ethnocentric nature of what constitutes 'the folk' discussed above, it is useful to consider what is *not* folk-related as we formulate our definition. The way that cultural markers are transmitted becomes a key characteristic in our understanding of what constitutes the compound and oft-used term 'folklore'. Issues around the uses of tradition are addressed in detail below, where we find that folklore is what gives form to tradition (Bronner 1998: 480). Moreover, the cultural practices that the nineteenth century intelligentsia viewed as remnants of the past will be reconceptualised as functioning resources that are characterised by creativity and adaptation (Bronner 2017: 11).

The compound term 'folklore' itself was first introduced by William Thoms in his famous letter to *The Athenaeum* in 1846; Thoms urged the editor of *The Athenaeum* to encourage its readers to gather the 'manners, customs, observances, superstitions, ballads, proverbs etc. [. . .] which are scattered over the memories of its thousands of readers, and preserve them in its pages' (1846: 863). For Thoms, then, 'the lore of the folk' includes a wide variety of expressions that today are collectively referred to as 'intangible cultural heritage' (ICH). Although the focus of the present book is ICH, the subject area of folklore is broader than just the intangible elements of our cultural expressions. Games, dances, 'solo folklore' and folk drama can also be studied under the folkloric lens (for examples, see Mechling 2006, Dundes 2007a: 55, 156; Martin 2013: 616). Sadly, there is an air of desperation in Thoms' original letter when he talks of 'how much [folklore] may yet be rescued by timely exertion' (1846: 863). This anxiety around the preservation of ICH was still being experienced by Hamish Henderson a hundred years later when he championed the 'urgent work of recording, preserving and safeguarding the native traditions of the people' (2004: 46). However, Thoms' letter highlights a crucial element of folklore (or ICH) that resists the need for a 'rescue ethnology' approach, particularly considering the issues being addressed here.

Referring to Jacob Grimm's *Deutsche Mythologie* first published in 1835, Thoms observes that Grimm's work amounts to 'a mass of minute facts, many of which, when separately considered, appear trifling and insignificant' (1846: 863). Crucially, though, Thoms realises that 'when taken in connexion with the system into which his [Grimm's] mastermind has woven them, [they] assume a value that he who first recorded them never dreamed of attributing to them' (ibid.). Aligning with the English anthropologist Edward Tylor's observation that 'in anthropology nothing is insignificant' (1881: 265), Thoms recognises that seemingly inconsequential folkloric utterances can be immensely valuable if given the correct treatment. The correct treatment is to examine the items of folklore that interest us with as much contextualisation as possible and to make our observations and interpretations from there. As Joseph Jacobs realised as early as the 1890s, 'survivals are folklore, but folklore need not be all survivals' (1893: 237). Jacobs' point is that folklore is an ongoing process of retention and invention, a key component of our discussions throughout this book. Specifically, it is argued that items of folklore are not to be viewed as calcified objects being dumbly handed down through generations. Instead, such expressions are living, malleable artefacts that are constantly adapting in negotiation with cultural change. In the forthcoming analytical chapters below, examples of how this adaptation manifests within the Travellers' storytelling traditions are presented to the reader, investing the stories with meanings that reflect the social location of the tellers. Jacobs' early conceptualisations of folk traditions being an ongoing process have percolated through the centuries and continue to underpin contemporary ethnological scholarship. Moreover, as Neill Martin has pointed out, 'the extra information imparted by observation is classically ethnological; we want to collect and understand not just the surface form, but the impulse which generates it', and most importantly for our purposes here, 'the *context in which it is performed and used*, and how it fits into the wider tradition of comparable forms' (2013: 624, my italics).

Before moving on to consider examples of how this theory works in practice, it is worth thinking about how items of folklore – such as oral narratives – function when they circulate in society. William Bascom's important essay, 'Four Functions of Folklore' (1954), provides a solid platform on which to begin. In his essay, Bascom is concerned with the social and cultural context of folklore, and how these elements are connected to its function. Although Bascom's discussion centres on the folklore of non-literate societies, his essay provides insights that are useful to the study of folklore in general. This is primarily because Bascom frames his discussion with a quote from Irving Hallowell – discussing oral narrative and its recording by anthropologists, Hallowell suggests that, historically, there has been a 'failure to exploit fully the potentialities of such data' (1947: 544). Hallowell argues that this failure stems from anthropologists, and scholars from other disciplines, viewing oral narratives as a literary-historical problem (ibid.: 545). That is, when oral narratives are viewed as 'historical texts', the central concern had been to discover what they reveal about the (historic) environment from which they came. This is undoubtedly a worthwhile scholarly enterprise, except that the literary-historical method neglects the relationship between culture and oral narratives as items of folklore. Put another way, the literary-historical method can neglect viewing items of folklore as reflexive expressions of the contemporary culture in which they are expressed. And this is the issue that Bascom addresses when he considers the social and cultural context of folklore. Bascom is ultimately interested in discovering what role folklore plays in the daily lives of the individuals who use it (1954: 334).

A dilemma recognised in recent folkloristic scholarship between folklore and tradition arises at this point. Bronner suggests that 'tradition in folkloristics is revealed as both continuous and changing, obvious and elusive, and therefore in need of explanation' (2012: 92). To begin to formulate such an explanation in the Scottish context, it is worthwhile considering the relationships between the cultural expressions we know as folklore, and the complex nature of the traditions that condition these expressions. And, specifically, to focus on the unique relationships that Scotland's Travellers have with their shared history, and how these relationships manifest themselves in their storytelling traditions. In terms of narrative traditions, tracking the development of Traveller communities as distinct social groups is most productively limited to the relatively recent past – the past 150 years or so – as identifying stories as conclusively 'Traveller' before 1860 would be problematic. This is because at the time of writing, the author is not aware of any stories, in print or in manuscript, that are explicitly attributed to a Traveller storyteller prior to 1860. This period, though, provides useful insights into Travellers' lived experiences by showing how the nature and content of narratives reflects the socio-political landscape in Scotland. As we have already seen, socio-political trends and anxieties can manifest themselves in Travellers' anecdotes and stories. And, as Shari Stone-Mediatore puts it, although 'not a replacement for theory or empirical data, stories have an irreplaceable function of their own insofar as they sensitise us to yet untheorised human and historical significances of political phenomena' (2003: 67). By viewing stories in this way, it is possible to access the wealth of information that they represent. This material is then utilised within a critical framework to deliver insights into the communities where the stories are being told.

For our purposes, and returning to Bascom's functions of folklore, Bascom's focus on the social aspect of folklore echoes the applications of socio-narratology that were introduced in Chapter 1. The reader will recall Frank's suggestion that 'stories and humans work together, in symbiotic dependency, *creating the social*' (2010: 15). Both Bascom and Frank are concerned with what folklore *does* in societies and communities and the present study is also concerned with how Travellers' folk narratives function during transmission from one generation to the next. Moreover, the examinations of the stories focus on both the social context and the cultural context of the narratives. The social aspect of Travellers' lives is crucial in terms of their relationships with the settled or mainstream population, and how these relationships are negotiated through narrative. As to the cultural aspect, focus is being directed more specifically on how Travellers' folk narratives condition and then represent their worldviews *as Travellers*. In terms of function, Bascom concludes that folklore 'operates within a society to insure [sic] conformity to the accepted cultural norms, and continuity from generation to generation' (1954: 348–349). This much is true, but Traveller narratives also embody a fusion of the social and the cultural to form complex expressions of distinctive identities. This complexity is anticipated by Bascom when he highlights 'the basic paradox of folklore' (ibid.: 349), suggesting that while folklore can function to maintain the stability of a culture, it can also function as a socially sanctioned outlet that questions imposed societal conventions.

Intimated throughout these opening chapters is the notion that Traveller narratives are infused with a shared set of values and beliefs. In the present context, these values and beliefs have been collectively described as a distinctive Traveller worldview. As was noted above, the collective term 'worldview' represents the 'subjective interpretations of perceived and experienced reality of individuals' (Dégh 1995: 132). Again, it is important to stress here that Travellers' worldviews are by no means homogeneous, and the aim is not to describe a 'unified field' of Traveller worldview or to engage in a *comprehensive* overview of Traveller storytelling. Broadly, the Travellers' storytelling traditions share characteristics with wider European traditions, including Irish and Scandinavian cultural spheres. We find many examples of international tales from the Aarne-Thompson-Uther (ATU) index. An international tale is a story with a theme, specific and identifiable events and/or characters (motifs), and recognisable overall structures that appear in a wide variety of cultural contexts across the globe. The overall structures, or 'tale-types', of international folktales were classified by Antti Aarne in 1911, then augmented later by Stith Thompson in 1955 and again in 1981. More recently, the overall structures were updated by Hans-Jörg Uther in his 2004 work *The Types of International Folktales: A Classification and Bibliography*. In terms of our purposes in this book, this type of identification and classification, or taxonomy, is eminently useful because it allows us to compare similar narratives that are found in a wide range of cultural contexts and socio-political settings.

ATU 591 – *The Thieving Pot* (Thompson 1946: 185; Uther 2004 Vol. I: 348), for instance, is examined and, elsewhere in the corpus collated for this book but not examined, are versions of ATU 470 (TAD 65859), ATU 403 (TAD 65438), ATU 910B (TAD 31634) and ATU 331 (TAD 67502). What this book does is take a close look at the types of narratives that negotiate themes specific to the Scottish Traveller context. For example, the Burker tales examined below are singularly Traveller, and the narratives involving 'folk onomastics' are similarly culturally specific to Travellers' traditions. Although the stories under examination are shown to share themes and characteristics with narratives found in a variety of other storytelling contexts, our interest here is in the stories that set the Traveller traditions apart. The novelty of the methodological approach being deployed means that detailed analyses are based on a relatively small number of narratives that showcase the uniqueness of the traditions from which they come.

A further important and related point to make during the explanation of the critical underpinnings is that the Travellers' storytelling traditions share characteristics with non-Traveller narrative traditions. One of the most extant examples that the forthcoming analyses demonstrate is an empathetic attitude to the natural environment. That is not to suggest that such laudable attitudes to our natural world are exclusive to the Traveller storytelling communities. The relationships with international tale-types cited above are evidence of common themes shared by a multitude of oral storytelling communities. Thompson recognises this commonality when he stresses that 'there is an unmistakable historical connection among the traditional narratives of all the peoples extending from Ireland to India [and] an obvious common store of narrative motifs and even of formal elements' (1946: 14). It is no surprise, then, to find motifs and environmental concerns, that are common among international tale-types, within Traveller storytelling traditions. When it comes to an affinity with the natural environment, Ní Fhloinn recognises one such instance when she points out that Irish seal-traditions 'reflect an infinitely more refined and sophisticated understanding of the delicate balance which exists between mankind and the natural environment' (1999: 241). Again, the present study is aware of commonalities within the context of separate storytelling traditions and my purpose is to elicit the culturally specific examples found within the Travellers' traditions. Examples of the interconnectedness with other storytelling traditions is provided throughout our discussions.

Beforehand, a strong Traveller tradition-bearer, Stanley Robertson, who features heavily in forthcoming chapters, gives a concise summation of cultural specificity. After telling a story he calls 'The Traveller's Parchment', Robertson explains that 'no two Travellers would tell that tale the same way twice [. . .] it builds to your creative imagination' (TAD 38319). The key points to note here are that that tale is culturally specific, it is a *Traveller's* parchment, and the narrative is open to invention, given that the basic structure is in place. The 'basic structure' can be considered here as the tale-type, with the specificity embodied by the nature of the protagonist. On the same note, and following Dégh's notion of individuality (1995: 132), each narrative is viewed as an individualised expression of worldview that is informed by a shared sense of cultural identity. What this means in practice is that we find common themes and assumptions, or worldviews, embodied within Travellers' narratives. To clarify the relationship between worldview and cultural identity further, Dundes' conception of 'folk ideas' (2007a: 185) is useful. For Dundes, folk ideas are 'traditional notions that a group of people have about the nature of humanity, of the world, and of life in the world [. . .] the building blocks of worldview' (ibid.). The 'group' is a discrete element in this formulation, with each group having sets of folk ideas. Folk ideas are understood as products of their social, political and economic environments. Dundes goes on to explain that 'worldview will be based upon many individual folk ideas' (ibid.), and this is the crucial point because the combination of a group's environment interacting with multiple folk ideas produces unique and discrete worldviews.

We have been thinking about how narrative expressions are being conceptualised as manifestations of shared assumptions and worldviews, and how the Travellers' narrative traditions represent a unique example of such manifestations. The reader will recall that 'tradition' is being defined here as a process by which contemporary narrators voluntarily acquire, modify and sustain an inherited pool of cultural resources, or Dundes' 'folk ideas'. More significantly, this narrative tradition is infused with a culturally significant aesthetic that underpins the impetus of the present study. Expressions of a shared cultural identity are revealed within the content of the Travellers' narratives, and the narrators' accessing and expressing their inherited cultural resource is the process of tradition. Another function of the narratives, then, is to house these shared cultural identities and worldviews, allowing them to be accessible to future generations. Again, for the purposes of this book, it is argued that the Travellers' narratives function as ciphers, and its purpose here is to decode the narratives and offer plausible interpretations of their meanings. As Betsy Whyte explains, 'all of the stories had some special meaning [. . .] *if you pay attention*' (TAD 82457). R.M Dawkins also addresses the meaning of folklore, proposing that ostensibly simple stories can be the carriers of complex allegorical or symbolic meanings that negotiate human nature and experience (1951: 418). More recently, Bronner asks 'what does folklore connote?' (2017: 83). Bronner promotes the concept that folklore can be analysed from many different perspectives – such as historic-geographic, functionalist, psychoanalytic, feminist – and that the analysts of folklore collaborate with practitioners to construe the 'meanings, connotations, and consequences of traditional knowledge' (ibid.: 142). The observable characteristics of stories – both their manifest and latent meanings within specific cultural contexts – are therefore the central focus of our discussions here.

Discussing the issue of 'whose meaning?' when interpreting folklore, Holbek refers to groups of 'interested parties' (1987: 191). It is not necessary to recreate Holbek's list of said parties here, however two of these parties are relevant to the search for meaning within stories. The first of these parties is the interpreter, the critical approach to which has been described above. Secondly, when it comes to the narrators themselves, Holbek suggests that narrators of folklore have deliberately 'remembered the [. . .] tales and carried them on to new generations because *they themselves* appreciated them', and that the tales 'meant something to the narrators [. . .] regardless of what they had meant to narrators in the distant past' (ibid.: 192). This view is also held by Dawkins: 'that a story should have lived for certainly centuries and been found valuable and interesting', says Dawkins, 'does suggest that it must in some way be more than a mere stringing together of the fantastic and incredible' (1951: 419). This book takes the position that this sort of appreciation – or more accurately *understanding* – of stories applies to the interpreter of the narratives, and that a lack of direct experience of a thing does not necessarily deny its meaning.

The key differentiator is the analyst being cognisant of the cultural context of the story under analysis. The analyst evaluates 'the ideological as well as teleological implications of *their position* in relation to the material or people being studied' (Bronner 2017: 142, my italics). Consequentially, the forthcoming analyses deliver interpretations of the stories that are mindful of the many perspectives from which we can view folkloristic expressions. The process of contemporary narrators acquiring, modifying and sustaining inherited cultural resources, or stories, discussed above is a key consideration as this discussion progresses. Holbek goes on to provide a useful analogy for this transmission in the form of a contemporary craftsperson: although their tools and procedures may be of considerable age, our narrators' knowledge and skills are contemporary (1987: 191). This view is consistent with the description of tradition-bearers and their differing roles that we encountered in Chapter 1. We saw how passive, active and strong tradition-bearers all contribute to the survival of the Travellers' narrative traditions. Moreover, expanding upon Holbek's analogy, the active and strong tradition-bearers become the verbal craftspeople of their generation, learning the stories and applying their own unique knowledge and experience to them.

TRAVELLER STORYTELLING – THEORY IN ACTION

The type of analyses that this study undertakes are not unprecedented. There are two significant previous studies, by authors writing around the turn of the twenty first century, who have been introduced in the preceding chapters; John Niles and Donald Braid, whose works set a benchmark for the present study. It is therefore both necessary and useful to consider in some detail Braid's *Scottish Traveller Tales: Lives Shaped through Stories* (2002) and Niles' *Homo Narrans: The Poetics and Anthropology of Oral Literature* (1999) to establish our research context. Braid's study sets out to explore the complex relationships between Travellers and the stories that they share. His overarching hypothesis is that the Travellers use their stories for entertainment, as vehicles for education, as reminders of who they are and as a way of comprehending their experiences in the world more generally (2002: 37). Braid is not the first author to make this point about the storytelling traditions of Scotland's Traveller communities. Niles makes an equivalent summation when he reflects on the function of the traditions; for Niles, the Travellers' 'lore is an expression of their reality. The oral narratives of the travellers [sic] provide sauce for their life, true. They also yield spiritual nourishment' (1999: 172). Braid goes further than this, suggesting that 'Travellers use stories as a way of responding to the social, political, and historical issues that affect their lives' (2002: 46). These various functions of storytelling could be said to be true of practically any ordered narrative in any given social context. However, like the impetus of the present study, Braid recognises that Scotland's Travellers have a set of unique identities that are based on their distinctive worldviews.

For instance, Braid sees 'the premium Travellers place on freedom and autonomy, and the choice they make for family over economic success' (ibid.: 105) as expressions of Traveller worldview. It is important to note here that Braid conceptualises worldviews in terms of similarities and differences. The Travellers' veneration of personal freedom can be viewed as opposed to members of the settled or mainstream population whose worldview is perhaps more attuned to the accumulation of wealth and property. Moreover, Braid's arguments rest on the assertion that Traveller storytelling represents a creative process that summons and adapts traditional resources to create meaning (ibid.: 107). At the same time, Braid informs us that Traveller storytellers engage with international tale-types, transforming well-known stories to 'embody Traveller identity, worldview, and style [. . .] giving listeners an experience of the coherency of their own identity and worldview' (ibid.: 148). As demonstrated in Chapter 1 when discussing the roles of tradition-bearers, this study adopts the complementary premise that traditional material is deliberately acquired, modified and then sustained as a collective resource. Preceding Braid, it is worth quoting Niles at length when he articulates this point precisely:

> Songs and stories are not just handed down, like heirlooms, from one generation to the next. If a singing or storytelling tradition exists, then it is re-creative at every stage. [. . .] This process of re-creation will continue so long as the world presented in the narratives and the worldview of singers and storytellers coincide, if not in literal detail then through an algebraic set of equivalencies that is implicitly understood. As long as this happens, successive generations of people will learn a body of traditional narratives, will remake them, and will find in them a system of belief and perception by which they can live in the midst of a changing world.
>
> (1999: 172)

Building on the insights of Niles and Braid, the present book offers new evidence regarding the transmission and filiation of the Travellers' stories. The overarching purpose is to utilise previously unexplored evidence to demonstrate *how* these stories function to condition and then represent the Travellers' distinctive cultural identities.

Based on these two already established premises – that the Travellers possess distinctive worldviews and identities, and that their stories are carriers of these worldviews and identities – Braid's monograph considers the Travellers' stories within the context of the storytellers' lives, and vice versa, hence Braid's subtitle. As a demonstration of what happens when we begin to apply these theoretical positions to the stories themselves,

Braid's study offers several useful examples. One such is Duncan Williamson's performance of 'The Traveller and the Hare'. This short story tells of a 'local Travelling man [who] had never married, and he didn't have any family' (cited in Braid 2002: 110–111) and who one day decides that he has had enough of the Travelling lifestyle. After spotting a hare feeding in a field, the Traveller hatches a plan to seek his fortune in pig farming, starting with the capture and sale of the hare. In his excitement, the Traveller spooks the hare, it runs off and his plans are foiled. In the closing line of the story, the Traveller man laments, '"Well", as he turned away, "it could have happened"' (ibid.: 112).

Braid begins his analysis by reminding the reader that Williamson's 'story is more than a humorous anecdote', it is also a 'serious commentary on Traveller identity, choices, and values that transcends the boundaries of the performance event' (2002: 114–115). For example, to the Traveller-listener, Braid suggests that the narrative is indicative of a Traveller behaving in a marginal way because he has chosen a solitary lifestyle and has no family (ibid.: 115). Braid's interpretation refers to the strong familial bonds that exist between not only Travellers and their extended families, but also often extending to include the wider Traveller communities found throughout Scotland and beyond. In terms of Williamson's 'The Traveller and the Hare', the results of Braid's interpretation mean that the Traveller protagonist has effectively 'abandoned Traveller worldview and accepted settled worldview' (ibid.). With divergent worldviews as the central theme, Braid continues, Williamson demonstrates the relative validity of Traveller and non-Traveller worldviews (ibid.: 116). For the Traveller-listener then, when the object of the Traveller's desire is scared off by his enthusiasm, 'the illusion of comfort and security is humorously revealed to collapse at the slightest provocation [. . .] pointing out the absurdity of settled worldview and vindicating Traveller worldview' (ibid.). Braid goes on to 'double-check' his interpretation with Williamson who confirms that his protagonist's intentions amount to 'a non-Traveller idea [. . .] he chose the wrong way to start [. . .] that's the idea of the story' (cited in Braid 2002: 117–118).

By considering Williamson's story from a Traveller's perspective, Braid's interpretation supports our present critical approach. Firstly, filiation – an individual's conviction in the veracity and reliability of transmitted traditional material – is an important function of Traveller storytelling; and secondly, it is crucial to approach the stories from an emic perspective if we are to gain plausible understandings of their meaning. In the case of 'The Traveller and the Hare', Braid's emic conclusion is that Williamson's fictional story functions to explore 'differences in cultural identity [. . .] to argue the validity of deeply held cultural beliefs [that] should be understood as intentional aspects of meaning' (2002: 118) within the context of the story. As we will see, it is possible to elaborate on Braid's method to reveal not only the macro-meaning of these stories, but to uncover other significant meanings within the minutiae. Braid goes on to consider an etic interpretation of the story because an example of an outsider's perspective of 'The Traveller and the Hare' is instructive. From an outsider's perspective, such as the future-orientated planning that Braid says defines American worldviews (ibid.: 116), it seems reasonable that the Traveller would like to escape the state of penury in which he exists. Additionally, again from an outsider perspective, the Traveller protagonist's sacrifice of raising a family, and his imagined investment that begins with the sale of the hare, amounts to a non-Traveller worldview. Given the protagonist's poverty and isolation, the outsider perceives his aspirations to wealth and security as admirable. When the Traveller ultimately fails in his ambitions, the outsider would perhaps view the story as tragic and find pathos in the protagonist's final lament. However, the logic of the story casts such ambitions as absurd, thereby reinforcing the Traveller worldview that family and belonging are paramount when pursuing a meaningful life. Elsewhere in Braid's analyses, he identifies and engages with other outsider perspectives that are negotiated within Traveller storytelling. During the analysis of one unnamed narrative involving a Traveller and a gentleman, Braid argues that the protagonist 'masterfully plays on the prevailing stereotype of Travellers as ignorant and potentially irrational' (ibid.: 211).

The following chapters of the present study expand such emic perspectives further, considering wider socio-political and economic discourses that enhance the plausibility of the interpretations. We will consider a wider range of contextual factors and apply a broader range of methodological approaches to the stories. We will see how literary criticism and structuralism are potent allies when searching for deeper meanings within ostensibly simple narratives. Braid deployed a similar strategy and his questions to contemporary Travellers revealed careful thought about, and understanding of, the nature of the stories being told (ibid.: 287). The present study draws on primary source material that has, thus far, not been considered in the scholarship surrounding Scotland's Traveller communities. These contexts not only situate the narratives within the wider European folkloric tradition, but in the unique lived experiences of Travellers in Scotland. Braid concludes that 'Travellers themselves are capable of thinking about stories in analytical ways although they may not choose to do so on a day-to-day basis (ibid.). Braid's discussions are plausible and persuasive, giving the present work a reliable foundation on which to expand.

These opening chapters have served to situate the Travellers in terms of their status in Scottish society, giving a nuanced picture of Travellers' socio-cultural history, and mobilising the contemporary debate about the uses of tradition. Such perspectives are rarely applied to oral narrative and conspicuously so when it comes to Scotland's Traveller traditions. The central argument here has been that one function of Traveller storytelling is to provide an arena where cultural continuity can be sustained. This function represents the process of tradition wherein communities store cultural capital, making it accessible to future generations of tradition-bearers. Under these conditions, as we will see, it is possible to distil plausible meanings from a given traditional resource, providing clearer understandings of the communities to which the resources belong. The following chapters begin to examine different varieties of narratives, delving deep into their inner workings to reveal a singular folkloric idiom.

Notes

1. Translation by Angus Matheson and Derick Thomson https://calumimaclean.blogspot.co.uk/2017/06/the-man-with-cassock.html [accessed 18 March 2024].
2. The author has sought and received reflections on his interpretations from tradition-bearers from within the communities. My sincerest and ardent thanks go to Cathie Laing, Jess Smith BEM, Jimmy Williamson, Davie Donaldson and Shamus McPhee.
3. These ethnocentric evolutionary views were reflected in America by authors such as Lee J. Vance who suggested that study of the folk 'reveals the evolution of modern culture from the beliefs and usages of savages and simple-minded folk' (see Bronner 1998: 74).

3

Cultural Identity and Storytelling

IDENTITY STRATEGIES WITHIN TRAVELLER STORYTELLING

IT HAS BEEN RECOGNISED for some time that storytelling practices are intrinsically linked to the educational and cultural development of individuals within their communities. Niles observes that storytelling amounts to the maintenance of 'social equilibrium by strengthening the bonds of affection between individuals while affirming the beliefs and values on which the continuing existence of a community depends' (1999: 171–172). Before moving on to Part II of this book and looking at examples of Traveller storytelling in some detail, this chapter sheds light on debates around individual and group identity formation, and what this means in the context of the Travellers' unique identities. Given the mostly twentieth-century-based perspectives of the opening chapters, this chapter goes on to furnish the reader with insights and perspectives from more contemporary members of Scotland's Traveller communities. We bring together the discussions from previous chapters to think about how Traveller storytelling traditions set themselves apart. Within a Traveller-centric, humanistic framework, it anticipates the detailed discussions of Part II by showing how the Travellers' storytelling traditions represent a singularly Traveller cultural conceptualisation.

Lauri Honko has suggested that, within identity research, 'the mainstream is towards analysing the identity of the individual, not necessarily in isolation from groups but as the final result of different group experiences, [and] shared values' (1988: 14). This is an important insight from Honko which suggests that we can tap into the overarching values and beliefs of the group by looking closely at the identities of individuals from within the group. However, Honko perceives problems with this approach, in that the resulting analysis may reveal more about the individual than the 'identity strategies of a collective body' (ibid.). 'Identity strategies' is a useful term for our purposes and one that may help to mitigate Honko's reservations around drawing conclusions about group identity that are based on expressions of individual identity (ibid.: 15). Considering Travellers as a group in the broadest sense, an example of one identity strategy is their fundamental differentiation between themselves and the settled population. The settled or 'mainstream' Scottish population, as outsiders to the group, are variously referred to by Travellers as 'scaldies' (J. Robertson TAD 10285; S. Robertson TAD 42990), 'hantle' (J. Robertson TAD 10285; Whyte TAD 39610; Stewart TAD 56424; S. Robertson TAD 38124), 'flatties' (Whyte TAD 76669) and 'bucks' (J. Robertson TAD 10285). From this perspective, Traveller communities have specific nomenclatures for anyone *other* than Travellers and can therefore be said to operate an identity strategy. Clark also recognises such strategies in Traveller families, asserting that 'at heart there is a profound sense of "self" and importance attached to being part of a community that knows itself, and *flatties* (non-Travellers), very well' (2018: 108). On the surface, this strategy may be viewed as isolationist, however, as we will see, there is compelling evidence to suggest that this isolationism was enforced, and then enacted by the Travellers themselves to ensure their survival through centuries of hostility. A short excerpt from an interview with Stanley Robertson will serve as an example of this isolationist strategy in practice. Robertson tells us that his father 'couldnae speak tae the Aberdeen scaldie folk, he just had nothing in common with them, and he remained aloof fae them' (TAD 42990). Robertson goes on to suggest that 'with him [his father] being like that, every one of the family became like that, ken? We've a' got this same way wi' us [. . .] I'm very much aloof, I dinnae mix wi' scaldies' (ibid.).

The transmission of shared values and beliefs can also be viewed as an identity strategy, and one that explicitly manifests itself in the Travellers' storytelling traditions. Stories, then, are an ideal medium through which to examine the distinctive cultural identities of Scotland's Travellers. We might ask at this point, then, what is it that makes these stories 'Traveller tales'? If the characters of the story *and* the narrator are explicitly identified as Travellers, then the story is considered 'Traveller'. If the narrator identifies as Traveller, but the characters within the story are not explicitly identified as Travellers, close attention must be paid to details of the story to categorise it as a 'Traveller' tale. However, if the characters within the story are identified as Travellers, but the narrator is not, then this approach is problematised. For instance, the non-Traveller Reverend Norman MacDonald (TAD 8571) tells a story in Gaelic, similar to one told by Duncan Williamson. Williamson's story tells of a Traveller baby who is given to and raised by wealthy but childless landowners. When grown up and out walking with his adoptive father, the Traveller boy recognises the makings of a spoon in an old cow's horn, thereby affirming his Traveller roots. Williamson's story about the finding of the cow's horn and its significance is considered in more detail in a later chapter. Meantime, in MacDonald's version of the story, a childless Duke meets a Traveller family with many children, and the Travellers agree to give the Duke a young girl to raise as his own. The Traveller girl is raised accordingly and becomes a 'Gentlewoman'. Many years later, the Traveller-Gentlewoman is out walking, encounters a group of Travellers and is never heard from again. MacDonald then informs us that this story is the origin of the Gaelic phrase, 'Thoir bò gu ruige taigh mòr is iarraidh i don bhàthaich' [Take the cow to the big house and it will want the cowshed]. At the conclusion of MacDonald's story, the Traveller-Gentlewoman is married to a Traveller man: 'agus phòs i fear aca' [and she married one of them] (TAD 8571) could be read as an affirmation of Traveller values relating to family, in that the protagonist instinctively knows where she will feel happiest. The parallels with Williamson's story are clear. However, the focus of MacDonald's story is the opposite – where Williamson's story is an affirmation of the protagonist's latent, inner Traveller identity, MacDonald's story carries a similar message about an inner identity, but the implication is negative – the cow does not know what is good for it, or you can take the Traveller off the road, but you cannot take the road off the Traveller.[1] MacDonald's story may be read as positively affirming the Traveller protagonist's self-awareness *as a Traveller*, but its context as the origin of a condescending proverb remains.

In another example, one cautionary tale that Andrew Stewart tells us was 'handed down from Tinker tae Tinker, and I jist heard it the same way as I'm tellin' it here' (TAD 13847), a poor Traveller becomes wealthy after a supernatural helper tells him where gold sovereigns are buried. The Traveller ultimately squanders his wealth drinking, and being overly generous, giving his money away to 'Tom, Dick and Harry' (ibid.) whilst 'spending more than what he was earning' (ibid.). The moral of the story is clear; wealth can appear unexpectedly and disappear likewise. To make the best use of unforeseen, fortuitous events, a person must exercise prudence and discretion. This sort of didacticism is by no means unique to the Travellers. What is unique, however, is that the protagonist is named 'MacPhee'. Some Travellers harbour superstitions concerning the MacPhee Travellers, with the northern branch of the family being considered unlucky, or unpopular (TAD 38906; TAD 10279; TAD 35360; Henderson 2004: 230). From this perspective, Stewart's injudicious protagonist, MacPhee, embodies everything that a Traveller should not be. Ironically, the northern MacPhees have been described by Traveller Lizzie Higgins as 'the first travellin' lot in Scotland, they're the real folk, authentic Travellers' (TAD 38906; cf. Henderson 2004: 230) and are associated with rescuing Scottish clansmen from British soldiers after the Jacobite rebellion (Henderson 2004: 230). Higgins goes on to suggest that all the other Travelling families in Scotland today are descended from intermarriage between the MacPhees and members of the hunted clan folk (TAD 38906). The ambivalent nature of the MacPhees – altruistic progenitors on one hand, foolish drunkards on the other – is just one example of how social change and straightforward didacticism can intermingle in Travellers' narratives. Again, we return to examine Stewart's narrative about Geordie MacPhee in greater detail in a later chapter to draw out the intricacies of his story.

In these introductory examples, the differentiation in meaning concerns what the story *is doing* in the context in which we find it. This contextualisation is at the heart of the interpretations being carried out in this book, a process of contextualisation that facilitates meaningful engagement with stories from the Travellers' traditions. At the same time, an awareness of stories about Travellers that we hear from other sectors of society is important. As was demonstrated in the example from MacDonald above, it is the *meaning* of the story that aligns it to the Traveller tradition. In the same way that *Orwellian* is evocative of dystopia, or *Swiftian* speaks to political satire, *Nackian* storytelling traditions conjure up sophisticated negotiations of perennial folkloric themes, all the while leavened by the socio-political realities of the Travellers' status as unwelcome misfits, with irony and ambivalence as staple features. The information held within Travellers' storytelling traditions is at the heart of this study, yet the way we are *using* this information must be distinguished from its uses and functions within the communities themselves. For the outsider, stories, ballads and songs represent a body of intangible cultural heritage that can help us to understand more about the inner lives of the communities who share them.

For many Travellers, oral narratives are a central part of their early education and upbringing. Niles makes a point of foregrounding the educational function of stories in Travellers' lives, propounding that 'stories provided them with lessons in life more useful than anything that they were taught in school' (1999: 165). The concept of education being delivered through storytelling as part of the intellectual developments associated with childhood is affirmed by Stanley Robertson. Robertson explains that growing up, 'nearly a' the auld Traveller women telt ye stories' (TAD 50189), and that 'you needed a spiritual training, and you needed a physical training, and one was as important as the other' (ibid.). Robertson elaborates on his point of education through stories, revealing that during storytelling sessions, 'when you were there, it became part o your character an makeup. You were being shaped and moulded' (cited in Niles 1999: 165). Stories, then, not only function to impart 'training', as Robertson puts it, but can also be seen as the transmission of knowledge, character and experience from one generation to another. Elsewhere, discussing the intergenerational transmission of stories in Traveller communities, Geordie Stewart confirms that stories have been passed around for 'generations, aye, generations', and that after supper, he and his family would tell 'stories the whole night' (TAD 81408). More evidence of storytelling practices being central to Travellers' domestic and social lives comes from John Stewart – storytelling 'played a big part' in day-to-day life, explains Stewart, 'because there was no televisions' (TAD 65775). Stewart goes on to describe 'when Travellers would stay beside one another [. . .] they sat up late at night and they would swap stories round the fire' (ibid.). Moreover, Stewart articulates the difference between stories learned at school, and stories learned around the Travellers' camps: 'we couldnae be bothered wi' the likes o' Jack and the Beanstalk', Stewart tells us, 'they were too schoolified [sic] for us, there wisnae enough depth in them' (ibid.). The sense of a depth of meaning within Traveller storytelling, alluded to by Stewart, is something that will be thrown into sharp relief during the forthcoming examples.

As we heard from Robertson and others above, the process of intergenerational transmission among Travellers can also extend to emotional and intellectual levels, further strengthening the deeply rooted familial and community bonds that Travellers have with one another. The strong emotions evoked through sharing stories in this way has been eloquently described by Betsy Whyte. Whyte tells us that when she is telling stories to children, 'the whole thing comes right back, instead of you tellin' your mother the story, you're sittin' there listening to your mother telling you the story, but the words are comin' oot of your mooth' (TAD 67341). Commonly held values and beliefs are included in this process of transmission, the sum of which becomes the conveyance of 'cultural capital'. 'Culture', in this this sense, is defined as the outward expression of commonly held values (Jacobson-Widding 1983: 14) and 'capital', as a resource to be drawn upon when negotiating the wider world. Stories are the cultural capital of the Travellers; they are at once the outward embodiment of a shared set of values and beliefs, and simultaneously an inner reservoir of experience that can be drawn upon at need. Testament to this conceptualisation of the central importance of stories to contemporary Travellers comes from Traveller storyteller

Jess Smith BEM: 'stories are the way forward for the Travellers to learn about their past', Smith remarks, 'many Travelling families have kept these stories, crucially important gems, and they've shared them down through the years [. . .] stories are so important' (*Gypsy, Roma, Traveller History Month* (GRTHM) 2021).

There are also more material uses for the stories. John Stewart tells us that as children, Travellers would use stories as a form of currency, to be used in exchange for things that other children had (TAD 65775). Duncan Williamson shares a similar experience where he once 'walked intae Coupar Angus for an ounce o' bacco [tobacco]' (TAD 30610) to exchange it for a story from Johnnie MacDonald, who was 'a great storyteller' (ibid.). Williamson goes on to declare that he 'would listen to a story better than go to the pictures [cinema]' (ibid.). The value that Williamson places in the receiving of stories – along with Stewart's more materialistic example – makes tangible the importance of storytelling in Travellers' lives. Furthermore, the notion that stories represent a form of capital that can be stored, freely given, and exchanged, illustrates a worldview that stands in contradistinction to the possession-driven ethos of high-capitalism. This contradistinctive worldview can also be witnessed through depictions of conflict with the state, or the dominant elite and their ideologies. It seems sensible to assume that this unsympathetic view of capitalism is anachronistic, and that modern Travellers 'embrace' the system. However, it must be recognised that there are other factors to consider; it is not 'capital' or money, *per se*, that seems to be the problem for the Travellers and the protagonists of their stories. It is more the recognition of the greed and inequality that the capitalist system engenders. As we move on to close examination of examples of Traveller storytelling, we find that deceptively simple stories can contain sophisticated messages about the nature of family and society, negotiating what it means to be a Traveller within a capitalist society that is often hostile to communities and individuals who harbour alternative worldviews. Our examples also demonstrate a connection with the environment that speaks to a more reverential relationship with the landscape and echoes an identity that has perhaps been renounced under the auspices of progress.

When it comes to interpretative close readings, it is vital to note that we are affording here what Braid has described as 'careful generalizations' (2002: 32–33), proceeding on the premise that, viewed from a certain perspective, individualised narrative expressions can provide insights into the formation of collective identities. The narratives under analysis are drawn upon to explore the identities of the narrators as *individual* Traveller storytellers, offering plausible interpretations of Traveller culture and tradition more generally. Therefore, it must be stressed that each narrative is being viewed as an individualised expression of worldview that is informed by a sense of a shared cultural identity. However, the analysis of one individual's narrative and the broader context of storytelling are not mutually exclusive, they supplement each other (Lüthi 1982: 125). Edward Spicer's (1971) notion of individual and collective identity systems is useful from this perspective. For Spicer, an individual system is a person's recognition of certain symbols, and what those symbols stand for; the collective system amounts to the 'display and manipulation of the symbols', which in turn 'calls forth sentiments and stimulates the affirmation of beliefs on the part of the individuals who participate' (1971: 796). Spicer's summation is redolent of the concept of ideological imperatives introduced in preceding chapters. For our purposes, items of folklore, such as oral narrative, represent the 'display and manipulation' of symbols within these identity systems. The *recognition* of these symbols is the tradition, with tradition being understood as 'a dynamic, multivalent body of meaning that preserves much that a group has invented and transmitted' (Foley 1992: 227). The individuals who participate to sustain and modify this body of meaning are the various degrees of tradition-bearers that were introduced in Chapter 1 above.

Spicer's concept of 'identity systems' is reminiscent of Honko's 'identity strategies' (1988: 14). The reader will recall Honko suggesting that we can tap into the overarching values and beliefs of groups ('identity strategies') by looking closely at the identities of individuals from within the group. However, Honko voiced concerns about making assumptions about group identity based solely on the utterances of individuals (ibid.). This seems to be a rational position, given that members of a group each have a unique, individual identity and can therefore only speak for themselves. Of course, this position creates a theoretical barrier; if no one individual can absolutely speak for the group with any authority, then how do we study the group at all? The group would disintegrate into unconnected, isolated individuals. In practice, this is patently not the case, and the keystone is an individual's acquisition of traditional material through volitional participation. To mitigate this disintegration of connected communities, the concept of 'filiation' – an individual's conviction in the veracity and reliability of transmitted traditional material – plays a central role in the formation of collective identities. Consequentially, Spicer's symbols and Honko's strategies can be seen to complement one another; oral narratives are the vehicles for the transmission of the symbols, with the strategy being the deliberate participation in the transmission of codified information that is enthusiastically received. Put another way, oral narratives, when viewed as 'manipulated and displayed' items of folklore, function as expressions of a shared collective identity, and in this case, one that is distinctively 'Traveller'. Moreover, the expressions of individuals from within this collective identity operate reflexively. Folklore, as Bronner propounds, can be 'malleable according to varied contexts, and individuals could even construct their own identities based upon the creative manipulation of traditions' (2017: 11). The folk narratives explored here are a two-way street from this perspective – the individual identity can be informed by the traditional material, and the traditional material is consistently updated during the creative process of tradition-bearing.

MODERN PERSPECTIVES AND THE STATE

Much has been written about Travellers and their relationships with the various manifestations of the state in Scotland. It is not the intention to add to this body of grey literature here. It is useful, however, to highlight certain examples and comment on the present situation, to summarise the salient points and provide an overview of the changing relationship between Travellers and the state. It is also important to take a somewhat long view here – incorporating the notorious '1895' report, for instance – because historical conceptualisations of Travellers have a demonstrable impact on their storytelling traditions. This material also shows how attitudes towards Travellers have evolved over the last hundred years or so. Our purpose here is to elucidate the important interactions between Travellers and the central government to highlight the relevance of such discourses to the contemporary communities. At the same time, the discussion here provides further context for the forthcoming interpretations and underlines the ideological differentiation that remains at the core of this study.

Previously, in Chapter 1, we saw how the evidence found in TSAS reveals a distinctly problematic relationship between Travellers and elite members of society in the past. What is clear from the evidence presented is that the Travellers' alternative lifestyles led to their demonisation in the eyes of the ruling elite during the late eighteenth century, and persisted into nineteenth century. The Scottish Government's *Advisory Committee on Scotland's Travelling People* (ACSTP) have provided a useful chronology of the State's interaction with Travellers. 'Earlier central government initiatives in Scotland, where a search for effective information as a basis for policy either specifically on, or at least including, Travellers', we are told, 'now stretch back more than a century'

(ACSTP 2000: Section 10.1). These initiatives include: 'The Report of the Departmental Committee on Habitual Offenders, Vagrants, Beggars, Inebriates and Juvenile Delinquents' (1895); the 'Report of the Departmental Committee on Vagrancy' (1906); the 'Report of the Departmental Committee on the Tinkers in Scotland' (1918); and the 'Report of the Departmental Committee on Vagrancy in Scotland (1936). The more modern committee's recent aspiration towards the collection of 'robust and objective information' (ACSTP 2000: Section 10.1) was not always extant. It is apparent from the titles of the historical reports, cited above, that the officials conducting the reporting were not entirely sympathetic to the situations or lifestyles of their subjects. For Travellers in particular, it soon becomes clear that the official line was to attempt to eradicate them by targeting their children. As Dualta Roughneen points out, legislation and policy-making often encroach on nomadic peoples' liberty and autonomy (2010: xi).

In a 1905 report prepared by Inspector J. Boyd for Education (Scotland) – which is missing from the ACSTP list above – evidence from a 'Mr Macdonald' regarding 'the problem of tinker children' in the Caithness district during the year 1904 is presented (Boyd 1905: 9). Macdonald reports that 'the children seem to be trained to regard their fellow creatures as natural enemies; they grow up as outcasts without ambition to rise above the squalor of their surroundings' (ibid.). Given the evidence of the persecution of Traveller from TSAS and elsewhere, the aversion of the Traveller children to officialdom is perhaps understandable. Macdonald goes on to assert of the Traveller children that it is 'impossible with the present *machinery of compulsion* to bring them within the range of the Education Acts [. . .] even if an educational *net of smaller mesh* be provided' (ibid.). The rhetoric of such governmental reports frequently reduces Traveller communities to unthinking and insidious pariahs. Within the context of Inspector Boyd's ostensibly objective report, Macdonald is vying for additional funds to tackle 'the problem' or attempting to wash his hands of the Travellers altogether. According to Macdonald, the educational authorities in his district cannot be 'reasonably expected to trouble themselves and burden the local rates with the education of a class that contributes nothing to the parish but work for the police' (ibid.).

The earlier and now notorious 1895 report – prepared for the then Scottish Secretary, George Otto Trevelyan – titled 'The Report of the Departmental Committee on Habitual Offenders, Vagrants, Beggars, Inebriates and Juvenile Delinquents' anticipates Macdonald's fiscal concerns. Commenting on the compulsory education of Traveller children, the Committee concludes 'that one of the chief reasons why the law is not enforced is because to do so would entail expenditure on the parish enforcing it' (in Cameron et al 1895: xxxii). The Committee provide an example from Perthshire where the lack of enthusiasm for the law is obvious, and where the Magistrates presumably did not consider the Traveller child worth the expenditure (ibid.). However, the Committee become insistent and recommend that 'powers should be given to School Board districts and parishes in a county or adjoining counties to unite in enforcing the attendance at school of the children of nomadic parents' (ibid.: xxxiii). The effect of this new power, the Committee explain, would be 'to enable to be borne by an extensive area the expense of contributing to the maintenance of children liable to be sent to Industrial Schools' (ibid.).

In other words, School districts were being officially encouraged to remove what were deemed to be neglected and/or delinquent children to Industrial Schools – government institutions where children would be educated with trades – regardless of their opinions around whether it would be 'worth it'. In the 'Minutes of Evidence' section of the same 1895 report, William Mitchell – the Vice-Chairman of Glasgow School Board and Juvenile Delinquency Board – when asked how the Committee might accommodate the Travellers in his district suggests that the Travellers' 'movable dwellings should be registered and brought under the control of the Local Authority for inspection' (in Cameron et al 1895: 9). Mitchell's rationale is that such dwellings would be found to be insanitary and therefore uninhabitable, especially for children. In Mitchell's scheme, when the Travellers' camps are consequentially struck by the authorities, the families would be offered accommodation in custom made 'Refuges'. This done, Mitchell believes that the Travellers 'might gradually be absorbed with the labouring population', and 'their children looked after and sent to school, and the whole tinker clan thus gradually brought into association with the other labourer' (ibid.). Mitchell's class prejudice was likely compounded by his membership of the Glasgow School Board Attendance Committee (1873–1903) and his published views on the centrality of scholastic education: 'Education is the leading spirit of the age', declares Mitchell, 'children must have the natural and material wants of the body supplied ere the benefits and blessings of education can be either received or valued' (1885: 16).

Again, the rhetoric here is that of forced assimilation to eradicate the Travellers and their way of life. Mitchell's venom is clear when he states that 'the tinkers I speak of and their children are positively just like cattle. They have no moral training or teaching of any kind whatever' (in Cameron et al 1895: 10). Similar sentiments are expressed by other witnesses throughout the report's 'Minutes of Evidence' section. Chief Constable John MacPherson of Perthshire states that 'the only way of dealing with them is, after having them compulsorily educated, to send them away out of reach of their tribe' (ibid.: 210). MacPherson explains that he is 'certain that, if allowed to join their friends, even after spending some years in an Industrial School, they will just relapse into their old habits' (ibid.). Elsewhere, Colonel Williamson of Crieff puts his feelings bluntly: 'speaking for myself, as an individual', says the Colonel, 'I think the law ought to step in and declare that camping out or living in camps is an illegal form of life' (ibid.: 214). The vitriol continues in the appendices of the 1895 report where the Committee of the School Board of the Burgh of Wick and Pulteneytown submit that:

> The tinker community is composed of a tribe or family quite alien to the local population, among whom they do not mix in social life or intercourse, neither work nor help in any way to alleviate the burden of local taxation, but by their mode of life, their obscene ways and conversation, their squalor and drunken habits, are a menace to our very civilisation.
>
> (ibid., Appendix LXII: 606)

The above submission to the 1895 report is a striking example of the sort of ideological discourses that concern us here. The 'obscenity and menace' that the Traveller communities represent is couched in their alternative lifestyles; the sedentarist ideals of social intercourse with 'the locals', working and paying taxes, are set against what the committee sees as an inherently 'uncivilised' way of life. Similarly, the implications of the Children Act (1908) meant that the children of parents who led 'alternative' lifestyles could be forcibly removed from their families to promote the children's 'reformation'. The 1918 governmental report is little better in terms of the hostility it displays towards Travellers, suggesting that through the segregation of the 'Tinker' children at school, their teachers may be able to induce them to a desire for a 'settled' occupation, and encourage cleanliness (cited in Taylor 2014: 149–150).

As with TSAS, the details found within the governmental reports cited above are often underpinned by misunderstanding and paternalism. Similarly, the housing scheme at Bobbin Mill, Perthshire established by The Church of Scotland in 1947 was a misguided and poorly executed attempt to 'socialise' a select group of Travellers, who had previous connections to the site (Taylor 2008: 172–173; cf. Taylor 2023). The scheme was taken over by Pitlochry Council, where it was described as an 'experiment' with the buildings 'not in conformity with the Building Bylaws' (ibid.: 173).

An official review of the scheme in 1957 deemed the 'experiment' unsuccessful due to 'constant difficulties with additional members of the clan overcrowding the houses' (ibid.). In a documentary film titled *The Forgotten Experiment*, Bobbin Mill resident Shamus McPhee described the scheme as 'a way of normalising people who were regarded as social misfits' (2008). The site exists to this day under the auspices of Perth and Kinross Council. As demonstrated here, governmental reports and attempts at assimilation by local councils contributed to the marginalisation of Travellers in Scotland and many of the officials involved were openly advocating cultural genocide. Moreover, the blatant and pervasive hostility that Travellers have experienced at the hands of an unsympathetic state has undeniably influenced their storytelling traditions, as observed above by Henderson, and evidenced through the examples provided in the present study.

There were oases of understanding, however. Discussing approaches to educational reform in Scotland, one author writes in *The Scotsman* that 'many of them [Travellers] perform a circuit in the year, with more or less regularity, and have their customary halting places' (1893: 4). Armed with this knowledge, the author suggests that rather than uprooting Traveller children from their families to be educated, an educational reformer might consider sending educators to the families at given times throughout the year. This approach is, however, then deemed untenable by the author as 'any scheme of appointing teachers with roving commissions [. . .] is not to be thought of' (ibid.). The appointees concurred, with one volunteer from a Perthshire welfare committee – designed to 'engage' with Travellers during the 1920s – reporting that she was forced into her work and hated it (Taylor 2014: 156–157). *The Scotsman*'s author goes on to wax poetical when he empathises with 'this much-neglected class', who represent 'one of the last relics of the picturesque and the unconventional that has been left to us in a world that, according to some, is only too much bound down with rules and fashion' (1893: 4). In terms of the education of Traveller children, the author ultimately concludes that as 'important as education is, it is not the only sanative thing in human life' (ibid.). The implication being that there is merit in 'the outdoor training and knowledge of nature' (ibid.) that the Traveller children receive at the hands and minds of their own family groups. The conceptualisation of an organic form of education anticipates what we now understand about Travellers' upbringing. In one more modern survey, it was found that 'Traveller parents do not for the most part consider the formal education system to be the prime means of passing on their cultural capital, viewing the family as the arena in which that is achieved' (Bancroft et al 1996: 14).

Further progress was made later in the twentieth century with the introduction of the policy of toleration and non-harassment of Travelling People in 1977 (ACSTP 2000: Section 5.1). Unfortunately, the committee's choice of terminology, with the use of the term 'toleration', further betrays the fundamental misunderstanding of the issues by the state. Specifically, the ACSTP reported that many Travellers resented the implication that they were to be 'tolerated', rather than accepted, by society and the state (ibid.: Section 5.6). Much of the reporting executed over the years by these state-funded committees is motivated by gathering statistical information, with little or no regard for the humanitarian aspect of such activities. It is therefore not difficult to conclude that there is an element of control at the core of the various committees' activities. Hugh Gentleman's report on Travellers, submitted to The Scottish Office in 1993, makes this element of control clear when he alludes to 'potential *users of information*' (1993: 3). Given the nature of the previous committees' involvement with Travellers, it would be safe to assume that the Travellers would not exactly welcome intrusive questioning from representatives of the central government. During his introduction, Gentleman observes that Travellers 'have always been reticent about providing information to officialdom' (ibid.: 5), and that this situation has been exacerbated by the state's focus on collecting information of a fiscal nature. In Gentleman's defence, he does state that the use of the updated information that he collected 'was strongest in the context of community nursing and health visitor services' (ibid.: 4). Gentleman also questions the accuracy of his report when he observes that 'the only way in which this kind of information can be obtained with any degree of reliability is by traditional social anthropological approaches involving spending a lot of time building up trust and acceptance' (ibid.: 5). It is ironic that the very attitudes that the state expects from Travellers are the same ones that the Travellers themselves have been consistently denied. As Marcus puts it:

> It would seem that the project of othering, demonising, and exclusion continues and arguably has succeeded in criminalising and fragmenting one of the oldest nomadic communities in Britain. However, Gypsy/Travellers in Scotland continue to exist, resist and unite as communities on the periphery; and in understanding this periphery, the living legacies of power at the centre also come into view.

(2023: 109)

The most recent engagement between Travellers and central government is the *Race Equality Action Plan 2017–2021*, in which the Scottish Government has included the Ministerial Working Group on Gypsy/Travellers

(MWGGT). As noted in Chapter 1, the term 'Gypsy/Traveller' represents a conflation between two distinct ethnic groups, Gypsies and Travellers. This compound term was created, Traveller Sheila Stewart explains, 'a good few years ago' (2002: 188) when Stewart and a Member of Parliament from Dundee approached the House of Commons. Stewart goes on to say that their approach had the intention of updating the Race Relations Act (1976, amended 2000) to replace the derogatory term 'Tinker' with the term 'Traveller' (Stewart 2002: 188). At this time – presumably sometime after 1976 – Gypsies already had legal rights under the Race Relations Act, and so Stewart and the MP went further. According to Stewart, the term 'Traveller' was then recognised by the government as the preferred ethnic descriptor for Stewart's people – in the same way that Gypsies were recognised as having a distinct ethnicity – and were therefore protected under the Race Relations Act (ibid.). Consequently, The Scottish Executive's *Equal Opportunities Committee's* 'Inquiry into Gypsy Travellers and Public Sector Policies' (2001) officially sanctioned the compound term, stating that 'all legislation and policies should be framed on the understanding that Gypsy Travellers [sic] have distinct ethnic characteristics and should therefore be regarded as an ethnic group' (2001: Recommendation 2). This recognition was then crystallised in 2008 when an employment appeal tribunal set a legal precedent in Scotland, ruling that Scottish Gypsy/Travellers are to be considered an ethnic minority (Cemlyn et al 2009: 211).

Unfortunately, as Stewart explains, this resulted in Travellers being referred to as Gypsies, and as 'Gypsy Travellers'. For Stewart, this 'did a lot of harm in Scotland' (2002: 188) in terms of the Travellers' distinctive identities being misrecognised by other members of society. Despite this, the term 'White: Gypsy/Traveller' was then deployed as an ethnic category by the National Records of Scotland during their 2011 census (2014: 2). Although, from a grammatical perspective, the punctuation mark '/' can represent 'or', its presence in the census implies a homogeneous ethnic category and has the potential to corrupt the resulting data. Rebecca McKinney has pointed out that some Travellers in Scotland reject any associations with Gypsies, even when the Travellers in question have ties of kinship with Gypsy families (2003: 17). From the perspective of both Stewart's testimony and the Scottish Government's attempts at counting Travellers, it is a lamentable conflation of terminology. In an academic context, there is also disagreement around nomenclature when discussing Scotland's Traveller communities. For McKinney, 'it is not possible to treat Gypsies and indigenous [Scottish] Travellers as entirely separate, or separable, populations' (2003: 16). McKinney's assertion is based on the notion of the supposedly unavoidable 'practicalities of life on the road' (ibid.) resulting in intermarriage between various groups that, historically, shared an itinerant lifestyle. The present study resists contributing any further to this complex debate and proceeds on the Travellers' self-identification as Scottish Travellers, or Nacken and Nawken. However, it must be noted that 'while the intangible nature of ethnicity may now be taken for granted among present generations of social scientists', as McKinney goes on to suggest, 'this understanding has not necessarily filtered down into either the public consciousness or the pragmatic minds of policy-makers' (ibid.: 19).

The example of the MWGGT cited above demonstrates that the conflation between Gypsies and Travellers persists in the government's official literature. The MWGGT state that their 'remit is to drive forward cross-government actions which will improve the lives of Scottish Gypsy/Traveller communities' (2018). Despite the rhetoric remaining somewhat paternalistic, further reading into the ethos of the group reveals a movement towards a more equitable relationship between Travellers and the state. The MWGGT state that they will 'consider how to improve engagement with Scotland's Gypsy/Traveller community and their participation influencing and shaping policy' (ibid.). Such engagement with the communities echoes Gentleman's earlier suggestion of a more socio-anthropological approach, and demonstrates a significant step forward by the Scottish Government. The modern media has unprecedented reach and influence through the internet and, unfortunately, most people's only experience with Travelling communities or Travellers is what they see in the media. A further crucial step forward, therefore, comes from the MWGGT's commitment 'to tackle discriminatory portrayals of the [Traveller] community by the media' (ibid.).

Close engagement with the Travellers' storytelling traditions addresses the underrepresentation and misunderstanding that is evident in mainstream media and politics. Happily, within an academic context, it is an underrepresentation of the Travellers' stories that are addressed here, not any misunderstandings. Scotland's Travellers continue to attract the attention of scholars from across the globe who have also perceived this underrepresentation. For example, writing for the National Museum of Ethnology in Osaka, Japan, Ryo Yamasaki recently examined how 'Traveller characters communicate their distinct worldview and value system by telling stories' (2020: 535). Yamasaki drew upon Stanley Robertson's published work, *Exodus to Alford* (1998), to conclude that Traveller storytelling has the power to 'relativise the mainstream, non-Traveller worldview and value system, thereby helping to raise awareness of presenting cultural diversity within Scottish society' (ibid.: 553). In Robertson's work, says Yamasaki, the urban and the rural are juxtaposed to highlight the discrimination that Travellers faced in built-up environments (ibid.: 547). Like Yamasaki, the examinations and contextual details of previous chapters revealed a Traveller identity that negotiated conceptualisations of the urban and the rural. This binary is perhaps unsurprising considering what we know about the Travellers' chosen lifestyles in the past and the concomitant bonds with the natural environment.

Despite lifestyle changes, these values persist to the present day. *Gypsy, Roma, Traveller History Month* (GRTHM) is an annual event that 'recognises the history and celebrates the cultures, traditions and contributions of Gypsy, Roma and Traveller communities in Scotland and elsewhere in the UK' ('About' 2017). GRTHM is a national event, endorsed by the Scottish Government, that involves a variety of collaborations between advocacy organisations and members of the communities. Minority Ethnic Carers of People Project's (MECOPP) Community Arts Worker, Peter Ross, curates a series of podcasts entitled 'No Less a Traveller' in which Travellers talk about their lives and experiences. In the first podcast of the series, 'No Less a Traveller: My Gypsy/Traveller Identity', we hear from two Travellers, Samantha and Lucinda, discussing their identities (GRTHM 2020). When asked what culture means to her, one speaker responds that 'it means shared values, knowledge, experience. Just your place in a society' (ibid.). It is clear from the speakers' discussion that part of their place in society is the recognition that they are different; 'the real problem that Travellers face today is acceptance from the wider society', we are told, 'because in their world, we're so different [. . .] because we act a certain way or think a certain way' (ibid.). The concept of a distinctive Traveller ideology is revealed here in that these twenty-first century Travellers recognise that their very thinking sets them apart from mainstream Scottish society. Moreover, the speakers suggest that 'perceptions, obviously, things like stereotypes' (ibid.) need to be challenged so that Traveller culture in Scotland is better understood.

One expression that continues to resurface is the story of James Macpherson, who was hanged at Banff in 1700 merely for 'being a Traveller'. In a modern retelling for 2021's GRTHM celebration, Maggie McPhee's version negotiates the same deep-seated anxieties about the systemic injustice perceived by contemporary Travellers. In 'Heartbreak Through Her Eyes', Maggie McPhee recounts the story as a first-person narrative that nullifies the temporal gap between generations. 'I want to tell you about my son, Jamie Macpherson', Maggie begins, 'back then I was a young Traveller girl' (GRTHM 2021). Maggie goes on to describe how she has a son, Jamie, with a Highland laird and how the boy is taken from her and raised in Invereshie House, near Kingussie in the Scottish Highlands. After his father's untimely death, the narrator explains that Jamie 'came looking for me and my people', and 'we took Jamie into our clan and he fitted just right' (ibid.). Unfortunately, Jamie fell in with a 'puckle of nae yoosers [a bad crowd]', eventually attracting the scorn of 'the sleekit [deceitful] Lord Braco' (ibid.). Maggie is referring to Alexander Duff of Braco, born around 1650, who is described by one chronicler as 'certainly a good countryman in all national concerns, and a very useful member of society in the North of Scotland' (Baird 1869 [1763–73]: 52). Braco was further distinguished by the 'care he took to have all the Highland robers [sic] and thieves who pestered the low Country at that time, apprehended and brought to justice' (ibid.).

Maggie's Jamie is soon to feel the sting of Braco's justice; the same chronicler describes Jamie as belonging to a band of 'notorious breakers of the peace in all sort of villainy' (ibid.). In Maggie's narrative, Braco and his men eventually catch Jamie at a market in Keith, and he is imprisoned at Banff awaiting trial. Soon, Maggie continues, 'Judge Dunbar, a friend of Lord Braco, sentenced my Jamie to be hung just for being a Traveller' ('Heartbreak Through Her Eyes' GRTHM 2021). A record of the trial itself was printed in the *Miscellany of the Spalding Club* in 1846, where the defence claims that the case brought against Macpherson is based on laws that 'have no coherence, nor contingence, with the pretended crimes' (Geills and Fraser 1846: 179). The defence goes on to point out that the Sheriff, Nicolas Dunbar, is not a 'judge competent' in cases of robbery and reiving, of which Macpherson stands accused (ibid.). Citing several Acts of Parliament, the defence ultimately argues that Macpherson's 'villainy' amounts to petty crime and that execution is therefore excessive. However, the Sheriff and jury disagree, and Macpherson is condemned to death by virtue of his status as an 'Egyptian [Gypsy, Traveller]' and person of 'pessima fama [bad reputation]' (ibid.). The fact that this narrative appears in contemporary Traveller tradition is testament to its continuing relevance to the communities. More significantly, Maggie's choice of narrative voice is a poignant evocation of how proximate the story is to her experience; much like Jamie's renowned fiddle that the narrator 'locked [. . .] in the family kist [chest]' ('Heartbreak Through Her Eyes' GRTHM 2021), so too the story and its poignancy endures.

THEY DINNAE HAE THE DEEPER WISDOMS

On the surface, the stories discussed above have been shown to engage with themes of persecution, familial bonds, and social and cultural otherness. However, we have also seen that these stories explore wider social and environmental concerns. Within these stories, there is an intangible yet indelible force at work. Andrew Stewart's narrative about the precarity of wealth, or Maggie McPhee's account of Jamie Macpherson's execution, offer tantalising glimpses into the ideological negotiations that are at work in the Travellers' storytelling traditions. Or, as Robertson puts it, certain stories can 'give a very materialistic training [. . .] but they dinnae hae the deeper wisdoms' (TAD 50189). As noted above, we must not infer from these stories that Traveller identity is considered to be genetic. Instead, the figurative meanings within the stories must be sought to better understand their functions. Considered in this way, the question of a genetically inherited Traveller identity can be reconceptualised. What the stories explore is not some metaphysical connection between Travellers and their offspring that stands for a predetermined Traveller identity. Rather, the stories ask us to consider how we act, and how we interact with others and our environment. The Travellers' stories also contemplate perennial truths and anxieties, confronting the dualities that are inevitable during human experience (cf. McDermitt 1980: 140).

What the above opening examples demonstrate is the singular way in which Traveller storytellers go about negotiating such themes. The stories discussed above function to transmit codified information that affirms a collective, intergenerational cultural identity and ethos. Or, as Williamson so eloquently puts it, 'as long as they are there in their stories, they're alive. We can bring them back' (cited in McDermitt 1980: 141). This ancestral evocation is the heart of it then; the seemingly anachronistic worldviews negotiated through narrative can be viewed as manifestations of the accumulated wisdom of generations of highly adaptable and successful Travellers. Within the stories, value systems, viewed as identity strategies, mean that Traveller identity is fixed, while the changeable socio-cultural conditions are used as a platform on which to negotiate anxieties around loss of identity. Deeply entrenched familial bonds, a close affinity with the natural environment and a sophisticated awareness of relationships with wider Scottish society are the hallmarks of the stories that the Travellers continue to share. Although these hallmarks have been described and recognised in Traveller communities before now, the forthcoming analyses demonstrate explicitly the ways in which the cultural identities of the Travellers manifest themselves during the transmission of oral narrative.

Note

1. A variant of the same proverb runs: 'Thoir leat a' bhò do'n chaisteal, 's thèid i dhachaidh do'n bhàthaich' [Take the cow to the castle, and she'll go home to the byre] (Nicolson 1882: 368).

Part II

4

Negotiating Cultural Identity

Oral narratives can and should be interpreted in the same way as artistic texts. In the same way as printed literature, oral narratives can embody sophisticated negotiations of contemporary social and cultural issues. This elevates the stories to a position where their contents shift from 'vestigial' understandings of an apparently simpler world to sophisticated negotiations of cultural identity. A central function of Traveller storytelling is to provide an arena where cultural identity and continuity are represented, conditioned and sustained. To demonstrate how this function manifests, Part II begins by examining a series of 'identity strategy' stories from two strong tradition-bearers who we met in Part I – Stanley Robertson and Duncan Williamson. What these stories represent are meaningful negotiations of Traveller identity through nuanced explorations of superficial appearances. What we find in these stories is the theme of an enigmatic *inner* Traveller identity, an identity that is juxtaposed with a specious outward identity.

As a recurring theme in Travellers' stories, Braid propounds that the inclusion of this contrast functions to 'strengthen the bonds between Travellers [. . .] and to maintain autonomy and identity in the face of pressure to assimilate into settled culture' (2002: 46). The core duality within these stories is that of Traveller and non-Traveller, and the function within each story is to articulate this very distinction.[1] These stories juxtapose dualities from a distinctly Traveller perspective, where we encounter themes of justice and injustice being negotiated through protagonists with seemingly contradictory identities. We also find the concept of immutable familial bonds being used to expose the oppositional forces inherent to social existence. It is important to note that we should not take stories involving inner Traveller identities literally to mean that Travellers view their identities as genetically inherited. Instead, stories involving the miraculous reawakening of an innate Traveller identity should be viewed figuratively as an expression of how deeply 'Travellers experience their culture' (ibid.: 37). This chapter also introduces the reader to examples of how Traveller storytellers engage with more familiar narratives that cast the identity net further; here we discover well-known themes, in this case Cinderella and Faust, being negotiated within the traditions.

THE TRAVELLER-JUDGE AND A LOVELY SPOON

Our first example comes from Stanley Robertson. Robertson recalls a story that he 'remember[s] ma grandda' telling when I wis a bairn, and I've also heard it reiterated again by ma mither' (TAD 38131). The story involves a young Traveller couple who have a baby but cannot afford to feed it properly. Crucially, the child has a 'most unusual birthmark, just right doon tae the back o' his neck, an' it was a black mark like a black mole, and it had a red scar that went 'roon it' (ibid.). Fearing for the child's life, the young, starving couple decide to leave it 'right at the door of this toff [wealthy] folk' (ibid.) in the hope that the child will be saved. Twenty-five years later, the couple are accused of poaching on private land and sent to trial, where they fear they will be hanged. It is important to note at this point that Robertson places his story at a time when a person could indeed be hanged for poaching on private land. More importantly for the narrative, Robertson explains that at this time 'it was illegal to be a Traveller, and you could've been hanged, 'cause Macpherson was hanged in Banff for being a Traveller' (ibid.).

This mention of James Macpherson – executed in 1700 at Banff and who we encountered with Maggie McPhee in the previous chapter – places the chronology sometime before 1783, when capital punishment of Gypsies and other itinerant individuals was still being recorded (Okely 1983: 4). In framing his narrative in this way, the theme of Robertson's narrative becomes, ostensibly, the persecution of Travellers and Gypsies. Macpherson, having been accused of various capital crimes, was executed mainly based on his illegitimate birth to a Gypsy mother, and his subsequent associations with Gypsies (Mackenzie 1878: 28; Whyte 2013: 221; Duff, in TSAS Banff 1845: 23). During the eighteenth century – and up until the late-nineteenth century – Travellers ('Tinkers' at that time) and Gypsies were widely regarded as synonymous.[2] It is therefore plausible that James Macpherson's mother could have been a Traveller, or a Gypsy. At the conclusion of Robertson's story, the young couple are saved from the gallows when the judge at their trial – who was 'known to be a hanging judge' (TAD 38131) – inexplicably lets them go free. As the couple are released, they encounter the judge and notice the distinctive birthmark on his neck. They ask the judge why he set them free, to which he replies '"I don't understand it, I've never been known to be like this", he said, "just when I looked down to you, I had the cold shivers running up and down my spine", he says, "I think you're putting some sort of curse upon me"' (ibid.).

This statement from the judge warrants closer scrutiny. If the judge is being cast here as symbolic of a state that unjustly persecutes Travellers and Gypsies, it seems only fair to consider the narrative from the perspective of the state. As noted in the opening chapters above, the changing perception of Travellers from useful members of Scottish society to maligned non-conformists appears to have taken root sometime around the middle of the eighteenth century. It is not surprising that a people who, in Timothy Neat's words, display 'an almost pathological aversion, not to hard work, but to habitual labour and the discipline of the clock' (1996: 224), would not fit in to the mechanical repetition of a newly industrialised Scotland. The evidence presented in preceding chapters affirms that the settled, or mainstream, population's perceptions of Travellers and Gypsies in Scotland suffered a marked change for the worse during this period. The peripatetic lifestyles of Travellers and Gypsies not only did not fit with the prevailing winds of industrialisation, but this lifestyle became associated with criminality, immorality, and anti-social behaviour in general. Predictably, this hostility, coupled with the Travellers' resistance to assimilation, led to conflict. Such misconceptions about Traveller culture are borne out by the words of the judge; the supernatural 'curse' of the Travellers, so feared by the judge, betrays the prejudicial attitude of the state towards the perceived insidious mysticism of the Travellers and Gypsies that stands in stark opposition to the rationality of modernising industrialisation. In this sense, Robertson's story takes place in an all too real historical setting that effectively places the protagonists at opposite ends of an ideological spectrum; the reader will recall Olrik's law of contrast (1992: 50) from Chapter 2, a common feature of oral narrative, and perceive it here, clearly at work.

The judge is, of course, the Travellers' grown-up child. In Robertson's narrative, then, the judge has a dual persona: On one hand he is 'a very harsh looking young man, donned with his wigs and pomp and splendour' (TAD 38131); on the other hand, the judge's Traveller persona is symbolically represented by his birthmark. The 'black mark' of the Traveller is representative here of some inherent disfigurement, or otherness, that differentiates and distances him from the establishment.[3] The juxtaposition of the 'pomp and splendour' with his disfigurement becomes the corporeal representation of the judge's dual nature. The disfigured and impoverished Traveller child is thrust into a world of privilege and power by his parents, and reluctantly so. By the conclusion of this short story, when the Traveller child has matured, his resulting pompous appearance as a court judge is ironically lambasted on two fronts. Firstly, the outward disfigurement of the innocent Traveller child is mirrored by his grotesque appearance in adulthood. After being raised in the 'rare big huge toff mansion hoose' (ibid.), his 'unattractive' qualities become his propensity for hanging people and his ignorance of the ideological imperatives of those he perceives as beneath him. The duality revealed by the plot of this story is clear: what is deemed outwardly ugly or repulsive is betrayed by the inner rectitude provided by the Travellers' culture. Braid also recognises this theme of outward appearances being deceptive and meaningful in Travellers' stories, arguing that deceptive appearances within Travellers' narratives demonstrate 'deeper ways of perceiving and understanding the world' (2002: 37).

The harsh judge, given to hanging, in his pomp and splendour is therefore symbolic of the injustice that Travellers and Gypsies faced at the hands of the state. In Sheila Stewart's printed collection of Traveller stories, *Pilgrims of the Mist*, she explains that the stories in her volume come from Travellers all over Scotland and that her selections reflect the fact that the tellers 'think in the same way I do' (2008: vii). The opening narrative, titled 'The Hanging' and framed as an oral history, engages with the same themes as Robertson's – lethal persecution based on identity. In Stewart's story, a Traveller named Andy Campbell is accosted by a man on horseback who accuses him of lying about having no tobacco to spare. '"All you damn tinkers are the same"' (ibid.: 1), blurts the aggressor, and he proceeds to strike the Traveller with his horsewhip with such force that he falls from his horse. '"How dare you unsaddle me from my horse! You will pay for this, tinker"' (ibid.: 2), the horseman shouts, before he drags Andy to jail. Not only is Andy persecuted in this account, but his persecution occurs in such a way that he himself is to blame for it. When Andy's family arrive at the jail the next morning, they are told that he is being hung that day; '"because he is a tinker"', the jailors tell the family, '"we need to get rid of tinker scum"' (ibid.: 3). Andy's family duly protest, identifying themselves as 'Tinkers', and are sentenced to suffer the same fate on the gallows. In Robertson's Traveller-Judge narrative, the symbolic content cooperates to convey the meaning of the story by challenging such blind persecution. Regardless of his establishment upbringing, the Traveller child grows up to display an inherent sense of justice, despite the tension that this creates with the immorality and prejudice associated with the establishment's persecution of Travellers and Gypsies. The 'cold shivers and curses' that the judge persona experiences in the presence of his biological parents galvanises his latent Traveller persona to win the day. The judge remains unaware of his Traveller heritage throughout the narrative, and resorts to superstition to explain his actions. The judge's perceived lack of agency ultimately reflects the fate of the many doomed Travellers and Gypsies who were executed based solely on their identities.

Both Robertson's and Stewart's stories remind us that the lethal persecution that Travellers faced at the hands of the state has not been forgotten and has passed into the oral traditions shared by Travellers. Robertson concludes his narrative by explaining the deep, unconscious familial bond that transcends the material transformation of the abandoned child: 'mother nature's ties of the cord must still be there', Robertson tells us, and that 'there are things that can testify to ye a blood kin, withoot actually haein' to be telt' (TAD 38131). Thus, the abandoned child's Traveller identity is immutable, despite his alternative upbringing, his resulting high social status and the power over life and death that he wields in adulthood. The incorruptibility displayed by the abandoned child demonstrates the Travellers' ability to negotiate an unfair system of justice – embodied by the state – through narrative.

In a 1949 lecture titled 'The Role of the Artist in Society', Henderson explained that 'folk art is an implicit and in many respects explicit challenge to the ruling class way of looking at the world[:] we have more to learn from them than they from us' (cited in Neat 2007: 236). Robertson's narrative embodies this sort of challenge to the ruling class in a particular way; there is no explicit defiance, confrontation or belligerence on the part of the Travellers. Instead, the challenge comes through the Travellers' affirmation of their worldview and the ideological commitments that underpin this view. Notwithstanding material and intellectual transformation – not to mention access to power over life and death – the Traveller child ultimately remains loyal to his family. The 'hanging judge' is ironically cured of his persecutory ways when he exclaims to his Traveller parents, '"I think you're putting some sort of curse upon me"' (TAD 38131). Robertson's use of dramatic irony, by way of 'the curse of the Travellers', demonstrates a level of sophistication that typifies Traveller storytelling. In Robertson's story, the deeply entrenched sense of persecution felt by Travellers to this day is vitiated by their ability to morally transcend their persecutors. Moreover, Robertson's plot structure, narrative technique and characters collaborate to challenge persecutory behaviour whilst simultaneously affirming aspects of Traveller worldview. In terms of the ideological imperatives being enacted here, we return to this point in the next chapter, where Robertson's story is revisited in further detail.

A narrative from Duncan Williamson engages with the same theme of an immutable, inner Traveller identity and strong familial bonds. This story also demonstrates the theme of deceptive outward appearances playing a pivotal role in the plot. In Williamson's untitled story, the two sets of protagonists are referred to as 'the Travelling People', and 'this lady and gentleman' (cited in Braid 2002: 35–36). By depersonalising his protagonists, Williamson effectively creates a binary between Travellers and members of the settled population as discrete groups. From this perspective, the protagonists of Williamson's narrative embody the entirety of the two disparate social groups and are symbolic of opposing ideological commitments. Williamson's story can therefore be viewed as an encounter between the Travellers and the settled or mainstream population, regarded as discrete social units. For ease, the two sets of protagonists are referred to as the 'Travellers' and the 'Settled People' henceforth. Williamson explains that the Settled People liked the Travelling People, and so allowed them to camp on their land. One night, the Traveller woman is begging for food at the Settled People's mansion and discovers that the Settled woman is unable to bear children. The Traveller woman, on the other hand, is fecund and tells the Settled woman that she has already borne six children (ibid.: 35). Given these further details, the binary aspect of Williamson's narrative comes into sharp focus: Settled and Traveller, have and have-not, infecund and fecund. Of course, the first two binaries exist outwith the narrative, they exist in reality and are routinely observed in the lived experiences of both sets of protagonists. However, the final binary is not so visible, and it is here at the familial level that the narrative is played out. The Traveller woman's inner fecundity and outer poverty is juxtaposed with the Settled woman's outward material wealth and her inner dearth.

During their meeting at the mansion door, the Settled woman proposes that the Travellers give the Settled People one of their children, imploring to the Travellers that 'I'll give you anything that you want' (ibid.). After a consultation together, 'naturally, the Travelling People went on their way. And they left the wee baby, which was a wee boy' (ibid.). Giving away a child in such a way is anything but natural, and as we will see, the baby in Williamson's story has an allegorical function. What is conspicuously absent as Williamson's story continues is evidence of any transaction having taken place; the Travellers simply hand over their child and the Settled people 'reared it up to be their own' (ibid.). The Travellers stood to gain materially by giving the Settled People one of their children, yet they do not. Whether it came in the form of money, land, animals or something else, the material wealth on offer to the Travellers is refused. In the context of Williamson's story, ill-gotten material wealth is denounced as the Travellers effectively refuse to sell their child, but it would be difficult to argue that Williamson's story is a comment on avarice. For instance, Holly Tannen recorded a version of this story from Williamson in 1986; presenting this version in his book, *Webspinner: Songs, Stories, and Reflections of Duncan Williamson, Scottish Traveller*, Niles points out that the versions differ significantly in their detail (2022: 152). One such detail is that in this version, Williamson narrates that the Settled People 'gave them [the Travellers] some money' (cited in ibid.: 153). Despite this variation, the premise and trajectory of the narrative are the same and the theme of have and have-not remains central to the advancement of the plot. The fact that the Travellers can give something as precious as a child – with all that that carries in terms of Traveller worldviews around family – without receiving anything in exchange is perhaps a safer reading in this respect. Moreover, the Settled People's *perception* that the Travellers are the have-nots in the situation is a more revealing consideration. By refusing the offer of 'anything you want', the Travellers affirm that there is nothing the Settled People have that they want.

This presents the question, what *is* it that the Travellers have? The answer comes at the conclusion of the story where we meet the Traveller child at five years old, out walking with the Settled man and their pet dog. The dog picks up an old cow's horn and the Traveller child exclaims, '"Daddy, wouldn't that make a lovely spoon!"' (ibid.). There is evidence that, in the past, Travellers were known for fashioning spoons from animal horn (for example, TAD 82053). Discussing Traveller handicrafts in 1972, Traveller Belle Stewart remarks, 'horn spoons they used to make. My father could dae a' these things' (TAD 100320). There are also mentions of Travellers being referred to as 'Horners' in TSAS (Auchterderran 1791: 458), and Macritchie also cites the Horner appellation when discussing Travellers (1894: 1). In Campbell's *Reminiscences*, he tells us of Travellers he knew in his youth who 'made spoons out of the horns of rams and cattle' (1910: 24). Elsewhere, Isabel Grant, curator of the Highland Folk Museum, describes how the 'Tinkers' she knew would fashion spoons from horn (2007: 128).[4]

Consequentially, the conclusion of Williamson's story explicitly aligns the child with a handicraft known to be practised by Travellers. The implication being that, in spite of his upbringing, the child remains a Traveller. The Traveller child with artisanal aspirations encourages us to make use of what is provided by nature, and to avoid the trappings of living solely for the pursuit of material gain. As Roger Leitch has pointed out, 'the material culture of the travelling people demonstrates a marvellous ingenuity and awareness of natural resources' (1988: xxviii). The environmental awareness of the Travellers identified by Leitch is playfully represented in Williamson's narrative, when the Traveller child imagines a spoon within the old cow's horn. From this perspective, the focus of the story is shifted away from the Travellers 'naturally' giving up their child and is refocused on the Travellers' relationship with their environment. This may go some way to explaining why the child in the story was so willingly given away – the meaning of the story lies in the ethos of the young boy as a representative of Traveller culture and identity. The fecundity of the Traveller couple is aligned with the fecundity that Travellers recognise in nature; the revelation of the child's 'inner' identity performs an allegorical function when he recognises the regenerative power of nature in the potentiality of the lovely spoon.

Like the judge in Robertson's narrative, the child in Williamson's story has a Traveller reawakening. Crucially, both stories are linked in that each reawakening is intimated by the presence of blood relations. In Robertson's story, the familial presence is literally the appearance of the judge's biological parents; as we heard from Robertson, 'there are things that can testify to ye a blood kin, withoot actually havin' to be telt' (TAD 38131). In Williamson's story, the familial trigger is the presence of a cow's horn. Although the horn could be read as an allusion to a handicraft practised by Travellers in general, Williamson specifically casts the child's father as the artisan, explaining that the child's father 'used to make spoons, you see?' (cited in Braid 2002: 36). In the variation cited above – recorded by Holly Tannen in 1986 – Williamson concludes his narrative in a similar fashion; when the Traveller child identifies the potential spoon, the Settled man pronounces, '"Of course, it's in your blood" [. . .] "In your blood it will remain"' (cited in Niles 2022: 153).

THE CINDERELLA MASTERPLOT

As early as 1893, Marian Roalfe Cox's *Cinderella: Three Hundred and Forty-Five Variants* laid out the basic premise of this all-to-familiar set of stories. 'In arranging the variants belonging to the Cinderella type', says Cox, 'the *essential* incidents of each group may be seen as follows' (1893: xxv), going on to delineate three main categories – 'Cinderella', 'Catskin', and 'Cap o' Rushes' – that, effectively, constitute the tale-type. The core elements of the Cinderella tale-type are a persecuted protagonist; magical aid or a helpful animal; and a 'happy ending'. However, as Cox goes on to point out regarding Cinderella stories:

In compiling this collection of variants the difficulty has not been in tracing resemblances, but rather in determining what degree of family likeness or relationship shall constitute eligibility. Numerous "as the sand and dust" are the stories which have received their share of a family heritage. A particular folk-tale incident may recur in an endless number of permutations and combinations with other sets of incidents, and hopeless is the task of comprehending a series whose term is infinity.

(ibid.: xxxiv)

Much and more has been written about this ubiquitous narrative since Cox's pioneering study and insight, notably Anna Birgitta Rooth's *The Cinderella Cycle* (1951). Rooth's comparative study included some seven hundred versions, and both Cox and Rooth were 'especially interested in distinguishing the separate but seemingly related forms of the story' (Dundes 1982: xiv). Furthermore, as Thompson reminds us, incidents from Charles Perrault's 'Cendrillon' are 'so familiar through two-hundred-and fifty-years' use as a nursery tale that we are likely to think that all the details which he mentions are essential' (1946: 127). On the contrary – when viewed as a perennial plot that amounts to a transformative process, or rejuvenation, stories within the so-called Cinderella Cycle can function as useful platforms for the negotiation of cultural identity. For our purposes here, then, rather than embark on a comparative exercise between tale-types and their many hundreds of versions and variations, it is useful to consider the so-called 'Cinderella Cycle' as what H. Porter Abbott calls a 'masterplot'.[5] For Abbott, a masterplot can be viewed as a set stories that 'we tell over and over in myriad forms that connect vitally with our deepest values, wishes, and fears. Cinderella is one of them' (2008: 46).

The below examples demonstrate such vital connections within the Travellers' traditions and show how their negotiations of cultural identity manifest in unique ways. This type of nuancing was recognised by Carl von Sydow when he referred to 'special types, ecotypes' (1934: 349) within wider fields of tradition. A narrative ecotype is a version of an international tale-type that has adapted to be meaningful within a certain socio-cultural environment – it fits in, necessarily, to its cultural 'ecosystem'. The nineteenth-century folklore collector John Francis Campbell anticipates Von Sydow when he remarks of one story that 'it bore the stamp of the mind of the class, and of the man, who told it in his own peculiar dialect, and who dressed the actors in his own ideas' (1860–62: xlvii). This important concept of storytellers' 'own ideas' – or ideologies – being inculcated in their narratives is a trenchant observation about the nature of folkloric expressions, and becomes the central theme of the below discussions, and those of the following chapters.

At the same time, the Travellers' storytelling traditions do not always exist in isolation from the global community; in fact, they very much belong to that community and are expressive of international tale-types, manifesting themselves in specific ways, and, as Campbell knew, with culturally specific meanings.

Stories belonging to the Cinderella Cycle – Aarne-Thompson-Uther (ATU) Tale-Type 510A, 510B and 511 – can be found throughout the globe with each variant having its own flavour and context. James Danandjaja concludes that in one Indonesian variant, having patience through adversity ultimately allows the persecuted heroine to acquire 'the emotional placid stability which is considered to be civilised [. . .] by the Javanese value system' (1982: 177). Elsewhere, A. K. Ramanujan identifies the consumption of food as playing a central role in an Indian version of the story; Ramanujan observes that food 'appears at least five times' (1982: 272) in a version from Kannada and highlights the 'central importance of food in Hindu ritual and worship, and of food transactions as markers of caste-rank' (ibid.). Duncan Williamson's repertoire of stories can also be seen to include themes and motifs found in a variety of international tales. In his introduction to Duncan and Linda Williamson's *A Thorn in the King's Foot: Folktales of the Scottish Travelling People*, Henderson notes that 'Duncan does not consider himself in the category of "creative" storyteller [. . .] and accordingly it is possible, with fair confidence, to attach AT [ATU] numbers to most of his tales' (1987: 20). As we have witnessed throughout this book, many of Williamson's stories also exhibit a certain idiom that is underpinned by his cultural identity as a Traveller. As noted above, this idiom manifests itself in the fusion and nuancing of recognised international tale-types to create ecotypes of narratives.

The 'deepest values', recognised by Abbott cited above, can be found in nuanced Traveller renditions of the Cinderella masterplot. Henderson points out that the story named '"Mary Rashiecoats an the Wee Black Bull" is AT 511A [. . .] is related to the Cinderella Cycle, and has been found widely distributed throughout Europe' (1987: 20). AT 511A – which was amalgamated by Hans-Jörg Uther (2011 Vol. I: 296) ATU 511 – *One-Eye, Two-Eyes, Three-Eyes* – is ostensibly a Cinderella-type story except that the persecuted heroine is a persecuted hero. Thompson points out that, in variations of ATU 511, 'there is always a youth instead of a girl as the principal actor. He is helped by a bull' (1946: 129). In Uther's updated classification of AT 511A to ATU 511, his plot synopsis does not include the heroine being replaced by a hero. However, in Uther's description, the animal magical helper remains, as does the persecution of the protagonist. Betsy Whyte, a Traveller tradition-bearer we heard from in previous chapters, tells a version of ATU 511 where the persecuted protagonist is female (TAD 36559). The narrative trajectory – a persecuted protagonist who transforms, with magical help, and welcomes a 'happy ending' – aligns Whyte's version with the Cinderella masterplot and represents a more conventional version of the tale.[6] However, Williamson's version, 'Mary Rashiecoats an the Wee Black Bull', his narrative does not fit squarely with ATU 511 as suggested by Henderson. Although Williamson's version may fall into the Cinderella masterplot, there are events and motifs that differentiate it from the stock ATU 511 tale-type whilst simultaneously embodying ATU 511's central theme of persecution and transformation. Moreover, these examples bring the distinction between active and strong tradition-bearers – introduced in Chapter 1 above – into focus. Whyte's Cinderella story is evidence of her actively bearing the tradition, whereas Williamson's version represents a nuanced version that includes perennial themes whilst being artistically manipulated to produce more culturally specific meanings.

At the beginning of 'Mary Rashiecoats an the Wee Black Bull' we are introduced to the protagonist, Mary, whose mother and father have been killed in an accident. Mary is taken in by her grandmother who was 'a nice an kindly old soul an she loved Mary dearly' (Williamson 1987: 62). However, Mary has no companions at her grandmother's house, so the grandmother procures an unwanted bull calf from the auctioneer at the local market, and Mary and the bull become inseparable. Meanwhile, when Mary needs a new coat, her grandmother asks Mary to 'cut me some rashes like the rashes I want, I'll make ye a coat' (ibid.: 67). As an aside in the narrative Williamson explains the manufacture of this coat; 'rushes, we call them "rashes" [. . .] people long ago used tae split the rushes up, they wove them, they could make cloth fae them like they do wi the flax' (ibid.). Mary is then clad in 'the most beautiful green coat that you ever seen in your life' (ibid.: 68) and becomes known as Mary Rashiecoats. Years later, when money is short, Mary's grandmother insists that they sell the bull. Mary and the bull therefore run away into the forest where the bull becomes the magical helper and feeds Mary using a magic cloth. Eventually, the pair come to the edge of the forest where they stray into the territory of an ogre. The bull will 'make such a wonderful supper fir me' (ibid.: 72) proclaims the ogre as he takes the pair captive in his castle. However, the wee bull has been here before and instructs Mary to spill three drops of his blood that serve to distract the ogre while they make their escape.

At this point a magic flight occurs, with Mary riding on the back of her bull while it swims through a lake. With the ogre in pursuit, the bull tells Mary to throw salt into the water and 'there came a iceberg o salt' (ibid.: 75) that impedes the ogre. The ogre is finally stopped by a magic pea from the bull's ear that causes a narrow valley to collapse around the ogre when Mary tosses the pea to the ground. At the conclusion of Williamson's narrative, we find out that the bull was previously the ogre's unwilling apprentice and had escaped. He tells Mary that '[the ogre] reared me up an taught me all these wonderful things, but all these things were evil, I didna want none of his evilness anymore' (ibid.: 76). As the ogre is trapped in the rubble of the collapsed valley, the bull convinces him to 'set him free'. The ogre complies and the bull transforms into the 'most handsomes [sic] young man in the world you ever saw stood there dressed in green' (ibid.). The transformed bull then kills the ogre and lives 'happily ever after' in the ogre's castle with Mary and her grandmother. Williamson's story does contain elements of ATU 511, such as Mary Rashiecoats' bull as the persecuted protagonist on account of his unwilling apprenticeship at the hands of the ogre. Following Thompson's and Uther's descriptions of AT 511A and ATU 511 noted above, Williamson's Mary Rashiecoats story holds little else in common with that tale-type. Instead, what we find in Williamson's story is an amalgamation of several motifs and tale-types that place his version of the Cinderella masterplot firmly within the unique folk idiom of the Traveller storytellers. Williamson's story contains elements from across the Cinderella Cycle; Dundes (1982: xiv) notes that the cycle's subtypes include AT 510A. 'Cinderella', AT 510B. 'The Dress of Gold, of Silver, and of Stars', AT 511. 'One-Eye, Two-Eyes, Three-Eyes', AT 511A. 'The Little Red Ox' and a combination of AT 511 and AT 510A. Of Dundes' list, Williamson's story has elements of all these tale-types except AT 511 (until Uther's update to ATU 511, mentioned above).

However, Thompson notes that the plot of AT 511 is 'so closely related in detail to Cinderella and Cap o' Rushes that it is frequently considered a variant form' (1946: 128). Uther's amalgamation of AT 511A and ATU 511 also reifies the close relationship between the two tale-types. From this perspective, Abbot's conception of a 'masterplot' makes sense when considering Williamson's story. The typological distinctions made by Aarne, Thompson and Uther (ATU) are useful, but it appears that it is the overarching theme of transformation that gives the Cinderella Cycle, or masterplot, its ongoing international appeal. Williamson's 'Mary Rashiecoats an the Wee Black Bull' displays the transformation of a young orphaned girl into an adult, with the prerequisite husband, home and extended family. Yet Williamson's story also showcases the more explicit transformation of the bull; the handsome young man rejects the evil he sees in his tutor and is rewarded through his meeting with Mary and their ultimate contentment as a couple. Mary's and the bull's transformations are linked at the conclusion of the story when we find the handsome young man is 'dressed in green' (Williamson 1987: 76). Mary's coat of green rushes thereby differentiates Williamson's story from other stock versions of ATU 510B – *Peau d' Asne* (previously The Dress of Gold, of Silver, and of Stars [Cap o' Rushes]).

The above analysis demonstrates an alchemical process that draws on elements from various tale-types to create a distinctive Traveller expression. For example, Alan Dundes highlights the antiquity of one motif within the Cinderella masterplot, the stepmother feigning illness – referring to Anna Rooth's work on the Cinderella Cycle in the 1950s, Dundes notes how Rooth perceives the motif of the '"stepmother who pretends to be ill and demands the liver or flesh of the animal to eat" [. . .] and specifically compares it to the Egyptian "Tale of the Two Brothers"' (2002: 382). Dundes reflects that the Tale of the Two Brothers 'appears to have been recorded in the 13th century before the Christian era, which would make it more than three millennia old' (ibid.: 378). Significantly, Dundes goes on to note that this motif is also 'found in Aarne-Thompson Tale-Type 511A [ATU 511], The Little Red Ox' (ibid.; cf. Dundes 1982: xiv). For Mary Rashiecoats, the seemingly antagonistic actors who seek to deprive her of her bull, as we will see, are connected at the conclusion of Williamson's tale. Not only does Williamson's story amalgamate motifs from across the Cinderella Cycle, but it also includes motifs from other tale-types. The magic flight that Mary Rashiecoats and her bull take from the ogre's castle is another example of hybridity in Williamson's story. In the international versions of ATU 313 – *The Magic Flight*, Thompson notes that 'in all versions of this story the hero comes into the power of an ogre' (1946: 88–89). This is true of the bull/handsome young man in Williamson's story, and Williamson's story is further linked to ATU 313 in terms of the drops of blood that Mary and the bull leave behind to distract the ogre while they escape from his castle. In ATU 313, Thompson describes how 'the young people prepare for flight and leave behind themselves some magic objects which speak in their place when the ogre talks to them' (ibid.: 89). The salt and the pea that Mary throws from the bull's back also align Williamson's story with ATU 313; Uther notes that in ATU 313 the heroine 'throws magic objects (comb, brush, mirror etc.) which become obstacles in the way of the pursuer' (2011 Vol. I: 195). The amalgamation of the various tale-types from the Cinderella Cycle, and the addition of elements from a seemingly unrelated tale, gives Williamson's story a distinctive Traveller idiom and therefore a nuanced set of meanings.

When it comes to the interpretation of Traveller stories such as Williamson's above, Braid has also recognised 'a distinct Traveller flavour' (2002: 194) in stories that follow the Cinderella masterplot. In another of Williamson's versions of the Cinderella masterplot, Braid asserts that his performance 'echoes aspects of the Perrault version of the story while simultaneously transforming the content and meaning of the story to fit squarely within Traveller life and worldview' (ibid.: 174). One example Braid provides – and that can also be observed from the synopsis of Mary Rashiecoats above – is the lack of the persecuted heroine. Braid suggests that this lack is 'because this abuse does not make sense within Traveller culture' (ibid.: 195). Braid goes on to suggest that 'consequently, the story cannot be interpreted as a rags-to-riches success story or as embodying a tension in social structure' (ibid.: 196) and that Williamson's story has a focus on 'issues of cultural difference and discrimination' (ibid.: 200). Braid's interpretations are based on the heroine, a Traveller named Mary, being married to a laird and consequently into wealth and domestic security for her and her family. For Braid, the lack of familial persecution and the lack of social discrimination means that Williamson's story ultimately advocates 'the validity of Traveller identity and worldview' (ibid.) to the otherwise discriminatory non-Travellers.

In 'The Travellers' Cinderella', recorded in 1976, Williamson tells a more familiar version of the masterplot - like Perrault's, grand ball, glass slipper, magical carriage and all – and ironically, it is the Traveller protagonists who validate the persecution. Throughout the narrative, the Travellers continually belittle their status, and are fearful of being 'shifted' [moved on] or 'quodit' [jailed]. '"Better ye think o a young traveller man tae yersel"', cautions Mary's father when she speaks of attending the ball, '"you'll never get nae laird's son"' (Williamson 1989: 164). When the supportive grandmother uses her 'magic wand' to transform everyday items, and Mary, so that they are ready for the grand ball, Mary's mother observes them and is terrified: '"shanness [shame on us], shanness, we're quodit [. . .] that auld wumman's sprachin [begging] 'em for looer [money]"' (ibid.: 165). The masterplot's central theme of persecution remains, but it is being negotiated in a self-reflexive way – the Mary-Cinderella does not suffer directly at the hands of her (step) family and instead comes from a nurturing environment. However, anxieties around cultural practices such as regular winter camping grounds, itinerant bagpiping and reading palms are also expressed in this environment (ibid.: 162–163). Mary-Cinderella's function within the narrative is to undermine intergenerational attitudes towards persecution and embody cultural legitimacy. When Mary-Cinderella's foot 'fits the shoe', her transformation amounts to the legitimisation of the nurturing culture where she comes from. Not only this, but her doubtful mother, father and Mary's family are able to camp on the laird's land in perpetuity, without fear of persecution, with a safe and comfortable place to spend the winter (ibid.: 172). Williamson himself, as a strong tradition-bearer, somewhat anticipates this interpretation in his commentary of his story: 'the Travellers had their ain way o it and the country folk [mainstream population] had their ain way. I just liked the way I heard it [. . .] I mean the real Cinderella could be taken aff the Travellers' story, couldn't it?' (ibid.: 173).

It is useful to consider these interpretations of Williamson's Cinderella story in light of our understanding of 'Mary Rashiecoats an the Wee Black Bull'. If we treat these stories as belonging to the Cinderella masterplot, such interpretations can be expanded upon to give Williamson's Mary Rashiecoats story a more nuanced meaning. As was noted above by Braid, there is similarly no persecuted heroine in Williamson's Mary Rashiecoats narrative. On the contrary, we are told that when staying with her grandmother, Mary Rashiecoats 'begint tae feel she wis at home at last, she'd found someone who really did love her' (Williamson 1987: 62). However, Mary's familial bonds are broken; at first by tragedy through the death of her parents, and then by conflicting loyalties when she and the bull run from the grandmother who wants to sell the bull to slaughter. From this perspective, Mary's initial flight with the bull speaks of a different type of loyalty and demonstrates the characteristic individualism of Travellers that we have experienced throughout this study. Mary's individuality is explicit when Williamson describes the coat of rushes that gives Mary her name, 'nobody in the village had a coat like this' (ibid.: 68). Moreover, the fact that her grandmother made the coat using an ancient technique invests Mary's coat with the knowledge of her ancestors. In this sense, Mary is both an individual and a product of many generations of her ancestors.

The sense of continuity through a connection to the past is paramount in Travellers' identity formation, as expressed in the stories under discussion. Dressed in her coat of rushes, Mary Rashiecoats is distinctly 'other' to the villagers. Williamson describes how 'Mary visitit the village many times an the people in the shops used tae call "Mary Rashiecoats", not when she was there, but they said, "Oh, here comes Mary Rashiecoats again wi her wee black bull' (ibid.). As with all Cinderella masterplot narratives, the core themes are persecution and transformation. Mary's initial transformation through her coat allows her individuality to overcome her familial bonds and escape with her beloved bull. As noted above, Mary's transformation and her bull's transformation are aligned by their both being clothed in green. Mary's ultimate transformation is thereby implicitly bound to the bull's transformation from the outset. Furthermore, the grandmother and the ogre are also linked through their desire to have the bull slaughtered. At the conclusion of the story, the transformed bull explains how the 'ogre turned me into a calve an sent me to the market tea get slaughter, so that I could never indulge in his powers an tell anyone' (ibid.: 76). However, Mary's benevolent grandmother is keen to share the knowledge of her ancestors whereas the ogre wants to guard his secrets, even if it means murder. This parallel between the grandmother and the ogre complicates the stock plot of ATU 511. Williamson's Mary Rashiecoats story is the very definition of an ecotype; it showcases an aesthetic not only influenced by the storyteller's creative license, but also with the underpinnings of a cultural identity that stands in contradistinction to mainstream precepts.

Braid's observations around strong familial bonds in the Travellers' Cinderella plots remain, however, when Mary and her grandmother are reconciled in the 'fairy tale' happy ending. As we have seen, these versions of the Cinderella masterplot are linked in the Traveller tradition. Both stories involve a positive transformation that is underpinned by a certain set of cultural priorities, and legitimisation of those priorities. Alan Bruford and Donald A. MacDonald have pointed out that ATU 510B 'is much more usual than AT 510A, "Cinderella" proper [. . .] in the older tradition of Britain and Ireland' ('Notes' 1994: 446). For instance, another example of a girl with a coat of rushes appears in a story published in 1890 in the journal *Folklore* that was recorded from a Miss Margaret Craig of Elgin, Morayshire. This version stands in stark contrast to Williamson's Mary Rashiecoats in that the version named 'Rashin Coatie' (A. W. T and M .C. B. 1890: 289) has a persecuted heroine dressed in a coat of rushes by her antagonistic stepmother. In line with the Cinderella masterplot, the calf's magical aid ultimately allows Rashin Coatie to marry a prince and together 'they lived happily all their days' (ibid.: 291). In Williamson's version, the transformation is projected onto the persecuted hero rather than the heroine. What has also been demonstrated here is that, in Williamson's Traveller versions, the central themes of persecution and transformation – found across the Cinderella masterplot – can include sophisticated, self-reflexive negotiations, and transformations where understanding of the cultural context can significantly alter their meaning. In Williamson's Mary Rashiecoats story, elements from various tale-types are combined to offer a unique Traveller take on other more stable or mainstream versions of the international tale-types. While it is true that the bull's magical aid sustains Mary while they are on the run, and then also allows them to escape from the ogre's castle, it is the bull's transformation that ultimately provides the fulfilment of both protagonists. The Mary-Cinderella of Braid's example has the same fate as Mary Rashiecoats; both heroines are transformed, and through this transformation either retain their Traveller identities, or legitimise their cultural heritage, whilst simultaneously altering their, and their families', material position for the better.

ROBBIE HA' AND THE CANDLE

In one obituary for Stanley Robertson after his death in 2009, he was 'recognised as a wellspring of Scottish travellers' [sic] lore; renowned for his phenomenal memory, he could recall ballads and stories dating back through 500 years of oral history' (*The Telegraph* 2009). This sentiment was reflected by Robertson himself, 'having been brought up in a family of old traditional Travellers', he explains, 'I consider myself as an expert on their culture, lore, superstitions, habits and way of life' (*Reek Roon a Camp Fire* 2009: ix). Robertson also intertwines Traveller worldviews and beliefs with other aspects of his identity. His stories negotiate differing cultural identities with the addition of his own personal identity tropes. The central purpose of this chapter has been to demonstrate how cultural identity is being negotiated within the Travellers' storytelling traditions. Robertson's status as a Traveller, a strong tradition-bearer, and a self-confessed cognoscente of Traveller culture, makes him an ideal exemplar with which to conclude this chapter.

In his many recorded interviews, Robertson makes several references to his membership of the Mormon Church (TAD 65426, TAD 65165 and TAD 65425), making it clear that his faith played an important role in his life and informed his view of the world. However, Robertson explains that 'Mormon people don't believe in superstitions or ghosts [and] they thought it was really, really hilarious' (TAD 64651) whenever he referred to his superstitions as a Traveller. Robertson goes on to confirm that 'the [Mormon] Church tells ye not to believe in superstitions, but it doesnae tell ye to give up all yer customs and traditions' (ibid.). Robertson's status as a Traveller appears to come into conflict with other elements of his identity and he negotiates these conflicting elements of his identity through his stories. Robertson also reminds us of the importance of intergenerational transmission and filiation we encountered in preceding chapters: one 'story I wis telt came fi my grandfather' (TAD 44606), says Robertson, elsewhere remarking that his grandfather was 'very, very descriptive and so that's one trick I hid learned [from] him' (TAD 44613). Robertson's knowledge of Traveller culture, along with his own extensive repertoire, make him a significant source of information not only about cultural identity, but in helping us think about how stories cross generations and are re-imagined in the minds of gifted storytellers.

A good example is a story that Robertson refers to as 'The Story o' Robbie Ha" (TAD 44812). This is the story of a Traveller man who unwittingly becomes the agent of a malevolent spirit and is redeemed by his beliefs. In summary, the Traveller protagonist, 'Robbie Ha', is possessed by a recently deceased warlock; the warlock wants to take revenge on an undertaker who had helped a girl escape from him. The warlock therefore possesses Robbie and seeks out the undertaker to exact his revenge from beyond the grave. The warlock is denied when an old woman dies in the village and the warlock's spirit is put to rest, thereby releasing Robbie from his possession. Crucial here is the way that Robbie is released from the warlock's possession. At the beginning of the story, Robertson frames the narrative by telling us that a common belief among Travellers in Scotland is 'that when a person dies, they become the keeper o' the grave' (ibid.). At the beginning of the story, the warlock is the most recently deceased and is therefore the 'keeper of the grave'. Robertson explains that this role as keeper means that the warlock's evil spirit cannot rest until another person dies, at which point that person becomes 'the keeper of the grave'. However, what is ostensibly a story about a malevolent ghost, bent on possessing others, becomes more complex when we consider Robertson's membership of the Mormon Church, his metanarrative and his status as a Traveller. Robertson explains elsewhere that evil spirits cannot 'come and possess people withoot people deliberately wanting possession' (TAD 64940) in the Mormon belief system. According to *The Book of Mormon*, the corrupt individual is possessed 'because of their own iniquity, being led captive by the will of the Devil' (Smith, 'Alma' 1981: 40:13). The implication for Robbie Ha is that he is somehow party to his own possession and is therefore corrupt in some way. Robbie's sinfulness is symbolised by his name when Robertson tells us that being 'classed by "Ha" meant you were a [. . .] big hunger' (TAD 44812); that is, a glutton.

From this perspective, Robertson's story warns against sin, lest you be possessed by Satan or any of his agents on Earth. At the same time, Robbie's status as a Traveller means that, when the unfortunate old woman takes the warlock's place as 'keeper of the grave', he is released from possession and the potential to do evil in the world. There is an obvious contradiction here: Robertson's religious belief in Robbie Ha's sin of gluttony is set in contradistinction to the Traveller belief in the 'keeper of the grave' when his sinfulness is exonerated by Traveller belief systems that operate in isolation from Mormon scripture. In that case, arguably, Traveller beliefs and customs supersede religious doctrine and thereby make them void; the sinful Traveller cannot, in fact, sin. However, as we have seen throughout the examples presented in this book, there is a cultural legitimisation at work under the surface of this narrative. In terms of ideological negotiation in cultural expressions, such as Robertson's story, Fredric Jameson once described these situations as 'the imaginary resolution of a real contradiction' (1981: 77). Citing the work of anthropologist Claude Lévi-Strauss, Jameson's point here is that cultural expressions can be symbolic acts whose function is to embody an otherwise insurmountable contradiction. There is no *real* resolution at all. What is at stake within the narrative is Robertson's status as a Traveller becoming the defining element of his identity, despite his membership of the Mormon Church. This sort of narrative negotiation does not, necessarily, reflect the ideological commitments of the Traveller communities at large. What it does reflect is how a storyteller who belongs to the communities artfully negotiates their own cultural identity within a distinctive narrative arena.

A more precise example of this kind of artful negotiation in Robertson's storytelling are narratives where the Traveller protagonist overcomes some form of antagonist using their wits. Again, these types of narrative are by no means unique to Robertson or the Travellers' traditions, but the way that that narratives unfold often is. Within Robertson's repertoire, there are numerous stories where the protagonist 'sells his soul to the Devil' and plays out the popular legend of Faust. Robertson reinterprets Faustian tropes, embellishing the narrative with the distinctive Traveller folkloric idiom that we continue to encounter – a distinctive brand of storytelling that includes nuanced plots, or ecotypes, and motifs that offer insights into the ideological commitments of the storyteller. Before thinking about Robertson's story, it is useful to have some contextual information. Discussing the development of the Faustian myth, Philip Mason Palmer and Robert Pattison More argue that 'part of the material, like the compact with the Devil, is common property of the Christian Church. Other elements can be traced back to Hebrew and Persian sources antedating Christianity' (1936: 4). For Stith Thompson, 'the details of this bargain and the dealings between man and the evil one have interested not only men like Goethe and Marlowe but many other more humble bearers of tradition' (1946: 269). These observations – coupled with the antiquity of the Faustian myth – suggest that it contains perennial themes that stand outside of religion altogether.

Colin Falck describes the story of Faust as 'one of the most powerful and dominant myths of Western culture' (1994: 133) and goes on to suggest that 'in its later versions where Faust is saved rather than damned for his pursuit of experience [. . .] is in many ways an exact inversion of Christian teachings' (ibid.). What Falck is arguing here is that the Faust story can embody an intermingling of Christian theology with pre-Christian 'myths of a primal fall' (ibid.). The inversion of Christian teachings and links to primal anxieties of a spiritual fall are arresting concepts when we consider Robertson's version of the Faust story. Robertson's spiritual beliefs can again be seen to come into conflict with his status as a Traveller. In framing his version of the Faustian narrative, Robertson explains that he calls the story 'The Candle' (TAD 44606) and that 'Traivellers wir very superstitious [. . .] never ever to let a candle burn to the end and I think it wis through this particular story' (ibid.). From the outset, Robertson defines his story in terms of Traveller beliefs. As we saw in the previous story of Robbie Ha's possession, the framing of the narrative is key. For Robbie, his redemption through the 'keeper of the grave' is anticipated by Robertson's use of prolepsis in his contextual information before the story begins. Similarly, in Robertson's Faustian narrative, the candle plays a crucial role in the outcome of the story.

After being diagnosed with terminal tuberculosis, and with hopes to marry a girl that he has been courting, Robertson's protagonist Tam makes a pact with the Devil. The Devil tells Tam that 'I can promise you good health, and I can promise you wealth and prosperity' (ibid.). The Devil then tells Tam that he must 'bargain wi me that you will sell your soul to me' (ibid.). Tam is lured into the Devil's bargain by promises of good health and the financial means to marry the woman he loves. As part of the deal, the Devil tells Tam that 'I winnae come for you until you should let yer candle burn to the end' (ibid.). It is here that Robertson's name for his Faustian narrative becomes significant. The candle in Robertson's narrative becomes symbolic of Traveller superstitions and a means to outwit the Devil. In another rendition of this story, Robertson reveals the nature of the contest between Tam and the Devil; in this version, the Devil tells Tam, 'if you manage to beat me before you die, then I'll hae nae possession of yer soul' (TAD 64353).

At the conclusion of Robertson's narrative 'The Candle' (TAD 44606), Tam saves his soul from the Devil by going 'over to the candlestick, just as the last flame was comin', he poured it in his hand an' rolled it intae a ba' and swallied it' (ibid.). Tam then explains to the Devil that '"there's nae candle there", he said, "because that candle never burnt awa' tae nothing"' (ibid.). At this point the Devil is vanquished and 'disappeared just like a puff o' smoke' (ibid.). As with Robbie Ha, the protagonist's Traveller beliefs represent the means to overcome evil, and here in this ultimate case, the Devil. In a published version of the same story, Robertson explains that 'Tam had beaten the Devil wi his sharpness o mind and wit [. . .] Tam hid beaten the Devil by swallowing the candle!' (1989: 50). Robertson's engagement with perennial themes is conditioned by a commitment to his cultural identity. Moreover, Robertson's narratives negotiate these themes in such a way that they are connected to wider cultural spheres whilst retaining their own culturally significant aesthetic. Falck's ideas about the inversion of Christian teachings also play a part in Robertson's Faust story; Tam's health, wealth and prosperity are never compromised, despite his dealings with the Devil. On the contrary, Tam's Traveller wit allows him to dabble in 'the black arts' for his own material gain while never suffering a 'primal fall'.

Like Falck suggests, later versions of the Faustian myth do indeed invert Christian ideas about redemption and Robertson's version appears to be one of them. Thompson has also observed that in another rendition of the Faustian myth the protagonist 'is to pay the devil when the last leaf falls from [a] tree. It is an oak tree and the leaf never falls' (1946: 44). What Thompson calls 'other deceptive bargains' (ibid.) also appear in tale 'types 1182, 1184 and 1185' (ibid.). However, in Robertson's Traveller version the deceptive bargain is transformed so that it is the Devil that suggests the burning down of the candle as the conclusion of their bargain. What the Devil is not privy to is the Traveller superstition of not letting the candle burn down to the end, and it is Tam's knowledge and wit as a Traveller that ultimately provides his salvation. A candle being associated with life has also been identified as a recognisable folkloric motif by Thompson. More specifically, when 'motif K551.9 – let me live as long as this candle lasts' (Thompson 1955: 315) appears, 'a man who has sold his soul to devil thus escapes' (ibid.) and this is certainly true of Robertson's use of the candle motif in his story. Thompson suggests that motif K551.9 is 'Irish: O'Suilleabhain 36, Beal XXI 313' (ibid.) and so Robertson's use of it within the wider Celtic cultural zone is not surprising.

However, Robertson's version can be more specifically aligned to Uther's ATU 1187 – *Meleager*; in this tale-type, Uther explains that 'a man blows out the candle (eats up the candle) and is free' (2004 Vol. II: 68). Uther goes on to note that 'this tale-type has a strong connection to the myth of Meleager in Homer, Iliad [. . .] and can be found in Ovid's Metamorphoses' (ibid.). Considering the Homeric connection, Robertson's tale contains ancient and perennial motifs indeed. Furthermore, it could be argued that flames in general symbolise vitality for humans through life giving warmth and protection, or with an uninterrupted burning hearth that sustains the family. The way in which Tam uses the candle in Robertson's Faustian narrative resists this symbolism as the candle is extinguished. Ironically, it is in the extinguishing that Tam's vitality endures. Considering the contextual details of Robertson's life and his status as a Traveller, the candle motif takes on a specific complexion. For Robertson, it is the wit of the Traveller that ultimately conquers the Devil rather than a deception involving an everlasting candle or a tree that does not shed its leaves. The story Robertson learned from his grandfather is an example of how personal belief systems can operate in tandem with broader superstitions from the Traveller community, and indeed with perennial themes and ancient motifs. The brief opening examples included in this chapter demonstrate the efficacy of contextualisation and close reading techniques when we think about the cultural identity of storytellers. The forthcoming chapters delve deeper into the Travellers' traditions to present detailed interpretations.

Notes

1. For more details of how members of Scotland's Traveller communities articulate this contrast, see, for example: J. Robertson TAD 10285; S. Robertson TAD 42990 and 38124; Stewart TAD 56424; Whyte TAD 39610 and 76669.
2. Evidence of the mainstream homogenisation of Travellers, Gypsies, and any other 'undesirables', in Scotland can be found in TSAS Eaglesham (1792: 124), TSAS Bunkle and Preston (1792: 157), TSAS Borthwick (1845: 185).
3. Robertson remarks at the end of his narrative that in other versions of this story, the disfigurement comes in the form of a 'hairy knuckle' (TAD 38131).
4. The Highland Folk Museum opened in Kingussie in 1944 and is known as *Am Fasgadh* ('The Shelter') (Cheape 2007: 9). The museum contains all manner of artefacts pertaining to farming, fishing, crofting and domestic life in the Highlands.
5. Further reading around the Cinderella Cycle can be found in Alan Dundes' edited collection, *Cinderella: A Folklore Casebook* (1982), which includes a representative collection of essays, mostly from the twentieth century. More recently, Suzy Woltmann's edited collection, *Woke Cinderella: Twenty-First-Century Adaptations* (2020), offers a series of revisionist readings.
6. A Gaelic version of ATU 511, 'A Chaora Bhiorach Ghlas' [The Sharp Grey Sheep], can be found in John Francis Campbell's *Popular Tales of the West Highlands: Orally Collected* (1860–62), Volume II, pp. 286–289.

5

International Tales and Traveller Ecotypes

This chapter begins by considering what a narrative's form, or structure, can tell us about its function. We have previously encountered several so-called 'international tales' and the present chapter will continue discussing these to present the reader with further examples and interpretations. For instance, at the beginning of Robertson's 'Traveller-Judge' narrative discussed in the previous chapter, he remarks that he thinks that his story might 'come under some of the international tales [. . .] because you find that these Traveller tales are international tales' (TAD 38131). Considering the ATU classifications described above, Robertson's narrative does not appear to conform to the characteristics of any one tale-type. At the same time, Robertson's awareness of international tale-types is not surprising; strong tradition-bearers often combine, and reimagine, well-known international and local tales. Many Travellers' stories come to represent a mélange of international tale-types that are modified to reflect local conditions. These narrative mélanges are palpable demonstrations of the distinctiveness of Traveller storytelling that has been alluded to throughout this book. In the context of the combination of tale-types and motifs, Traveller storytelling can be viewed as a distinctive mode of orality where the narrators create narrative ecotypes (cf. von Sydow 1934: 349).

The reader will recall from the previous chapter that a narrative ecotype is a version of an international tale-type that has adapted to a certain socio-cultural context. This adaptation amounts to combining and manipulating various plots and motifs that can be shown to appear in other discrete socio-cultural contexts. It is not the purpose here to ask *how* or *why* these plots and motifs appear in discrete contexts, but to examine how the Travellers' stories become embedded with nuanced meanings that reflect *their* unique culture and lived experiences. We will also consider Williamson's narrative technique in more detail through an example that engages with an international tale-type; Williamson's Traveller version of an internationally-known story provides a germane contrast to Robertson's explicitly 'Traveller' narrative in further demonstrating the sophistication of the narratives that this book examines.

THE SECRET POWER OF FORM

With this process of combination and manipulation in mind, comparisons and analysis with common themes and motifs can offer complementary interpretations of folkloric narratives. Additionally, if Lüthi is correct and 'the secret power of the folktale lies not in the motifs it employs, but in the manner in which it uses them – that is, in its form' (1982: 3), then Robertson's Traveller-Judge narrative can provide a case study in which to explore this 'secret power'. Through the combination of plots and motifs found in international tales, Robertson's narrative engages with perennial themes from a different perspective. We find that the themes and motifs in Robertson's narrative reflect the Travellers' subaltern position in society, whilst simultaneously engaging with the very same familial tropes discussed in our analyses above.

As noted above, Robertson's narrative does not conform to any one specific international tale-type. However, the motifs that Robertson deploys do appear in the Aarne-Thompson-Uther (ATU) tale taxonomy.[1] Tale-type ATU 327A – *Hansel and Gretel* (Uther 2004 Vol. I: 212) – is a useful opening example. The themes, motifs and anxieties shared with Robertson's narrative are highlighted to offer interpretations based on the overarching premise of this tale-type. These discussions articulate how Traveller storytellers invert and manipulate international themes and motifs to reflect the Travellers' unique cultural identities. Before making any interpretations based on the tale-type classifications and motifs, it is useful to summarise the events which take place in Robertson's narrative, which are as follows: destitute parents abandon a child, said parents enter a crisis, the crisis is averted, the fate of the abandoned child is revealed, there is a recognition by birthmark, and finally, the parents and child are separated once more. The narrative shares characteristics with tale-types ATU 327A – *Hansel and Gretel* and ATU 850 – *The Birthmarks of the Princess*. Within the two tale-types, three identifiable shared motifs are present: in ATU 327A, S301 – 'children abandoned' and S321 – 'destitute parents abandon child'; in ATU 850, H51.1 – 'recognition by birthmark'. On the surface, Robertson's story of an abandoned child 'coming good' bears no resemblance to the plot of *Hansel and Gretel* and we are not suggesting here that Robertson's narrative is a version of the international tale-type ATU 327A. However, considering the central themes and motifs in conjunction with the plots of these stories, several similarities become apparent.

It is therefore useful to consider Robertson's story from a structural perspective to better understand its function. The structure of any given story can be seen as a specific set of principles that govern the plot, the characters and the motifs that appear within the narrative. Consider Olrik's position that 'storytellers have a tendency to observe certain practices in composition and style that are generally common to large areas', and that 'the regularity with which these practices appear makes it possible for us to regard them as "epic laws" of oral narrative composition' (1992: 41). As we saw in Duncan Williamson's narrative about a group of Travellers' experiences with a wealthy American tourist in Chapter 2, examples of Olrik's laws can, unsurprisingly, be found in the Travellers' traditions. In Williamson's story involving the American tourist, the law of contrast was identified as central to the meaning of the story. Olrik goes on to point out, regarding the epic laws, that 'a large part of the poetic tradition [. . .] looks to the preservation of the production of the individual poet, and is viewed as a tradition developed among specific peoples and within specific eras' (ibid.: 42). Olrik's 'individual poet' can be conceptualised as a strong tradition-bearer – such as Robertson or Williamson – and the 'specific people' as Scotland's Travellers.

From this perspective, the two stories under examination in this chapter are evidence for our argument that Traveller storytellers adhere to certain narrative compositional rules, while simultaneously *creatively engaging* with these rules. It is in such creativity that we find the distinctive folk idiom that Traveller storytellers express. We saw that the central theme of Robertson's Traveller-Judge story is the absent Traveller child and his sense of an immutable inner rectitude enjoyed by the Travellers. Robertson's narrative follows Olrik's 'Law of Centralisation' in that the narrative arranges itself around a central character (ibid.: 49); in this case, the absent child. Olrik's central character functions in tandem with the 'Unity of Plot' law, allowing him to reshape 'the given material, especially when it deals with the extraneous [for example, historical occurrences], in order to better place all of the episodes in relation to the main character' (ibid.). As in Williamson's story involving the rich American tourist, we also find the 'Law of Contrast' in Robertson's story, manifested in the dual nature of the Traveller-Judge. We have then at least three of Olrik's epic laws at work in Robertson's narrative: firstly, the absent Traveller child is the central character and therefore dominates the plot; secondly, the Traveller-Judge brings unity to the plot by embodying events that are external, yet pertinent to the narrative – the fatal persecution of Gypsies and Travellers in the past; and thirdly, contrast in character is also a function of the centralised Traveller-Judge, where the contrast in the characters is as explicit as possible. The distinctive Traveller folk idiom manifests itself in the way that Olrik's overarching narrative devices are rendered in the telling of the stories. In this way, the laws identified by Olrik provide a frame for the stories, but the details used to develop this frame into a coherent narrative are distinctively Traveller. Combining these positions with reference to the international tale-types described above is a useful way to reveal the 'secret power of form' within folklore.

THE TRAVELLER-JUDGE (REVISITED)

For the purposes of the present discussion, we will rely on the Grimm's version of *Hansel and Gretel* for comparison. As Thompson has pointed out, the central elements of the European versions of *Hansel and Gretel* are so simple and uniform that a theoretical discussion based on one version does not suffer for it (1946: 37). A brief synopsis of the Grimm's *Hansel and Gretel* is as follows: parents abandon their children in a forest due to lack of food; the children find nourishment but are captured by an antagonist; finally, the children escape their captor and return home with material wealth. Considering *Hansel and Gretel* alongside Robertson's Traveller-Judge story, the lack of food that forces the parents to abandon their children is a theme explicitly present in both narratives. Lack of food intimates the journeys of the children in both cases, and this is, ostensibly, where the similarities between the stories end. However, following Lüthi's (1982: 3) notion cited above that the import of a story lies in its form, rather than which motifs are present, *Hansel and Gretel* negotiates the very same anxieties and hierarchical relationships found in Robertson's narrative. The story is a narrative negotiation of basic human needs and motivations; Robertson's story shares certain impulses with *Hansel and Gretel* and the negotiations are tempered by singularly Traveller nuances.

During his discussion of *Hansel and Gretel*, Holbek asserts that the lack of food and the abandonment of children represent the socio-historical reality behind the fantasy (1987: 394). In Robertson's story, the socio-historical reality faced by Travellers can be viewed in the context of the Children Act (1908), which includes legislation aimed at persons who 'habitually wander from place to place' (Acts of Parliament 1908: Section

118). Under the provisions of the Children Act, parents were obliged to ensure that their children attended public elementary school during the months of October through to March on at least two hundred occasions (ibid.). According to Taylor, the Children Act was a part of reformers' belief that 'Travellers were capable of change, and that their characteristics were not inherent', and that the 1908 Act aimed to 'promote education as a prime tool in their reformation' (2008: 80). Moreover, the 1908 legislation gave the authorities the power, without a warrant, to remove children to 'a place of safety' should their living conditions contravene any part of the legislation. The Children Act could assert control not only over the education of Traveller children, but also their upbringing more generally. Essentially, the Children Act aimed to take control of the early scholastic and cultural education of Traveller children to integrate new generations of Travellers into mainstream society. This attempt to eradicate Traveller culture through their children did not entirely escape the public's eye, with sympathetic citizens recognising the cruelty of such oppression. Writing in protest to the editor of *The Scotsman*, G. A. Mackay propounds that 'to separate the [Traveller] children from their parents would be something like a death sentence [. . .] and would be one of the cruellest and most useless acts' ('The Tinker Problem' 1917: 10). Similarly, another contributor to *The Scotsman* writing after the Children Act was passed commented that educating Traveller children 'out of their natural instincts and traditions may be a greater form of cruelty than that which it is supposed to cure' ('The Wandering Tribes' 1918: 4).

We also have oral evidence of the impact that this had on Travellers during the first half of the twentieth century. Betsy Whyte reports that up until the 1930s, the authorities would take Traveller children away from their families and place them in homes:

> [the children] had to be taught fi that size [i.e., a toddler] to be wise for them [the authorities] ye see. If they [the authorities] thought you were hungry, [then] "they kids are neglected, we'll take them into a home". And these bairns that were taken into homes, when they come home they had to be looked after because they'd learned to steal, they'd learned to do things that we'd never even heard aboot [. . .] They [the children] were never any good, they never had much sense after comin' oot o' a home.
>
> (TAD 76578)

The anxieties expressed by Whyte come not only from the devastation of having a child taken away from a family, but of the negative impact that this has on the child during its formative years. In terms of our narratives, anxieties around the loss of a child are inverted so that it is the

Travellers themselves that facilitate the exposure. To put this inversion into context, Neat observes that in popular folklore – presumably within the mainstream population – Scotland's Travellers have long been associated with the theft, abduction and purchase of children (1996: 225). In terms of Travellers adopting unwanted 'settled' children, Neat goes on to suggest that 'over the years, guilt-twisted remembrance has turned "giving" into "taking", agreed "deals" into "theft"' (ibid.; cf. S. Robertson TAD 85577). As we have witnessed throughout this book, the sorts of lived experiences recalled by Whyte – and those perceived of in other sectors of Scottish society – are transposed into Travellers' narratives and thereby negotiated in specific ways. Given the family-centeredness of the Traveller communities, the *absence* of a child becomes a powerful motivator in the composition and sharing of stories.

With this in mind, and notwithstanding *how* the child becomes absent, the central theme of the Grimm's *Hansel and Gretel*, Robertson's tale of the Traveller-Judge, and Williamson's Traveller reawakening story is the absence of children. During an examination of the abandonment of children in literature from late antiquity to the Renaissance, John Boswell remarks that child abandonment is commonplace as a narrative turning point; a fact that he puts down to the ubiquity of the experience for ordinary people during that period (1988: 99). Boswell goes on to note that the pervasiveness of child abandonment also extends to 'Germanic and Celtic peoples', where 'Irish annals, folklore, and saints' lives include almost the same range of forms and motivations for abandonment as Roman literature' (ibid.: 212–213). Boswell's evidence suggests that the abandonment – and subsequent absence – of children is an ancient theme, one that taps into the very nature of human reproduction and the universal instinct that tells us to protect our young. Intriguingly, Boswell also found that 'the virtually unanimous testimony of literature is that the parents left with an abandoned child a token, sign, or symbol', where 'these tokens were often intended [. . .] to make it possible for the parents to identify the child with some assurance' (ibid.: 126). In Robertson's story, this identity symbol is made manifest in the unusual birthmark – the 'Black Mark' of the Travellers – a point to which we return presently.

Meantime, in the Grimms' version of *Hansel and Gretel*, the childhood fear of abandonment – or even infanticide – becomes the inspiration for the children's journey into the fantasy realm of the forest. In this realm, interprets Holbek, the 'children's anxieties and aggressions are openly expressed without offending any real person' (1987: 394). The fictional witch of the story becomes a projection of the children's fear that their mother wants them dead; therefore, according to Holbek, it is psychologically safe for the children to kill the witch (ibid.). At the conclusion of the Grimms' story, the antagonistic stepmother – the architect of the children's absence – is also dead and their benevolent father has been eagerly awaiting their return.[2] Unlike Holbek's interpretation where the children are the focus of the story, Regina Böhm-Korff's interpretation shifts the focus from the children to the adults. Böhm-Korff perceives that the central meaning of *Hansel and Gretel* is the abandonment of children viewed from the parents' perspective, and that this meaning reflects the treatment of children during the period that the Grimms were compiling their tales (cited in Zipes 1997: 46). Zipes agrees with this refocusing on the adults, arguing that the Grimms' *Hansel and Gretel* amounts to the rationalisation of abandonment on the part of the parents (1997: 46). Consequentially, the Grimms' version of the story can be seen to reinforce hierarchical relationships; consider the fact that it is the parents who choose to abandon their children in times of dearth, rather than sacrifice themselves in some way to ensure that their children thrive.

In terms of the adults' rationalisation of an absent child, it is important to note that the Grimms' children return home with pockets filled with jewels and pearls. It could be argued that the children's new material wealth is symbolic not only of their triumph over adversity, but of their transition towards adulthood because they can now make a material contribution to the household. However, as Zipes has pointed out, we must realise that in analysing the Grimms' *Hansel and Gretel*, 'we are dealing not with a "pure" oral tradition that may have mythic roots in German or European culture but with a literary fairy-tale tradition connected to folklore that was part of a civilising process' (ibid.: 42). The symbolic material wealth gained by the children becomes a literary addition that Zipes sees as an ideological function within *Hansel and Gretel*; despite the abandonment of his children, the 'happy ending' at the conclusion of the story sees the father not only as a wealthy man but absolved of the guilt of abandoning his children. The ideological commitment Zipes refers to is the quintessentially sedentarist position that views material wealth as a central indicator of 'civilised' society. By the conclusion of Robertson's story, however, the symbolic wealth that has been gained is not represented in material terms at all. On the contrary, the value that has been gained by the absent Traveller child comes in the form of a transcendental sense of natural justice. It is a *moral* gain that has resulted from the absence of a child in Robertson's story, and it is a moral perspective that is represented in his story as inherently 'Traveller'. The reader will recall that there is no reconciliation of the parents and the children in either Robertson's or Williamson's stories. Instead, the conciliatory aspect of the Traveller stories manifests itself again in what we have already heard Robertson describe as the 'deeper wisdoms' (TAD 50189). A sense of justice and moral rectitude are placed above the familial and material reconciliation that we find in the Grimms' *Hansel and Gretel*. It is in this way that the ideological imperatives of the narrative are revealed; family and morality are placed at the centre of the narrative so that their importance to the tradition are clear.

Moreover, Robertson's story contains nuances of plot and motif that highlight the refined nature of Traveller storytelling traditions. Robertson uses narrative devices such as anagnorisis – the critical moment of recognition – that can be found from Sophocles' *Oedipus Rex* (c. 430 BCE) to Charles Dickens' *Great Expectations* (1861). Similarly, Robertson makes use of peripeteia, a reversal of fortune, as a narrative technique. Peripeteia occurs where the 'action of an agent of a dramatic action is prevented from achieving its intended result and instead arrives at an opposite actual result' (Belfiore 2009: 634). The reversal of fortune and recognition occur when the Traveller couple are inexplicably saved from the gallows, and their miraculous reversal of fortune is made explicable only when the recognition by birthmark occurs outside the courthouse. At a basic level, this combination of anagnorisis and peripeteia performs a cathartic function for the listener; there is a moral cleansing when the persecuted Travellers' lives are spared and a sense of closure as to the 'hanging' Judge's unexplained leniency.

Lack of agency permeates Robertson's story: the persecution faced by the Travellers denies them agency; the Traveller-Judge has no agency when he releases the parents; and the prejudicial State's agency is nullified when the Travellers are righteously liberated. The anagnorisis and peripeteia, from this perspective, function not simply as catharsis, but as symbols of emancipation. Both literally and figuratively, Robertson's Traveller characters are emancipated from society's ills: the starving child is saved from hunger; the Traveller-Judge's cruelty is inverted when he is compelled to release innocent detainees; and the persecuted Travellers have their freedom. After careful examination, Robertson's allusion to international tale-types in the metanarrative of his story becomes clearer. Central themes from ATU 327A – *Hansel and Gretel*, and motifs from ATU 850 – *The Birthmarks of the Princess*, collaborate in his story to elicit a nuanced meaning. Robertson achieves this meaningful collaboration between theme (child abandonment) and motif (anagnorisis/peripeteia) by making the outcome of the story obscure to all but the Traveller parents who abandoned their child. As noted above by Boswell, parents leaving a token or symbol to assure future recognition is a pervasive motif in child abandonment narratives (1988: 126). In Robertson's story, the symbol that assures recognition is the unusual birthmark borne by the child. The 'Black Mark' of the Travellers is central to the meaning of the story because the birthmark is just that, an innate part of the Traveller child's constitution. The birthmark as a symbol is neither deliberately bestowed by the parents, nor has a function as a turning point in the plot. Viewed in this way, Robertson's short story about the Traveller-Judge is a representative example of how meaning within Travellers' tales is revealed.

It is important to cite Boswell's study of child-abandonment narratives – and the ATU tale-types – because Robertson's story is not a unique invention in terms of the overarching themes with which it deals. However, by unpacking the complexity of this narrative through close attention to the plot, motifs and characters, we can peer deep into the culturally significant meanings of deceptively simple stories. *How* the story means, therefore, is dependent on Robertson's narratological competence as a strong tradition-bearer; his use of international themes and motifs, coupled with his own social location as a Traveller, means that a plausible interpretation of his story is made possible. In Chapter 1, we thought about Frank's notion of an individual's 'social location' as a set of narrative resources that are based on their shared experiences, expectations and circumstances (2010: 13). We linked social location to ideology in the sense that experiences and expectations inform an individual's beliefs about the socio-cultural environment in which they live. In the present example from Robertson, the ideological commitment of the story, as a reflection of the Travellers' folk idiom, is the negotiation of a lack of agency experienced by the Travellers. As a social reality, this lack is projected on to the very pattern of the story and becomes a positive affirmation of the potency of the Travellers' inner identities and symbolic of their resilience in hostile situations. Using the character of the Traveller-Judge, the inner worth of the Traveller protagonists is ironically projected onto the very agent who denies them their agency.

THE HEDGEHURST

Duncan Williamson's version of ATU 441 – *Hans My Hedgehog* is another good example of how strong tradition-bearers manipulate perennial themes to render their narratives after the Traveller idiom. Williamson's version – entitled *The Hedgehurst* (TAD 36536) – is a further example of how his stories engage with themes such as familial bonds, individualism, and the Travellers' relationship with nature and their environment.[3] Furthermore, considering the Travellers' unique position in Scottish society, Williamson's story represents a narrative negotiation of isolation, marginalisation and how these anxieties are reconciled. Unlike Robertson's story about the Traveller-Judge, where the narrative connections to *Hansel and Gretel* were less obvious, Williamson's retelling of ATU 441 resembles recognised international versions. However, certain aspects of *The Hedgehurst* give Williamson's version a particular complexion and, again, nuanced meanings. As Jan Ziolkowski has pointed out, the essence of a story will of course differ from culture to culture, yet this characteristic variability does not mean that analysis of variations is futile (2009: 110). Instead, using flexible techniques during the analysis of such variations provides compelling evidence to support the central argument of this book that culturally significant meaning is deeply embedded within the Travellers' stories. The following discussion deploys comparative techniques to reveal how Williamson's story – situated as it is within the Traveller tradition – differentiates itself from other renditions of this international tale-type. We begin by comparing the symbolic meanings that are extant in several versions, then engage with these common meanings within the context of Traveller worldview and ideology. This demonstrates that the Travellers' storytelling traditions do not always exist in isolation from the global community; they sit comfortably on an international stage, manifesting themselves in specific ways and with specific meanings. The following discussion reveals what such ecotypes resemble in the Traveller tradition and discovers their ability to condition and represent the distinctive values and identities of the communities to which they belong.

In terms of the themes and motifs found in ATU 441 – *Hans My Hedgehog*, Uther describes the tale-type as follows: After a hasty wish, or a curse, a childless couple have a son who is a hedgehog; the hedgehog grows up to become a swineherd in the forest and is very successful; the hedgehog encounters a lost King to whom he gives directions out of the forest, and the King promises one of his daughters in marriage as a reward; the hedgehog rides his rooster to court to claim his prize; on the wedding night, the hedgehog's skin is destroyed, he is disenchanted and transforms into a handsome young man (2004 Vol. I: 263). In Williamson's version, the plot and characters are broadly similar to Uther's description of ATU 441: a woodcutter and his wife are childless until the miraculous birth of a particularly hairy baby boy, the eponymous Hedgehurst; the boy matures and sets off into the forest with several animals, where he becomes a successful carpenter and builder; Williamson's version includes a lost King, and a promised reward after the Hedgehurst guides the King out of the forest; the Hedgehurst duly rides to the King's court on his cockerel to claim his reward, the King's daughter's hand in marriage; Williamson's narrative concludes when the Hedgehurst's skin is destroyed, the spell is broken, and he transforms into a handsome young man.

According to Uther (ibid.), the oldest printed version of ATU 441 is to be found in Straparola's collection of stories, *Le Piacevoli Notti* [The Pleasant Nights], first published in Venice in 1551. Straparola's story tells of a childless King and Queen, and of 'one who was born as a pig, but afterwards became a comely youth' (1894: 58). In Straparola's story – known as *Il re Porco* [The Pig Prince] – three fairies cast spells on the childless Queen so that she bears a son who has beauty, every virtue under the sun, but who is born in the skin of a pig (ibid.: 59). For the disenchantment of The Pig Prince to take place, the fairies deign that he must marry three times. After The Pig Prince's third marriage, his pig's skin is removed and destroyed, he is crowned 'King Pig', and lives long and happily with his wife. Ziolkowski disagrees with Uther's provenance for this story, pointing out that 'Straparola's "Il re Porco" relates a tale substantially the same as that recounted by the male narrator of *Asinarius* [an anonymous Latin elegiac verse narrative composed c.1200 CE]', where 'an ugly animal who weds a princess turns out to be a handsome youth and becomes king when the animal skin in which he has been enveloped is burnt' (2010: 384). Ziolkowski goes further, suggesting that the animal-bridegroom motif and the general plot of ATU 441 have their roots in a Sanskrit myth named *The Story of Vikramāditya's Birth*; Ziolkowski's argument is that – during an unspecified time period – the Sanskrit myth passed into Europe, was divested of its Hindu pedigree, and then suitably altered in order to conform to its new Occidental circumstances (2009: 203, 224). Consequently, the animal-bridegroom transformation motif that is central to the plot of ATU 441 remained, whilst the circumstances of his transformation were adapted to be meaningful to new audiences. This process of adaptation during the transmission of stories is another way of describing a narrative ecotype, as described above.

Aside from Straparola and his influences, we also find other literary versions of ATU 441 published in the late seventeenth century. Marie-Catherine d'Aulnoy's *Prince Marcassin* [Prince Wild Boar] from her *Les Contes des Fées* [Fairy Tales] (1697) features an animal-bridegroom being transformed into a handsome young man at the conclusion of the narrative. Charles Perrault's contemporaneous version entitled *Riquet à la Houppe* [Riquet with the Tuft] (1697) has similar narrative patterning and motifs, with the exception that the protagonist, Riquet, is not explicitly described as animal at birth, instead being described as hideously ugly. Later, the Grimms' nineteenth century version – known as *Hans My Hedgehog* (trans. Zipes 2002: 361) – follows a similar pattern to that described by Uther. However, the four literary versions of this tale-type differ in two important ways. In the earlier versions from Straparola, Perrault and D'Aulnoy, the childless couple are royalty: Straparola's couple are 'Galeotto, King of Anglia [. . .] and his wife Ersilia, the daughter of Matthias, King of Hungary' (1894: 58); Perrault describes 'a Queen who was brought to bed of a son so hideously ugly, that it was long disputed whether he had human form' (1791: 75); and finally, D'Aulnoy's story begins with 'a King and a Queen who lived in great sorrow because they had no children' (1892: 481). In the Grimms' version, we are introduced to a farmer and his wife (trans. Zipes 2002: 361), whilst Williamson's oral version begins with a woodcutter and his wife (TAD 36536). The second difference between the various versions of ATU 441 cited above is that the miraculous birth of the animal-bridegroom, or hideous child in Perrault, is intimated by fairies in all but the Grimms' version.

The social position of the protagonist(s) is the first difference that alters the landscape of the narratives from the outset and is one that warrants discussion. If we understand ATU 441 as essentially a transformation narrative, then the fact that Straparola, Perrault, and D'Aulnoy *begin* with the protagonist in an elevated social position is telling. If the beastly child is already a Prince, the transformations of the animal-bridegroom in the earlier versions become biographies of an already privileged child ascending to the zenith of the social hierarchy. The presence of an innate privilege appears to fit well with the literary versions of ATU 441. Before his birth into royalty, it is prophesised by the fairies that Straparola's *Il re Porco* 'shall be gifted with every virtue under the sun' (1894: 59); similarly, Perrault's princely *Riquet with the Tuft* should be 'very amiable [. . .] since he should be endowed with abundance of wit' (1791: 75); and finally, D'Aulnoy's *Prince Marcassin* will be 'always powerful, full of understanding and of justice' (1892: 481). By the conclusion of the pre-Grimm literary versions of ATU 441, the climactic shedding of the outer animal skin falls flat, somewhat betrayed by the already charmed lives of the protagonists. The somewhat redundant transformations found in the literary versions of ATU 441 stand in stark contrast to the transformation of Williamson's protagonist.

It could be argued that these literary versions behave in this way because they were intended to appeal to certain strata of the social hierarchy at the time of their publication. This is the view expressed by Ruth

Bottigheimer when she contends that Straparola 'spoke to the longings of a reading public with a taste for stories that would compensate for a dreary daily existence [. . .] and introduced magic into brief tales that promised wealth' (2002: 132). Perhaps Straparola's audience – like D'Aulnoy's 'literary acquaintances, all titled or wealthy or both' (ibid.: 129) – 'read to one another in dazzling painted and tapestried salons', knowing that they 'differed fundamentally from the humble [. . .] readership for whom Straparola had composed his rise tales' (ibid.). As for Perrault's tale, closer examination of *Riquet with the Tuft* reveals that the presence of the animal-bridegroom motif *at all* is debatable; Riquet's transformation is made metaphysical when his Princess, 'having made due reflection on the perseverance of her lover, his discretion, and all the good qualities of his mind, his wit and judgement, saw no longer the deformity of his body, nor the ugliness of his face' (1791: 87). That love is indeed blind appears to be the key message from Perrault, whereas in the other literary versions of the story, the transformations into maturity, and inherited titles, are explicitly physical.

In contrast to the tales just mentioned, both the Grimms' and Williamson's versions of ATU 441 begin with childless couples who occupy markedly different positions in society. The Grimms' *Hans My Hedgehog* casts the childless parents as farmers who 'had plenty of money and property' (trans. Zipes 2002: 361); whereas Williamson's couple are cast as a 'woodcutter and his wife' (TAD 36536) who live on the edge of a forest. According to Zipes, 'though primitive in origin, the folk tale in Germany, as told in the late 18th century and collected by the Grimms in the early 19th, related to and was shaped by feudalism' (1975: 129). From the perspective of the inequitable socio-economic relationship of feudalism, particularly in the Grimms' version, a central theme of the narrative is upward social mobility, rather than the maintenance of the social status quo found in the earlier versions discussed above. However, by the end of the Grimms' *Hans My Hedgehog*, the protagonist is not only transformed into a handsome young man but is also transformed into a monarch. Hans My Hedgehog's animal skin is eventually destroyed by fire, and 'the old King bequeathed his Kingdom to Hans My Hedgehog' (trans. Zipes 2002: 364). Social *mobility*, then, is not the fate of the Grimms' protagonist; his fate involves a transformation from wealthy landowner to the pinnacle of the aristocracy. It is difficult to agree with Zipes that this upward mobility is necessarily a reaction to the 'loss of family [that] must be compensated by the recreation of a new type of family that incorporates a sense of the Grimms' own bourgeois ethics' (1991: 216). For the final event in the Grimms' *Hans My Hedgehog* involves Hans revealing himself to his father as a King, wherein 'the old man rejoiced and went back with him to his kingdom' (trans. Zipes 2002: 364). Given the son's new position as sovereign, the recreated family can hardly be described as bourgeois. Perhaps Zipes was closer to the mark with his contention cited above about the effect of feudalism on German folklore and the Grimms' collection – rather than reconciliation into a bourgeois lifestyle, *Hans My Hedgehog*'s metamorphosis amounts to a binary shift from ruled to ruler. On closer examination, the Grimms' *Hans My Hedgehog* is not so very different from the other literary examples of ATU 441. All four of these narratives share the same basic impetus: the desire for power over others.

To put this impetus into context, it is useful to consider some of the motivations and methods of the authors of these tales. In a letter distributed in 1815, Jacob Grimm expressed his goal to 'save and collect all the existing songs and tales that can be found among the common German peasantry [. . .] wherever possible with their very words, ways, and tones' (cited in Zipes 2002: 26). In their preface to the first edition of *Kinder- und Hausmärchen* [Children's and Household Tales] in 1812, the Grimms declare that they will not allow these 'morsels of poetry to be kept entirely hidden from poor and modest readers' (cited in Zipes 2014: 3). These statements from the Grimms suggest that their intentions were not only to collect their material from the peasantry, but to sell the peasantry's own cultural expressions back to them, repackaged in printed form. However, research based on documentary evidence from the Grimms' archives – curated by Wilhelm Grimm's son Hermann – has shown that many tales were gathered from educated members of the middle-classes residing in towns and cities, even including the Grimms themselves (Kamenetsky 1992: 114). Thompson agrees when he points out that a 'large number of the tales in Grimm came from educated persons of the Grimms' own social circle' (1946: 407). Viewed with this in mind, interpretations of tales like *Hans My Hedgehog*, such as those given above, gain credence. It was the educated elite – the social climbers – who both created and consumed the Grimms' *Kinder- und Hausmärchen* in the first instance. Similarly, the tales printed in Straparola's *Pleasant Nights* in sixteenth-century Venice were primarily consumed by individuals who could afford to buy them; it was the nobility, along with literate and prosperous merchants and their families, who were able to choose to buy books in addition to food (Bottigheimer 2002: 31). Bottigheimer also emphasises another important point about Straparola's readership; the *Le Piacevoli Notti* were composed and published in a highly urbanised society and were designed to appeal to a readership of would-be social climbers (ibid.: 17). It is not difficult to imagine similar motivations in D'Aulnoy, given Jennifer Schacker's contention that D'Aulnoy's 'approach to the *conte de fées* is obviously different from that later valued by the Grimms and the folklorists they inspired', because D'Aulnoy deliberately included the 'dynamics of salon conversation into her fairy tale writing' (2011: 254).

The key point here is that the other extant, and clearly literary, versions of *Hans My Hedgehog* are markedly different in motivation from Williamson's. Although the present discussion does not engage with every known version of this story – such as those recorded in Lithuania, Sweden, Croatia, Iran, Japan, and elsewhere (Uther 2004 Vol. I: 263) – we are focused on the details of Williamson's version in the context of the Traveller storytelling tradition. In Williamson's narrative, we find that although the central theme of transformation exists, closer examination of *The Hedgehurst* reveals that this story does not share the same impulses as the literary versions described above. During the metanarrative of Williamson's story, he explains of his version that 'where originally it came from, I don't know [. . .] I don't think it's a very popular story among the Travellers' (TAD 36536). Williamson goes on to say that he learned the story in his teenage years from an elderly Traveller named Johnnie MacDonald; he explains MacDonald's technique as follows:

> It wisnae exactly the story, it's the wey he [MacDonald] told it, you know? He told it the right Traveller way, everything was really original, so that they [the audience] could understand it the real way it was told.
>
> (ibid.)

Williamson's perspective here encapsulates the essence of the present study's argument in that the Travellers' stories are meaningful to them as a community because of the *way* that they are told and re-told. Williamson's claim to the originality of the stories and his evocation of the 'right Traveller way' of their telling is a fluent description of the way stories are adapted to suit a specific cultural context. Furthermore, considering Williamson's statement that *The Hedgehurst* story is less popular among Travellers cited above, its inclusion in his repertoire suggests that it has a personal meaning for him. The fact that MacDonald's version of ATU 441 – and consequently Williamson's – bears structural similarities to the literary versions discussed above is unsurprising given the length of time that the literary versions have been circulating in print. Pinpointing where and when the story entered the oral storytelling tradition of the Travellers in Scotland is outside our remit here. However, considering these literary versions by way of comparison supports the contention that the Travellers engage with well-known international tale-types, borrowing themes and motifs to craft their own unique versions of the tales. Like Robertson, it is Williamson's narratological competence and social location that facilitates the meaningful analysis of his version of the story.

As was noted in the brief synopsis above, Williamson's version of ATU 441 is broadly similar in plot to the international versions recorded by Aarne-Thompson-Uther, and the same can be said for its similarity to the literary versions of Straparola, Perrault, D'Aulnoy and the Grimms. Essentially, we are introduced to a childless couple who miraculously conceive an animal-human hybrid child, and that child goes on to marry a princess and transform into a handsome man. Williamson frames his story in his opening line, placing the narrative at 'the edge of the forest' (TAD 36536). An important distinction to note in Williamson's version of ATU 441 – as with Robertson's and Williamson's other stories discussed above – is recognising the situatedness of the narratives when seeking plausible interpretations. At the highest level, Williamson's narrative is undoubtedly a version of the international tale-type ATU 441, and Williamson is undoubtedly a strong tradition-bearer operating within the Traveller storytelling tradition. This means that we are dealing with a story that has meaning to heterogeneous cultures across the globe, as well as with Williamson as an active proponent of oral narrative. In the preceding analyses of Traveller storytelling, we saw that under close examination – and with proper contextualisation – nuances within Traveller storytelling can infuse stories with deeper, culturally significant meanings. The same can be said for Williamson's version of ATU 441 – *Hans My Hedgehog*. As Lutz Röhrich reminds us in the search for meaning within folklore, 'only what is important and affects people directly enters folk narrative and tradition. Only what is meaningful is passed on' (1991: 13).

From the outset, Williamson's *The Hedgehurst* is arranged in terms of boundaries. As mentioned above, one key aspect of Williamson's narrative that differentiates it from the literary versions is the childless couple's position in society. The literary versions cited above all cast the parents as belonging to the upper echelons of the societies in which the narrative takes place. Williamson's woodcutter couple, on the other hand, are not only cast as belonging to the 'lower orders' of society but they are also physically placed on the margins, with their home at the edge of the forest. Moreover, the childless couple are without social connections; unlike the Grimms' farmer who 'went into town with the other farmers' (trans. Zipes 2002: 361), Williamson's couple lead solitary lives in the forest. We are told that the wife was 'always left on her own [. . .] because her husband was always away durin' the day cutting wood', and when the husband implores his wife to '"get someone up from the village! Get a woman or somethin"', his wife exclaims, '"I don't want a woman [. . .] I don't want anybody, I want a baby"' (TAD 36536). Williamson's story takes place in a distinctly different social environment from the other versions of ATU 441 noted above. Like the Grimms' version, we are introduced to the protagonists in a rural setting, and the description that Williamson provides evokes a sense of social isolation. It goes without saying that tapestried salons and royal courts would be utterly alien environments to Williamson's Traveller audiences. Furthermore, as Neat observes of the Travellers he collaborated with, the 'values and satisfactions of the farmer are not theirs' (1996: 224). As a result, *The Hedgehurst*'s miraculous birth is situated in a socio-economic environment that exists in contradistinction to the earlier literary versions of *Hans My Hedgehog*. The protagonists of Williamson's story thereby embody the marginalised lives that so many Travellers experience. The narrative is situated in a setting that speaks to the Travellers' relationship with their environment and childlessness is depicted as emotionally painful, speaking to the importance of family in the Traveller context.

In his version of the story, Williamson negotiates this marginality through the journey of his Hedgehurst. As opposed to the literary versions of ATU 441, Williamson's Hedgehurst loses his family when, after he left the family home, his 'mother took to bed wi' a broken heart for her wee son and she died' (TAD 36536). Meanwhile, after his wife's death, the Hedgehurst's father 'remarried again and moved away to another country' (ibid.). For the Hedgehurst, there is no reconciliation with his family, particularly with the father who resented him from the outset; we are told that Hedgehurst's father 'despised him and hated the look of him' and referred to his son simply as 'beast' (ibid.). Conversely, the Grimms' Hans is eventually reunited with his father who was initially 'happy at the idea of getting rid of him' (trans. Zipes 2002: 361). Similarly, in Straparola, Perrault, and D'Aulnoy, the conclusion of the stories sees the protagonists ultimately embedded into a household, in one way or another. In this way, Williamson's Hedgehurst is very much the individual. Williamson himself places value in the sense of individualism and freedom that the Traveller lifestyle affords a person; 'among the Travelling People in this country', Williamson explains, 'every family is an individual family, even though they are connected [. . .] there's no bosses, no law, no king, no nothing [. . .] everyone goes his own way' (cited in Braid 2002: 32). Similar sentiments are expressed by Bryce Whyte when he tells us that his sons 'don't like workin' under a boss, they work for thirsels!' (TAD 76669). Whyte's statement here is a stark example of the interaction between active or strong tradition-bearers and Traveller culture at large; the values that are expressed in discussions with outsiders manifest themselves in the stories that the Travellers share. Whether or not Whyte was familiar with Williamson's story we will probably never know, but the essence of the story provides valuable insights into the way that Travellers negotiate their inner identities and their outer worlds.

This individualistic, self-sufficient ethos is expressed within Williamson's narrative. After leaving home, the Hedgehurst establishes his own dwelling within the forest, described as 'the loveliest house built of wood that you ever saw' (TAD 36536). When the lost King arrives, Hedgehurst tells the King that '"I need help from no-one [. . .] I've done all this myself"' (ibid.). The Hedgehurst's solitary journey into the forest becomes significant from this perspective; the sense of trepidation and danger usually associated with forests does not exist in Williamson's story, or indeed in any of the literary versions under discussion. Instead, the forest represents an environment where the animal-human hybrid can thrive. For Zipes, the forest can also be a place where 'society's conventions no longer hold true. It is a source of natural right, thus the starting place where social wrongs can be righted' (2002: 67). A similar reorientation of the forest comes from Ann Schmiesing, where she sees *Hans My Hedgehog* achieving 'a level of activity and success in the forest that he would not have realised in the socially oppressive environments of the town or his parents' home' (2014: 126). These conceptualisations of the forest are especially pertinent for Williamson's protagonist given that he is effectively an orphan who has no recourse to parental support. Moreover, as we will see, Williamson's protagonist ultimately transcends these perceived social wrongs, and the forest becomes not only the place where he thrives, but the place where he belongs.

The sense of innate social hierarchies that exists in the literary versions of the story are absent in Williamson's version; the idea that this hierarchy can be overcome or usurped is similarly absent. The socially determined boundaries that exist in the literary versions are of little concern for Williamson's Hedgehurst, an attitude that becomes apparent when the Hedgehurst converses with the lost King. '"I am a King"', exclaims the King who is lost in the forest, to which the Hedgehurst testily replies, '"And I am a King! [. . .] And I have not lost my way: you are now in my Kingdom and you're no longer a king to me"' (TAD 36536). The boundary of the forest that Williamson establishes from the outset of his story is transcended as the story progresses. At the conclusion of Williamson's story, the Hedgehurst does not inherit or claim ownership of the Kingdom that he was instrumental in restoring when he guides the lost King out of the forest. On the contrary, the Hedgehurst bestows wealth upon the King, giving him 'some of his fine animals' (ibid.), and returns to his own self-made Kingdom in the forest with the princess. Donald Smith also recognises this sense of boundaries being transcended in the Travellers' oral traditions. Discussing Traveller singer Jeannie Robertson's ballad *The Gypsy Laddie* – which tells the story of an aristocratic Lady who 'runs away' with several Gypsy men after being enchanted by their singing – Donald Smith observes that the 'narrative is clearly shaped on the frontier between settled and Traveller society' (2001: 148). Smith goes on to suggest that the ballad of *The Gypsy Laddie* is a 'passionate lament and protest on behalf of the Traveller culture which transcends rather than transgresses the social order, because it aspires to the freedom of nature' (ibid.).

This insight from Smith is a useful way to segue into the second key differentiation between Williamson's story and the other versions that were introduced above. We already know that the relationship Travellers have with the natural environment is based on respect and harmony; for example, in the story concerning the old cow's horn and its recycling into a spoon. That the narrative journey in Williamson's *The Hedgehurst* is situated in a rural environment is, again, unsurprising. It is the plot of the story, and the actions of the protagonist, predicated as they are on transcending boundaries that is of interest here. And what is it that intimates this peculiar story and the protagonist's affirmation of his inner identity? The couple's wish for a child is the impetus of the narrative in all the above versions of ATU 441 and this is indeed the first motif identified by Uther (2004 Vol. I: 263). However, the *way* the miraculous birth occurs is an important consideration in the context of Williamson's version. The boundaries being broken in Williamson's narrative stand in stark contradistinction to the other versions of ATU 441. Like Smith's interpretation of *The Gypsy Laddie*, the central impetus of Williamson's version speaks to an affinity with a natural order that dispenses with hierarchical power relations. In Straparola, D'Aulnoy, Perrault, and Williamson, the birth of the animal-human hybrid is the result of an intervention by fairies. Unfortunately, in the Grimms' version, we are given no explicit explanation as to how the previously childless couple suddenly become pregnant and are delivered of their unusual baby. In the Grimms' version of the story, the mother does accuse her husband of cursing the family – '"You see how you cursed us!"' (trans. Zipes 2002: 361) the mother exclaims, and it could be argued that the curse is laid on the father as punishment for his pride. When the father goes into town, the other farmers often make fun of him for his childlessness, and this makes him angry enough to ask for a child, '"even if it's a hedgehog"' (ibid.). It is the father who has ultimate agency in the monstrous birth, and from this perspective, it is the reflection of the father's wish to vicariously ascend to power through his progeny.

In Williamson's version, it is a fairy who intimates the birth of the Hedgehurst, and in this sense, his version diverges significantly from the Grimms'. Williamson's story begins to have more in common with the earlier versions of ATU 441 that we have used for comparison. Williamson explains that fairies are 'part of an Other World for Travellers that they love', and he goes on to illustrate that the 'people [fairies] of this Other World have the freedom, have the power, they are immune from persecution' (1985: 15). In *The Hedgehurst*, the fairy who intimates the Hedgehurst's birth is described as wicked, yet the boy is born with 'two of the loveliest blue eyes you ever saw' (TAD 36536). The reader will recall the virtues that are bestowed on the monstrous births by the fairies in the earlier literary versions of ATU 441; true to Traveller style, the Hedgehurst's virtue is not described using abstract concepts such as wit, or justice. Instead, the indicator of the Hedgehurst's virtue is literally written on his face. As we have experienced before in Stanley Robertson's narrative style, Williamson's stories also include elements of dramatic irony. Describing the Hedgehurst, Williamson explains that 'as the days went on the wee boy grew, and the more he grew the uglier he got' (ibid.), yet his inner beauty is betrayed by his lovely blue eyes. To facilitate Hedgehurst's transformation at the conclusion of the story, Williamson introduces a 'henwife'. Discussing the role of henwives, Williamson says that 'even in the stories, old-fashioned stories wi henwives [. . .] there were nae bad henwives', going on to explain that people 'went to them for cures, and they went to them for tasks' (TAD 30617). The wickedness of the fairy is contrasted with the benevolence of the henwife when, at the conclusion of the story, the henwife gives the Hedgehurst's bride 'a wee pitcher [and] no ordinary pitcher' (TAD 36536). The Hedgehurst's bride is instructed by the henwife to 'take this pitcher of cold clear water and you'll throw it over him – and if it's a spell it'll be broken forever' (ibid.). The spell is indeed broken – '"Darling"', shouts the Hedgehurst after the magical pitcher has been discharged over him, '"you've broken the spell that was cast on me many, many years ago"' (ibid.).

In this way, *The Hedgehurst* is framed by two supernatural interventions: on the one hand, the wicked fairy that cast a spell on the Hedgehurst at the beginning of the story is cast by Williamson as the agent behind his monstrous birth that ironically bestows him with virtue; on the other, the benevolent henwife provides his deliverance from his curse and allows him to return to his kingdom in the forest. Williamson explains that the 'people [fairies] of the Other World are part of nature – same as the Travelling folk' (1985: 15). In this sense, the purportedly wicked fairy – with the help of the benevolent henwife – is the ultimate arbiter of the Hedgehurst's fate. More broadly, the Hedgehurst's return to nature, where he can be immune from persecution, is facilitated by two agents that transcend boundaries and challenge urban sensibilities. Discussing D'Aulnoy's animal-human hybrid stories, Lewis Seifert argues that such stories explore 'what might be gained from a hybrid subjectivity in which human reason is conjoined with animal instinct and human vice is counterbalanced by animal virtue' (2011: 257). Seifert's perspective here speaks of the animal-human protagonist's exploration of an innate affinity with nature, and this is something that is affirmed in the story of the Hedgehurst. The Hedgehurst is at once passive, as both the narrative intimation and resolution are enacted by peripheral characters; at the same time, he is an active participant in his story as the builder of his sanctuary in the forest.

Perhaps it is Williamson's *individual* Traveller identity that is being expressed in *The Hedgehurst*, and the meaning for him is therefore personalised. Braid has observed that when discussing Traveller life and culture, Williamson often generalises beyond his own personal perspectives (2002: 33). However, as Braid goes on to assert, he has 'come to trust in [Williamson's] observations and portrayals of Traveller life because they have been corroborated time and again' (ibid.). From this perspective – viewed within the context of the previous readings and the testimonies of other Travellers quoted above – *The Hedgehurst* and the interpretations of the story are both personal and representative of a broader Traveller identity. Williamson's Hedgehurst transcends boundaries; the situatedness of the narrative and the deeds of its eponymous central protagonist collaborate to reveal this central theme of the story. Unlike the literary versions that involve a physical transformation that results in the usurpation of the reigning monarch, Williamson's Hedgehurst does not forsake his forest, or his identity. Instead, the Hedgehurst's physical transformation becomes incidental; his journey from birth to maturity is better understood as a symbolic representation of the marginalised individual overcoming adversity, transcending socio-economic boundaries and doing so as a self-assured individual that is in tune with the natural environment. The ideological commitment of the Hedgehurst is therefore aligned with the storyteller and the experiences of a real social environment where ascension to positions of power is neither desired nor sought. All the while, the sentiment of Williamson's story is tempered by the grim realities often faced by Travellers. In a song of his own composition,

The Hawker's Lament, Williamson captures this sentiment by evoking the deep social trauma of international warfare, setting such conflicts against the familiarity of a Traveller lifestyle. In this protest song, Williamson juxtaposes the Travellers' sacrifices during wartime with the closure of many of the Travellers' traditional camping places by the mid-1960s (Williamson 1994: 272–273). His verse captures not only the loss of life in the service of the national interest, but also the loss of life*style* that Williamson witnessed first-hand in post-war Scotland. The futility of war is expressed here from a quintessentially Traveller perspective.

> But what did they fight for and why did they die?
> For freedom to wander round.
> But where can we wander, we have no place to go,
> For they've closed all our campin' grounds down.
> Though we fought for wir country and we fought for wir king
> An some gave their life for this land,
> It's out there in Dunkirk it's many they fell
> With their blood mixed up with the sand.
> [. . .]
> But maybe someday when we're gone from this world,
> An' we're buried deep down in the ground,
> Will God make us welcome, will he give us a home?
> Or will he tell us just to keep movin' on?
>
> Duncan Williamson, 'The Hawker's Lament'
> (TAD 68649 and Williamson 1994: 273)

Notes

1. Based on the combined work of Aarne-Thompson-Uther, all ATU references and motifs in the present work refer to Hans-Jörg Uther's *The Types of International Folktales: A Classification and Bibliography*, 3 vols. (2004).
2. In the Grimm's original tale, it is the children's biological mother who dies. The stepmother was a later addition (Dundes 1991: 78–79).
3. *The Hedgehurst* is the title given to the transcription of this story – based on TAD 36536 – in Williamson's *Fireside Tales of the Traveller Children* (1983), pp. 21–32.

6

The Burkers and Ideological Resistance

CLOSE EXAMINATION AND CONTEXTUALISATION of Travellers' stories are potent allies when seeking meanings within the stories. Both personal and collective cultural identity strategies are at work; the stories of the strong tradition-bearers we have examined already display themes that other members of the Travelling communities can identify with – strong tradition-bearers can ventriloquise the sentiments and worldviews of broader communities of Travellers. We have focused our inquiries on the inner lives of the Travellers, and how these inner identities manifest themselves within the stories that they share. This is a theme that we return to in subsequent chapters. The present chapter scrutinises a macabre external factor that has had a demonstrable impact on Traveller storytelling. The Travellers' oral history and storytelling traditions are replete with references to the so-called 'Burkers'. The term 'Burker' is a reference to William Burke and his murderous activities as a provider of cadavers to Edinburgh's medical colleges in the early nineteenth century. A brief overview of the salient points of Burke's activities, to contextualise the term 'Burker', is where we begin. This overview clarifies how the term itself is understood within the Travellers' traditions and is contrasted with more mainstream representations of Burke and his associates. We see how a combination of factors affected the way that Burkean anxiety penetrated the consciousness of the Travellers and settled population alike.[1] The aim here is to gain a clearer understanding of the impact that such heinous crimes had on Scotland's collective imagination, then to take a close look at how the Burkers manifest in the Travellers' tradition to the present day, presenting a new way of thinking about what they mean.

BURKERS IN THE TRAVELLERS' TRADITION

The term Burkers refers to a group of individuals associated with the activities of the infamous William Burke, who, along with others, murdered people to supply bodies to the burgeoning anatomy schools of early nineteenth-century Scotland. Marginalised individuals and communities were perceived to be particularly vulnerable to such practices, the perception being that they would be far less likely to be missed than members of mainstream society (cf. John Stewart TAD 75777; and Braid 2002: 79). The fear and anxiety associated with Burkers has percolated through generations of Travellers. Speaking in 1979, Betsy Whyte explains that 'ma mother had been brought up [to believe] the Travellers wis terrified tae live wi the country people because of fear of Burkers, ye see, o' gettin' Burkit [abducted then smothered to death] through the night' (TAD 63443). Elsewhere, speaking in 1954, Maggie Stewart tells a story regarding her father that involves Burkers; in this story, the father stops to drink at a spring and sees the reflection of 'a Burker stande [standing], he see'd him, in the water, so he got feart [afraid] ken?' (TAD 10224). This portrait of the Burkers as spectres that lurk in reflections, with latent violence, is an indication of how they appear in the stories. These early examples are tangible evidence of anxieties that Travellers harbour regarding both the mainstream population and Burkers. The purpose of this chapter is to problematise the notion that the Travellers' Burker stories are simply narrative manifestations of a persecution complex. Viewed from a certain perspective, this underlying theme of persecution can certainly be perceived. However, on closer inspection these stories are more complex than basic expressions or warnings about the threat posed by outsiders. Moreover, careful analyses continue to demonstrate the sophistication of the narrative traditions being considered in this study. The Burker tradition represents not simply a negotiation of an understandable persecution anxiety, it also has significance for the narrators in terms of depriving them of that which they cherish most, their liberty. The fundamental loss of liberty is the central thread that connects the Travellers' Burker accounts. We will see how the loss of liberty negotiated within these narratives amounts to a resistance against ideological contamination.[2]

Henderson believes that the influence of Burke's activities on Traveller culture should be understood as a manifestation of the threat of persecution felt by Travellers throughout the centuries, and to this day. For Henderson, 'we must probably look further back in history in order to understand the deeper-lying reasons for this persecution complex' (2004: 230). Considering the evidence of persecution that we reviewed in TSAS and elsewhere, it is hardly surprising that the Travellers have developed a certain amount of distrust regarding members of the settled population. Henderson cites the law against being an 'Egyptian' – or wanderer, vagabond, or tinsmith of no fixed abode – that existed in seventeenth-century Scotland as one plausible root of this complex (1995: 2636). The reader will recall the case of James MacPherson from previous chapters who was hanged at Banff in 1700 merely for 'being a Traveller'. Henderson may be correct in suggesting that the real fear of premeditated murder has percolated down through generations of Travellers and crystallised as an emotionally significant element of Traveller culture. The forthcoming analyses show that the Travellers' Burker tradition can also reflect a sophisticated ideological negotiation of deeply-entrenched social inequities. Henderson himself alludes to this reflection when he suggests that 'the alien phantasmagoric world of scalpel-toting predators [Burkers] has a more than symbolic reality' (2004: 160).

TSAS and other historical sources provide an abundance of evidence that Travellers have suffered unjustified persecution over the centuries. Part of this persecution meant that Traveller families were often unaccounted for in public records. This lack of formal registration – coupled with the general enmity for Travellers that we have so far witnessed – meant that many Travellers saw themselves as easy targets for abduction. The rationale here is that nobody would miss them except their families and friends, with the authorities taking little or no interest in the disappearance of 'undesirables'. Braid cites evidence of this view noting that 'some Travellers said their ancestors felt they were particularly at risk from Burkers', the reason being that 'Travellers would neither be missed nor cared about in situations of foul play' (2002: 79). Duncan Williamson clarifies this vulnerability and mistrust of the authorities, explaining that 'the Travellers were not registered [. . .] and if [the Burkers] took a body, whether it be a man, woman, or child, they were never missed. The Travellers never reported it' (cited in Braid 2002: 80). According to Sheila Douglas, the inability to report unregistered individuals as missing is 'one of the reasons the Travellers became so punctilious about registering the births of their children, who consequently officially existed and could be reported missing' (1985: 200). Further evidence of anxieties around Burkers comes from their association with anatomists. Betsy Whyte explains that 'the idea of cutting somebody up just for the sake of finding oot things, it was just beyond us. They [the anatomists] were like a different race, like something that wisnae human' (TAD 77229). Whyte's proclamations here speak to a fundamental ideological conflict with scientific enquiry that could be viewed as anachronistic. However, when viewed in the context of the Burker tradition, Whyte's anxieties around medical dissection voices broader concerns about the motivations of non-Travellers. In this sense, the ideological conflict does not represent a retrograde attitude to the scientific method, but rather an emotive response to a perceived threat; recall Maggie Stewart's story about her father seeing a Burker reflected in his drinking water, for instance.

In their 1975 study, 'Scottish Travellers or Tinkers', the Rehfisches reacted similarly when they encountered the Burker stories, concluding that 'these stories express in concrete terms the view that the outside world is hostile and one must be wary of it' (1975: 279). This seems a sensible conclusion except that Burke's murderous acquisition of cadavers did not extend outside of Edinburgh and took place over a relatively short period of time. In terms of Burke's murders, Lisa Rosner lists sixteen victims in total, all killed in or around Tanner's Close in the West Port of Edinburgh over a twelve-month period (2010: 1). However, there is evidence that the close association between medical schools and murder was not a phenomenon exclusive to Edinburgh. As opposed to the act of 'Burking' – that is, murder by intoxication and smothering, specifically to supply anatomists with subjects – some anatomy schools outside of Edinburgh are more closely associated with grave robbing, or 'body snatching'. The social trauma engendered by Burke's activities – coupled with the prevalence of body snatching across Scotland – has left an indelible scar on Scotland's national consciousness. Add to this Traveller Belle Stewart's comment in 1978 regarding Burkers: 'Oh aye, Marischal College [Aberdeen]. There's a hell of a lot of young Tinkers in Aberdeen went and sold the bodies' (TAD 55956). Stewart's statement here seems to suggest that there were also *Travellers* selling cadavers to the anatomy schools in Aberdeen. Douglas identifies one such individual as 'Danny the Burker', the 'ultimate horror of the Traveller who sells his own people's bodies to the doctors in the college at Aberdeen' (1985: 264). Douglas is sceptical about the veracity of Danny's nefarious activities, noting that it is possible that Danny 'encouraged other Travellers to believe what was said about him [and] he may even have been the source of the tales; for this would have given him special status and power among his own people' (ibid.: 265).

The social trauma engendered by Burke was not bound exclusively to Edinburgh where the murders took place. Furthermore, the conflation between Burking and body snatching is a plausible explanation for the nation-wide terror felt after Burke was executed for his crimes in 1829. One contemporary observer, Thomas Ireland, reflected that 'murder perpetrated in such a manner, upon such a system, with such an object or intent [. . .] utterly transcends and beggars everything in the shape of tragedy' (1829: 1). Quite so: subsequent generations of writers have grappled with the unprecedented crimes committed by Burke and his associates. For example, body snatching and cadavers were ubiquitous features in *Blackwood's Magazine* throughout the nineteenth century (Rosner 2010: 3); Alexander Leighton aimed at 'narrating a series of tragedies unprecedented in the history of mankind' (1861: iii) in *The Court of Cacus; or, the Story of Burke and Hare* (1861); later, Robert Louis Stevenson's *The Body Snatcher* (1884) echoed the activities of Burke and the anatomists of Edinburgh whom he supplied; the twentieth century saw similar narrative efforts by William Roughead in *Burke and Hare* (1921), and on stage with James Bridie's play *The Anatomist* (1931); the twenty-first century has already seen John Landis' cinematic rendition, *Burke and Hare* (2010), yet another narrative account in Owen Dudley Edwards' *The True Story of the Infamous Burke and Hare* (2014); C. J Dunford's psychological drama *Burke's Last Witness* (2018); and *The Edinburgh Dungeon* entertainment venue currently features an exhibition centred on Burke and Hare ('Greyfriar's Kirkyard' 2024).

Nowhere is the deep-seated Burkean trauma more perceptible than in the oral history and storytelling traditions of Scotland's Travellers. According to Ewan MacColl and Peggy Seeger, the Burker tales that they experienced during their time with the Travelling Stewarts of Blairgowrie 'show little of the inventiveness that characterises so many of the older tales' (1986: 57). This appraisal by MacColl and Seeger is in one sense an accurate description of many of the Burker stories in the Traveller tradition in that the Burker stories do appear to follow a broadly similar pattern. This narrative patterning serves a specific function within the Burker stories. This function is perhaps an element that eluded MacColl and Seeger when they see 'plots that are depressingly hackneyed', including characters that 'are as stereotyped as the interchangeable cops and robbers of television drama' (ibid.). The hackneyed and stereotypical protagonists, and antagonists, are cast deliberately so that the narratives can function and deliver their meaning. As Sheila Douglas has pointed out, Burkers, the medical profession and body snatchers have all been fused within the Travellers' stories into one and the same thing (1985: 24). Douglas goes on to point out that Burker stories 'tend to follow a pattern, a fact that must have some significance' (ibid.: 254). This fusing of elements or patterning within the narratives is perhaps what inspired Henderson's assessment that the Travellers' Burker stories are manifestations of deeper anxieties involving people from the non-Traveller world (2004: 230; cf. Rehfisches 1975: 279, cited above).

The predictability of the Travellers' Burker stories disparaged by MacColl and Seeger is evidence of the rigidity of the functions of the characters. There is a distinction between the innocent Traveller and the nefarious non-Traveller within the narratives, with Olrik's 'Law of Contrast' (1992: 50) at work once more. As a result, many outsider interpretations of the Burker tradition are one-dimensional. Not that these interpretations are altogether erroneous, only that, as is often the case with the Travellers' traditions, there is more to these narratives than meets the eye. Henderson contends that the persecution complex he recognised finds expression in the 'gruesome folklore about "burkers" (body-snatchers) who were supposed to be continually on the wait to waylay and murder travelling folk' (1995: 2636). Henderson's conflation of Burkers and body-snatchers is an indication of his misperception of the stories themselves. In his synopsis of the Burker tradition, Henderson also describes how the sinister medical students 'drive the "burker's coach" into the countryside to try and find isolated tinker encampments' (ibid.). A significant number of the Travellers' Burker accounts do not involve a coach or deliberate waylaying. Furthermore, the Burkers in these narratives are not 'body snatchers', rather the antagonists *create* the bodies themselves, giving the murders their most execrable characteristic. The narratives often rely on the Travellers themselves approaching the would-be Burkers. Close analyses of such details reveal more sophisticated aspects of the unique values, beliefs and worldviews of the Travellers and their Burker tradition. The Travellers' Burker stories are a rare opportunity to examine stories from communities that can truly call the stories their own. It is safe to say that the nation-wide social trauma engendered by Burke and the anatomists has impacted Scotland's Travellers in a unique way. The morbid fascination with Burke that has inspired mainstream storytellers is negotiated differently within the Travellers' storytelling traditions.

As opposed to a simplistic binary 'us and them' negotiation of identity, this study reveals that the stories the Travellers share represent more complex identity strategies. The present discussion therefore focuses on what Sara Reith sees as 'representing Traveller identity from within' (2008: 99) by resisting ethnocentric approaches that limit the scope of the interpretations. Appraisals, such as those cited above, that the Travellers' Burker tradition is simply a manifestation of anxiety about outsiders can be augmented if we view the stories using new perspectives. By viewing the Travellers' stories from within, Reith recognises 'the powerful potential of folkloric contexts to create transformative spaces through which divisive boundaries between "self" and "other" may be renegotiated' (ibid.). In terms of the Burker tradition, what becomes clear is that as opposed to the biographical or fictional representations found in the more mainstream media, the Travellers' Burker stories are often related as having *actually happened*. In one interview recorded in 1975, Betsy Whyte exclaims that 'it was true, they did Burke the Travellers, they did [. . .] that went on all over. And although youse folk [settled communities] mibbe disnae believe it, it goes on as much now as it did in these days' (TAD 77229). Indeed, the Travellers' oral history and stories contain remarkable similarities to the methods used by Burke; the victims are lured into an ostensibly benevolent house and given drink until incapacitated, facilitating the victim's murder without inflicting unnecessary damage to their body. This verisimilitude is revealing. By blending reality and fiction, the Burkean narratives' function is to structure the latent *representational* meanings of the stories upon real situations.

EQUILIBRIUM AND CAPTIVITY

It has been argued that the Burkean anxiety that pervades Traveller storytelling has its roots in an earlier mistrust of the medical profession; Douglas suspects that 'Travellers feared doctors long before the Burke and Hare case, but this certainly intensified it beyond rational bounds' (1985: 24). The underlying historical fear of the medical profession could be extended to include a variety of 'authority' figures given that the Travellers have faced manifold forms of persecution over the last 250 years. The examples we surveyed in Part I above showed that TSAS are replete with evidence of the established order maligning the lifestyles of the Travellers in the past (for example, Auchterderran 1791: 458, Eaglesham 1792: 124, Monteith 1845: 1281, Knockando 1845: 81). There are many other more contemporary examples of the narrative negotiation of such conflicts held in the SSS Archives which will be referred to during the forthcoming analyses. What is revealed is that other negotiations of conflict do not share the same narrative patterning as the Burker stories. We might ask, what is it about Burke and his crimes that inspired a tangential tradition that deals with conflict? The understandable mistrust of authority figures from the settled population manifests itself elsewhere in a variety of narrative negotiations. Moreover, the specific mistrust of the medical profession amongst Travellers, observes Douglas, has long since subsided, with many Travellers visiting local surgeries and being admitted to hospitals (1985: 25). At the same time, Douglas acknowledges that Burker stories continue to be told among Travellers in an 'almost ritual manner' and that 'the explanation for this can be found only by examining the stories themselves' (ibid.). With all the above considerations in mind, the fact that Burker stories have persisted in the Traveller tradition warrants closer examination.

As Henderson observed, there exist versions of Burker narratives that include a 'Burker's Coach', but there are also examples from the Burker tradition where no villainous coachmen are involved. These variations are related, of course, by virtue of their link to the medical establishment. Citing *A Dictionary of English Folklore*, Martin Shaw points out that the motif of sinister black carriages roaming the countryside appears in other discrete folkloric traditions recorded throughout the nineteenth century (2006: 167). The appearance of a 'Burker's Coach' is therefore not necessarily unique to the Travellers' tradition. The Burker accounts where the coach *does not* appear seem to have escaped the attention of Henderson and will therefore be our focus. There are several key elements that identify the Traveller tradition of Burker stories and that give the accounts an overarching similitude. The central tenets are: the Traveller protagonists are on the road and somehow find themselves in a precarious situation; the Travellers are taken in by ostensibly benevolent hosts but are then held in captivity; the kidnappers that the Travellers encounter are somehow associated with anatomists or the medical profession; there is often an element of intoxication, by some means or another, involved during captivity; and, finally, the captured Travellers – more often than not – escape at the end of their encounter. The key incident to note, in terms of the synopsis above, is the element of captivity. As we will see, these high-level motifs collaborate to represent an overarching 'Burker theme' that is predicated on the loss of personal liberty.

The central tenets outlined above are the structural units of the Burkean stories, their morphology. As noted, we are concerned here by how these units are organised and what this organisation can tell us about the meanings of the stories; analysis of the structure of the Travellers' Burker accounts illuminate certain elements of their lives and experiences. At the same time, the details of the stories can be seen to reflect personal experience and therefore include nuances. The individualism that we experienced in the previous chapter's narratives continues to manifest itself within the oral histories and stories involving Burkers. However, the individual nuances of the encounters with Burkers develop into a recognisable pattern that helps us to understand the motivations of the storytellers and unlock the meanings within their testimonies. As Dundes points out, one advantage of structural analysis is that 'not all the variants of a given tale or myth need to be analysed in order to ascertain the structure' (1964: 46). Furthermore, the initial 'descriptive' task of structural analysis is made easier by the fact that the Burker tradition is prevalent among Traveller storytellers, where there are a multitude of examples to work with.

Our first example from the Traveller tradition comes from John (Jock) Stewart. Stewart recounts an experience from his childhood when his tinsmith father sent him, his sister and one of Stewart's nieces out on a business errand (TAD 11474). Stewart was born in 1870 in Blairgowrie, Perthshire, which places the chronology of his story sometime towards the end of the nineteenth century. Recorded in 1955, Stewart's story begins when the companions are unable to make the return journey home to Fraserburgh in the dark, so they seek lodgings at a farm that they come across. At first, the woman who answers the door at the farmhouse is reluctant to provide lodgings but asks Stewart and his companions to wait until her son comes home. 'When the son come in', recounts Stewart, 'he wis a tall chap aboot six fit high he wis' (ibid.). The son offers Stewart and company a turnip shed to spend the night in, but it has been snowing and the shed is full of blown snow: 'well if we had plenty o' straw we'd manage fine', Stewart implores, but the son replies '"oh you'll no need nae straw", he says, "before morning"' (ibid.). With Stewart protesting, the son leaves the Travellers and bars the door of the turnip shed from the outside. Stewart manages to pry apart the boards of the shed with his pocketknife and the company collect their goods and escape. Later, the company come upon a row of crofts and encounter the Burkers who snatch at Stewart's hair and rip the clothes from Stewart's young niece as they flee in terror. The Travellers eventually come to a shop where the shopkeeper tells them that she cannot offer them sanctuary, explaining that the Burkers are '"here every night of the week", she says, "lookin for folk [and] they sell everybody they get"' (ibid.). The connection to the medical school in nearby Aberdeen becomes clear when Stewart questions the motivations of their attackers; '"bless me boy"', exclaims the shopkeeper, '"they tak and sell them in Aiberdeen", she says. "The quicker you're aff the road the better"' (ibid.). Eventually, Stewart and his company reach a farm where the farmer knows Stewart's father. The farmer agrees to hide the Travellers in his dog kennel for the night, assuring them that if the Burkers approach he'll give them '"an ounce uh leed [shotgun pellets] in the backside"' (ibid.). Thus, Stewart and his family successfully avoid the Burkers and Stewart's account ends.

Stewart's encounter with Burkers consists of a few key incidents – our structural units – and follows a discernible organisational pattern: whilst on the road, the Travellers involved somehow find themselves in a precarious position; they therefore seek refuge or a modicum of comfort before continuing their journey; during the suspension of their travels, the Travellers are taken in by malevolent hosts and held captive; during their captivity, or after their escape, it becomes clear that their hosts intended to murder them in order to sell their bodies; finally, the Travellers are delivered from their precarious situation or they escape by some other means. Consequentially, Stewart's account consists of the optimum narrative sequence, recognised initially by Aristotle in his *Poetics* as consisting of an appropriate beginning, a probable or necessary elaboration, and a dramatic resolution (2010: 94–95). Moreover, at an even more fundamental level, Jock Stewart's narrative amounts to a movement from a state of equilibrium, through disequilibrium, and then returning to a state of equilibrium.

Of course, this tripartite narrative sequence appearing in the present context is neither surprising nor revelatory. However, for the purposes of the present analysis and interpretation, Tzvetan Todorov's insights into the nature of this fundamental narrative sequence are useful. Using Boccaccio's *Decameron* as an example, Todorov describes what he terms a 'schematic formulation' to describe the commonalities between the four main plots within the *Decameron* (1969: 73). Todorov's scheme consists of a series of common elements that act upon each other to form a sequence of events. The scheme identified by Todorov amounts to a 'minimal complete plot [that] can be seen as the shift from one equilibrium to another' (ibid.: 75). The germane analogy of a sense of equilibrium – understood in the present context as 'a stable but not static relation between the members of a society' (ibid.) – effectively represents a shift in the balance of relationships between social actors. Todorov's examples from the *Decameron* involve the social relations between misbehaving monks and abbots, deviant nuns and abbesses, unfaithful wives and duped husbands. The nature of the relationships chosen by Todorov to illustrate his point are clear; they are inequitable power relations. In the examples cited by Todorov, there is a violation of a law by the subordinate actor – their celibacy or fidelity – which demands punishment from the senior actor (equilibrium). The punishment is avoided either because the subordinate reveals that the senior *also* violates the law, or that the senior is beguiled in some way into thinking that the violation never happened (both a state of disequilibrium). At the conclusion of the narratives, normality is restored but critically, says Todorov, the equilibrium will have a 'different mood or status [. . .] seen from different points of view' (ibid.: 74). The crucial shift within these relationships, concludes Todorov, means that the 'story is basically the description of an improvement process until the flaw is no longer there' (ibid.: 75). Put another way, inequitable relationships are negotiated within the *Decameron*, with the function being to alter the nature of the relationship and create a new equilibrium where the subordinate has new knowledge or power.

With the sense of inequitable social relationships and the function of narrative in mind, consider Jock Stewart's Burker account. Stewart's narrative, in terms of Todorov's shift from equilibrium to a new equilibrium, means the sequence of narrative elements can be described as follows: the everyday plying of the Travellers' trade as tinsmiths (equilibrium); a movement into the unknown and subsequent captivity (disequilibrium); a dramatic escape and safe return to familiarity (equilibrium). We are by now familiar with the Travellers' long experience of persecution and hostility from other sectors of Scottish society, past and present. Most significantly, the sense of an inequitable social relationship between Travellers and the state has been demonstrated from the outset; the impact that this has had on the Travellers clearly manifests itself in their various storytelling traditions. However, as we saw in the previous chapter, the ostensibly binary 'us and them' negotiations that appear on the surface of the stories can be enhanced through closer examination to reveal deeper meanings. What is important is the Travellers' ongoing fascination with accounts of Burkers, and why these narrative traditions continue to be shared among Travellers long after the very *real* threat has been extinguished. Or, as Douglas puts it, she 'became aware of the pattern of the stories and realised that their importance lay not in the facts they purported to relate but in the expression they provided for the Travellers' sense of insecurity' (1987: 10).

In Stewart's account, the reality of the protagonists' situation functions on two levels. Firstly, the details provided by Stewart – the plausibility of the cross-country errand, the description of their route, the physical description of the Burker, the blown snow of the turnip shed– collaborate to place the narrated events in a recognisable reality. The narrative is not merely an amusing anecdote or a tall tale. It is at once to be considered both a cautionary tale shared by a specific sector of Scottish society and a unique brand of oral history. The second functional level, and the one that we are concerned with here, is the historicity of the Burker accounts among the Travellers; the term historicity is being deployed here not in the definitional sense of a 'verifiable past', but in the anthropological sense that draws attention to the 'social moulding of perceptions of the past and the political contests between competing versions of the past' (Stewart 2016: 89). It is the *social* history of the Travellers that is being negotiated within the Burker narratives, but not in the straightforwardly binary sense that is being challenged throughout this chapter. Instead, the Travellers' social realities are captured within a narrative structure that speaks directly to lived experience, while contesting dominant worldviews that prioritise conformity to sedentary lifestyles.

Stewart's narrative is intimated by the quintessentially Traveller trade of the itinerant tinsmith, a way of life that literally spans generations in the premise of Stewart's account. As we know, rapid industrialisation in Scotland meant that the livelihoods of the Travellers were increasingly under threat due to dramatic changes to both mercantile and social relationships. This precariousness – or sense of insecurity, as Douglas has it – manifests itself during the disequilibrium of Stewart's Burker account. When the weary travellers reach out for help to members of the settled population, they are met first with distrust when the woman at the farmhouse denies them sanctuary, then with malevolence when they are held captive by the would-be Burker. A compelling detail included by Stewart is the height of the individual who imprisons the Travellers; Betsy Whyte informs us that 'according to the Traivellers, the Saviour [Jesus Christ] was pure red-heided and exactly six foot tall' (TAD 36470). It is ironic, then, that the figurehead of the ultimate form of sanctuary can appear in Burker accounts as the opposite. From this perspective, it is the *trust* of the Travellers rather than their *mistrust* that engenders their captivity. The disequilibrium of Stewart's account is indicative of the inequitable social relationship being negotiated through the narrative; the persecution complex recognised by Henderson is not solely at issue here, it is the underlying sense of the betrayal of one class over another. A new equilibrium is reached when Stewart and his company come under the protection of the benevolent farmer. The settled farmer's knowledge of Stewart and his family challenges the hostility of the malevolent farmers, signifying a more equitable social relationship that is based on understanding and empathy. Stewart's Burker account is therefore framed by a distinct sense of reality; the everyday activities of the Travellers are disrupted by the intrusive Burkers, only to return to everyday reality at the conclusion of the narrative. In her analysis of the same account, Douglas also recognises the distinct social reality that is being expressed by Stewart: 'For the farmer to protect the traveller', notes Douglas, 'is of course in keeping with what we know from the family history was the attitude of Perthshire farmers to tinkers' (1985: 262).

Davy Hutchison, a Traveller born in Meldrum, Aberdeenshire in 1899 (TAD ID 5207), tells a slightly different story involving Burkers.[3] Hutchison frames his account by telling us that 'it's quite true, there was such a thing, once upon a time, as Burkers', and elaborates that 'the doctors, once upon a time, they badly wanted bodies [. . .] they wanted fresh bodies, nae auld rotten bloody corpse [i.e. one that had been 'body-snatched']' (TAD 74614). Again, Hutchison's Burker story is framed in reality, including specific details that contribute to the verisimilitude of his account. The story proper begins with the introduction of a woman and her young son: 'There's a woman bide in Leadside Road, Aiberdeen and by goodness, she was a weedow [widow] woman', Hutchison begins; we then find out that 'at that time o day, there wis nae relief fir naebody', and Hutchison explains that the woman 'jist had tae mak a livin fir her ainsel' (ibid.). At the conclusion of his narrative, Hutchison places the date of his story at 'aboot a hundred an seventy year ago' (ibid.). Hutchison's narrative was recorded in 1955, which places the narrated events at around 1785, by his reckoning. This date of course precedes Burke's crimes by almost half a century. However, as was noted above, the commodification of human corpses existed before the infamous activities of William Burke (Richardson 1987: 52, 72). Indeed, it is not unreasonable to suggest that Burke was not, in fact, the first 'Burker'. Although no extant historical sources exist to provide evidence, it is certainly possible that committing murder to obtain cash from Aberdeen's anatomists had also occurred to other nefarious individuals outside of Edinburgh.

Returning to Hutchison's story, one Saturday, the mother and son leave their home in Leadside Road, Aberdeen, heading for the village of Whitecairns, which lies approximately ten miles to the north. Hutchison explains that the woman intends to sell her goods and make a small profit (TAD 74614); this practice is what is known as hawking, or brokering, an activity that many Travellers favour as it means they are free to work for themselves. Although Hutchison does not explicitly identify his protagonists as Travellers, details such as the woman's occupation as a hawker suggest that this is indeed the case. On arrival in Whitecairns, the woman leaves her son outside the grocer's shop window playing marbles and heads off around the village to ply her trade. When the woman does not return as expected for the four o'clock return bus to Aberdeen, the grocer sends the young boy home by himself. Back at home in Aberdeen, there is no sign of the boy's mother and a neighbour alerts the police; Hutchison highlights the sinister nature of the story when he comments that 'at this time o day, there wis big prices geein for bodies ye ken. Five pound apiece for bodies, it's awa back a while ye know' (ibid.). Presumably cognisant of the woman's peril, the police dutifully head to Whitecairns to investigate her disappearance, beginning their enquiries at a local hotel.

Crucially at this point, Hutchison describes the hotel's proprietors as 'aa reid-heeded folk that wis there at that time. The father wis reid-heeded, so wis the wife and so wis the daughter' (ibid.). This curious motif of the antagonists in the Travellers' Burker stories having red hair is linked to the identity of the Burker character from Jock Stewart's account; discussing the Travellers' Burker tradition, Duncan Williamson explains that 'Burkers wis a red-heided woman [and] a red-heided man' (TAD 36470). In a published collection of Williamson's stories, he includes a tale called 'The Boy and the Boots'.[4] In his preamble to the story, Williamson explains that there were people 'who used to steal people away and take their bodies, kill them and cut them up, and use them for research in colleges' (*Fireside Tales of the Traveller Children* 1983: 127). It is clear from the outset that the story is about Burkers and it follows the Burkean morphology described above. In 'The Boy and the Boots', the narrator recalls that 'my daddy had told me, "beware of red-headed people, especially farmers or land-owners" [. . .] he told me they were bad people' (ibid.: 132). The six-foot tall, red-haired antagonist dutifully appears to hold the waylaid Traveller protagonist captive, while the Burkers are summoned to claim their victim (ibid.: 131–133).

The taboo around red-headed people also appears in Andrew Stewart's story about a baker who accepts three pieces of advice rather than wages from his employer (TAD 31634). The second piece of advice given by his employer is '"never go intae a hoose", he says, "where there's a red-heided man an' a red-heided wuman' (ibid.). Stewart's protagonist encounters Burkers on the road and seeks sanctuary in a house belonging to a red-headed family. True to the Burkean pattern, Stewart's protagonist realises his peril and makes a cunning escape by hiding in a pig-sty. The reader will recall from Betsy Whyte's testimony cited above that, in the Traveller tradition, Jesus Christ was also red-headed. In the same interview (TAD 36470), Whyte goes on to point out that 'according to the wey some o the Scaldies [settled or mainstream population] has got it, it wis *Judas* that was red-heided' (ibid.). Whyte's observation here concurs with a multitude of depictions of Judas Iscariot, the ultimate betrayer, found throughout Western art and literature from at least the eleventh century (Baum 1922: 526). The parallels with Stewart's account and Williamson's story are clear, the Burker antagonists are ironically aligned with Jesus in both narratives. The motif of an ironically cast captor appears across the Travellers' Burker tradition and the use of dramatic irony is a trope we encountered in the examinations of previous chapters. The significance of these characters will be elucidated during the conclusion of the present chapter after further examples have been introduced and discussed. Meanwhile, the police in Hutchison's story do not uncover any evidence of the missing woman's whereabouts, despite further enquiries throughout the village. However, the grocer – where the boy was playing before his mother's disappearance – recalls seeing the woman going into the hotel with the red-headed proprietors. The police therefore return to the hotel and they 'go richt inside this time, they burst their wey inside' (TAD 74614). The police soon discover the woman 'lying in a box wi her throat cut, ready for the college in aul' Aberdeen. So, that was a very, very true story, it's a way back aboot a hundred an seventy year ago' (ibid.).

Despite any speculation around the chronology of the narrated events, Hutchison's narrative remains a valuable thematic example of the Burkean anxiety found within the Travellers' storytelling traditions. Given the contextual details offered by Hutchison, it is important to note that the woman's socio-economic situation places her and her son in a precarious position. As we saw in the case of Williamson's Hedgehurst and Robertson's Traveller-Judge – the forest dweller who would not forsake his home and the Judge whose reputation for injustice was subverted, respectively – the socio-economic situation of the protagonists plays a central role in many of the Travellers' stories. Without the benefit of the modern welfare system, the widow and her dependent in Hutchison's story would certainly struggle without financial support. Thomas Smout points out that the so-called 'Poor Laws' in post-Reformation Scotland had their foundation in the medieval concept of the 'able-bodied poor' and the 'helpless impotent poor': the able-bodied poor were to be scorned and punished as deliberately idle vagabonds whereas the helpless poor were seen to have a genuine need of the charity of society (1998: 84). Decisions on whether to provide relief for the poor ultimately fell to the Kirk Session, and it was often 'able-bodied' widows who suffered.

Based on the earlier synopsis of Traveller Burkean narratives offered above, it is clear that Hutchison's story shares many of the central motifs: the precariousness of the protagonists' situation; the capture and captivity by malevolent hosts, in this case, hoteliers; the victim's body is prepared for sale to the anatomy schools of Aberdeen; alas, in this case the woman did not escape, but her young son lived to tell the tale. Hutchison's inclusion of the details of the protagonists' socio-economic position is revealing. Similar to Jock Stewart's account explored above, an inequitable social relationship exists between the widow and a state that is unwilling to come to her aid. What is also clear is that from a structural perspective – equilibrium, disequilibrium, new equilibrium – Hutchison's Burker narrative does not precisely follow the same pattern as Jock Stewart's account. Instead, the conclusion of Hutchison's narrative sees the young son alone in Aberdeen without his mother. However, if we consider this conclusion in terms of the social relations under negotiation, a parallel exists. Specifically, the young son's safe return home is facilitated by the benevolent grocer, and his neighbour in Aberdeen takes pity on the boy and instigates the search for his missing mother

(TAD 74614). In the same way that Jock Stewart's protagonists are given sanctuary during their encounters with Burkers, so too is the young son in Hutchison's account saved by the benevolence of the grocer and the concerned neighbour. The same can be said for Andrew Stewart's Burker story, where the good advice of his employer ensures that the Traveller protagonist eventually escapes. The underlying structural principle, then, is the same across multiple Burker accounts: the betrayal of the Burkers is atoned by the benevolence of others. The narratives share a positive outlook and are expressions of an optimism that can prevail even in the direst of circumstances. Moreover, the combination of the pattern of the narratives and the interactions between the characters challenges negative stereotypes around the 'threat' that Travellers and their culture pose to the settled or mainstream population.

CONTAMINATION AND RESISTANCE

That the Travellers' Burker accounts are imbued with meanings that do not appear on the surface of the narratives has been suggested elsewhere. In one interpretation of a Burker account by the Traveller storyteller Jess Smith BEM, Martin Shaw concludes that Smith's story 'acts as a pedagogical and ideological tool, as it promotes the idea that women need to be independent in order to deal with the unpredictability of their economic and social roles' (2006: 170). In terms of structure, Smith's story follows the Burker theme already identified; after a fruitful day hawking, Smith's grandmother, and her infant child Maggie, find themselves alone on the 'vast expanse of Rannoch Moor' (*Jessie's Journey* 2002: 96); they encounter the dreaded Burkers and the villains demand possession of baby Maggie; terrified, and on account of an injured arm, Smith's grandmother briefly hands Maggie to the Burkers; through quick wits and sleight of hand, Maggie is retrieved from captivity; finally, the pair escape across the moor to the sanctuary of her cousin's camp on 'the far side of Loch Tulla' (ibid.: 99). According to Shaw, Smith's Burker story does not fit squarely within the Travellers' Burker tradition because it is usually adult Travellers who are threatened (2006: 168). However, the familiar Burker motifs, as described throughout the present chapter, are again present in Smith's account: a quotidian beginning, a precarious situation, an element of captivity and finally a return to familiarity, or sanctuary. Additionally, Smith's account is situated in lived experience, including a cast of female protagonists that are known to Smith, and with references to specific topographical features within the narrative.

Shaw's intriguing conclusion is based on the gender of the protagonists and the way that they act when confronted with mortal threat.

In Smith's account, we are told of her grandmother that 'there was no way she'd give up her child without a life-or-death struggle' (2002: 98). Both female protagonists are thereby placed in mortal danger – or the precariousness that is the hallmark of the Burker accounts – and it is the logic and experience of the grandmother that wins the day. The pair escape when the grandmother tricks the Burker into reining his horses, then uses the opportunity to snatch Maggie back and dash off into the boggy familiarity of Rannoch Moor, a place where the Burkers dare not follow. For Shaw, this means that the 'heroine or resistance figure of the story is [. . .] infused with knowledge of the environment that she operates in and [has] an advantageous knowledge of other ways of thinking' (2006: 170). Smith's Burker account is therefore more than a straightforward negotiation of a deep-seated-community-wide persecution complex, becoming what Shaw sees as a 'blueprint for how disempowered Traveller women [. . .] can use their wits to get through difficult situations' (ibid.: 169–170).

However, Shaw also suggests that the 'meaning behind Smith's story goes beyond the threat of the Burkers; it is a metonym for the perceived vulnerability of women and children in relation to unfamiliar others' (ibid.: 168). Thus, we are back in familiar territory. The point here is that close attention to the details within the Travellers' Burker accounts can reveal more nuanced, yet equally plausible, interpretations of their meanings. If what is at stake for Shaw, then, is the 'unpredictability of their [women's] economic and social roles' (ibid.: 170), Smith's narrative can be viewed from a different perspective. In Smith's account, the familiar Burker plot structure also speaks to the emancipatory qualities of 'local knowledge' and empowers the female protagonists to resist the Burker's naïve instructions to 'let her [Maggie] go, tinker, it's futile' (2002: 98). In Jock Stewart's Burker account, perhaps Shaw would comment on the untenable poor relief for the able-bodied widow. The widow's tenacious pursuit of her economic independence, fatally thwarted by an establishment that is ideologically opposed to her lifestyle, could be considered an act of resistance. Again, it is the social and economic realities experienced by the Travellers that are being negotiated within the Burker accounts. Any charge that these stories are either apocryphal or metaphorical loses credence from this perspective because, as is often the case with the Travellers' traditions, the more significant meanings are embedded below the surface.

The nuanced meanings within the Burker tradition are starkest when we consider the element of intoxication. The reader will recall the method of murder favoured by the narratives' namesake, William Burke. Burke and his accomplices would ply their unsuspecting victims with alcohol before smothering them, presumably to make the murder easier and to avoid any physical damage to the body. Speaking in 1954, Traveller Geordie Stewart tells a Burker story that he informs us happened to his 'mother's great-great-granny' (TAD 3817); with Stewart being born in 1930 (TAD ID 4842), this places the chronology of the story around the first half of the nineteenth century, or contemporaneous with the Burkean anxiety being felt throughout Scotland. Stewart begins his story by introducing us to a Traveller couple living on the West Coast of Scotland; 'he wis a real Tinker, he mended tin', Stewart begins, 'and she was a pedlar, she peddled with a basket' (TAD 3817). Finding themselves in a strange part of the country where they had never been before, the couple are at a loss for a place to camp for the night. With the weather turning and darkness falling, and the couple becoming desperate for a safe place to sleep, they see a farmhouse's lights in the distance and make their way towards it. In Geordie Stewart's account, we again find the familiar Burkean structure; Travellers going about their everyday business suddenly find themselves in a precarious situation and seek respite. The Traveller couple approach the house and ask for lodgings for the night. The farmer and his red-headed daughter, after some persuasion, offer the couple food and drink, and then allow them to sleep in a barn for the night. Again, the antagonist is red-headed, anticipating the theme of betrayal that can be found throughout the Travellers' Burker tradition. When the Traveller couple are led to the barn, the farmer tells them, '"dinnae worry yer heid nane", he says, "if ye hear a noise through the night", he says, "because there a coo ready to calf anytime" [. . .] "and we might be the go [be called into action]"' (ibid.).

So that the couple are 'not disturbed' during the night, the farmer explains that he will lock the door from the outside. At this point, the Traveller women's suspicions are aroused, and she becomes aware of a table in the barn with a small bottle and a cloth on it. The farmer retires and the Traveller couple are left alone in the barn. Presently, the couple hear 'scufflin' on the roof [. . .] so they look up tae the skylight an' they see a young lad's face' (ibid.). The young lad gives them a warning in the form of a song:

> Ochanee, lads, I darena tell,
> But if I wis you, I would rise and run.
> Do you see that bottle o' chloroform?
> It will be your death, oh, before the morn.
>
> (ibid.)

After hearing the song, the Traveller woman is left in no doubt that the couple are among Burkers. Their fear is intensified when the Traveller woman notices blood stains on the floor of the barn and the couple flee through the skylight, leaving all their possessions behind. The motif of intoxication – embodied by the chloroform in Stewart's account – also speaks to the theme of betrayal that underpins the Burker accounts. As we have seen, the Burker accounts employ ironically cast characters that amplify this sense of betrayal; the red-headed hosts, for instance, where the ultimate saviour becomes the ultimate betrayer. For Edwards, the 'murderous host is the most terrifying tale there is' (cited in McCracken-Flesher 2012: 19) and this is doubly so in the case of Burking, where the victims are first intoxicated then smothered. Stewart's account intensifies the Burker experience with the inclusion of the visceral details of the criminals' methods: first, the barn door locked from the outside; then the discovery of the chloroform and the lad's warning from above; finally, the previous victims' blood nonchalantly left for the ensuing victims to contemplate.

In an interview with the author, contemporary Nawken Davie Donaldson shares a Burker account that explores the very same themes encountered throughout this chapter. Donaldson's account begins with the recollection of the roadman's house that once existed in the Sma' Glen in central Perthshire; 'there's a story aboot my Great-Grandfaither, Willie, he wis oot hackin [hawking]', begins Donaldson, 'like many Burker stories they start with someone hackin [. . .] ye wouldnae hack the road if you were telt these stories' (Interview 2019). From the outset, Donaldson situates his Burker account in reality; the reference to his kin, for instance, and through his awareness of the tradition to which his account belongs. Donaldson continues to contextualise his account with topographical details; his Great-Grandfather and two companions were hawking in the Sma' Glen, which was 'the main road to the Highlands for a very long time, so that was the main route for Traivellers' (ibid.). This description of the road through the Sma' Glen – now the modern A822 – has indeed been the preferred route for some centuries, being the route favoured by General Wade for his military road in the first half of the eighteenth century, and earlier still by the northern cattle drovers heading south to market in the Scottish Lowlands (Haldane 1952: 32, 103). As we have seen previously, the richness of context in the Burker accounts firmly roots the narratives in a reality that is both recognisable and meaningful. Donaldson's protagonists are situated on familiar ground, but soon find themselves in a precarious situation when 'it's getting kinda dark, and they've no got nothin wi them' (Interview 2019). The company approach a farmhouse to seek lodgings for the night and are welcomed by the farmer and his wife. The Travellers are then given food and whisky and enjoy a pleasant evening with their hosts.

When it is time to sleep, the farmer offers the Travellers a space in his barn for the night and Donaldson's account takes a sinister turn. Under a dubious pretence of fire safety, the farmer insists on taking his guests' cigarettes, candles and lighters, so 'the boys all hand over their things' (ibid.).

However, a member of the company, Duncan Newlands, 'never trusted country-folk [non-Travellers]' (ibid.) so has kept a candle, the means to light it and a deck of cards. The captives soon discover they are not alone in the barn when Donaldson's grandfather finds a dead body and piles of the previous victims' clothing. At this point, the grandfather realises their danger when he 'kens, right there and then, ken aa these stories o Burkers comes right intae his heid' (ibid.). The Travellers then hear the voice of the farmer, assuming the captives are asleep after their food and whisky, '"they're up there boys"', the farmer whispers, '"gimme the payment noo and yis [you] can take them"' (ibid.). After hearing this, the company flee for their lives, suspecting that their antagonists are 'medical students, because Glenalmond College is just doon the road from Sma' Glen' (ibid.). Eventually, the companions come to the roadman's house where 'they don't have to say anything. The roadman's like, "right boys, I ken exactly, come here an I'll hide yis"' (ibid.). Donaldson tells a further 'auld story, it was actually [. . .] somethin to dae wi my folk up north, roond aboot Baff' (Interview 2019). The story begins with a young Traveller who has been out hawking for the day and becomes unable to reach his camp before nightfall. The lad comes across a likely house to pass the night and is invited in by an old couple. The inhabitants were 'lovely folk', Donaldson goes on, and there was a 'big roaring fire, a really cosy, bonny wee place' (ibid.:).

Both Donaldson's stories follow the Burkean masterplot; a wayward Traveller, or group, is enticed into supposedly safe accommodation, before becoming aware of a threat to their person in the form of Burkers and make an escape with the violence unconsummated. Donaldson's version aligns with a version told by Stanley Robertson – (TAD 65216), recorded in 1979 – where the protagonist is saved by an ally within the house who sings a song in 'Cant' to warn him of his peril. Cant is a language, used by some Traveller communities, that is formed of a large vocabulary from a variety of sources including Gaelic in the north of Scotland, and Anglo-Romani in the south (Clark 2006a: 16). In Donaldson's version, the ally is fleshed out further to include details of how he came to be in the settled house; 'back in they days', explains Donaldson, 'if your mother and faither croaked [passed away], you would go to work for other folk [. . .] you would either do that or go to a poor hoose, and naebody wanted to go to a poor hoose because it was a shan [bad] place to grow up in' (Interview 2019). The ally's parents had previously perished in a fire and the orphaned boy had been indentured to the settled people's homestead as a way of 'earning his keep'. This is an important point in Donaldson's narrative because it encapsulates the theme of the story. In his metanarrative, Donaldson explains that the point of the story is 'to teach you the importance of the Cant' (ibid.), before going on to disclose that 'we're taught from a very early age, whatever way, to protect the Cant and treat it wi a lot a respect. An one of the ways we done that wis through stories' (ibid.). The fact that this use of Cant is embedded within a Burker story is significant; its use here makes the narrative quintessentially Nackian because it delivers its meaning using a Traveller-centric language.

More specifically, this aspect of the Travellers' Burker legends demonstrates a resistance to ideological contamination. In Stanley Robertson's version, the listener is warned, 'dinnae sloch the hantle's slab [do not drink the non-Travellers' tea] (TAD 65216). There are other examples from international folklore of singing being used as a warning of peril. In ATU 1419H – *Woman Warns Lover of Husband by Singing Song*, a woman sings a lullaby to warn her approaching lover that her husband is at home and that he should flee (Uther 2004 Vol. II: 211). Elsewhere, in ATU 958, when a shepherdess is accosted by a band of robbers, she plays a trick and manages to sing a song that alerts her friends further along the valley (ibid. Vol. I: 598). In Scotland, the Gaelic song *Aoidh, na Dèan Cadal Idir* [Aodh, do not sleep at all] (TAD 86108), is sung by a young girl being held captive; she sings the song to a man, Aodh, who happens by the house where she is being held, with her assailants planning to murder Aodh in his sleep. Aodh escapes, brings help for the kidnapped girl and they are subsequently married. In Donaldson's story, a verse is sung by the ally to warn the visiting Traveller of his peril:

Deek how the hashie govels,
Deek how the hashie hah.
Shan cowels, shan pottie,
Bing avree and feck awa.

Ha aa the hantle's habben,
Ha aa the hantle's hah.
Feek the neddies tae yer naggin,
Dinnae sloch the hantle's slab.

(Interview 2019)

Donaldson offers the following translation of the key elements: 'look how the people eat, look how the people eat. Bad people, bad house [. . .] eat all the people's potatoes / do not drink the people's tea' (ibid.).[5] Discussing cultural differentiation and ethnic origins, Okely points out that the use of a certain language cannot be regarded as a signifier of 'race' or ethnicity (1983: 8). Okely's argument goes that the 'underlying assumption is that language is transmitted or learnt only through biological descent' (ibid.). I do not argue here that the use of Cant in Traveller storytelling indicates an exotic racial lineage, or that Cant encompasses the cultural differentiation between Travellers and the mainstream population.

However, in the present context, the *way* that Cant is *used* supports the argument that distinctive cultural identities are being negotiated within the stories and that an ideological position is being espoused. When the ally finishes his warning song in Donaldson's story, the lady of the house protests: 'ah'll no be haen [having] any a that Gaelic song in ma hoose' (Interview 2019). The settled woman's misapprehension of the language being used announces her role in the narrative. She stands for the basic misunderstanding of Travellers by the settled population and her status as a Burker becomes incidental. Moreover, the ally's Cant song functions to create a connection between the singer and listener, engendering trust between the two Travellers in the story. Donaldson's version of this story evokes a clear sense of fraternity between the two Traveller protagonists at the individual level. Their linguistic recognition serves to defuse the tension in the ally's indentured status because it gives the ally emancipatory agency when he finds his compatriot in peril. Donaldson's testimony and story represents further evidence that the personal autonomy prized by Travellers is negotiated within their Burker tradition. The present example demonstrates that this negotiation is achieved by linking autonomy with a shared cultural identity using Cant. The ally's autonomy is symbolically removed by his indenture with the settled people, only to be validated *in extremis* when he frees his cultural relative from the existential threat of the Burkers.

In Chapter 2, I intimated to the reader that Traveller stories share characteristics with stories from other cultural spheres, and here we find a striking example. In Irish oral tradition, the historical figure Daniel O'Connell is surrounded by a wealth and variety of folklore (uí Ógáin 1995: 1). O'Connell was an important figure during the Catholic Emancipation of the early nineteenth century, contributing to a landmark measure that allowed Catholics to sit as Members of Parliament. One of the most prevalent anecdotes about O'Connell's life – with over one hundred and forty versions documented – tells of an unsuccessful attempt to poison him and where he is saved by a warning spoken or sung in Irish (ibid.: 150, 153). The story, 'A Dhónaill Uí Chonaill, an dTuigeann Tú Gaeilge? [Daniel O'Connell, do you understand Irish?]', resembles the pattern of the Burkean stories from Robertson and Donaldson: the protagonist finds himself in a precarious situation; an unexpected ally warns him of his peril using, relatively, esoteric language; the protagonist then escapes the intended violence unharmed. In the story, O'Connell is usually in London and in the company of Protestants sharing a meal. A serving girl becomes aware of his peril and warns O'Connell, variously, that there is 'something in your dish', or 'pepper in your porridge', and 'as much in your glass that would kill hundreds' (ibid.: 151). The conclusion of the narrative sees O'Connell's would-be poisoner killed by sleight of hand and O'Connell and the serving girl escape together. The parallels with the Traveller Burker story are clear, and the underlying ideological imperatives more so. The protagonist and ally undermine the dominant language of their hostile hosts while simultaneously embodying a symbolic victory for O'Connell's Catholic cause.[6] The similarities between the anecdote about O'Connell and the Traveller Burker stories are indicative of relationships between cultural spheres and highlight the unique ways in which common motifs are utilised.

As with the previous examples cited above, Donaldson's accounts share the fundamental Burkean structure: an everyday situation evolves into a precarious one; the protagonists seek refuge and are subsequently held captive by malevolent hosts; and finally, the captives escape and find true refuge with a benevolent host. Similarly, Donaldson frames his account in a reality that is at once socially, historically and geographically situated. During Donaldson's contextual introduction to his Burker account, he explains that 'in those days, you could go an chap a door of a fairmhoose and they'd let ye in because fermers relied on Traivellers so much, they were quite good to us' (ibid.). Here again, the premise that the Travellers' Burker accounts are predicated on a persecution complex is undermined. In Donaldson's account, the protagonists have no reason to suspect that the farmers mean to murder them and sell their bodies. The poignancy of Donaldson's account lies in the very opposite, where the weary Travellers place their trust in their hosts and are betrayed. When Duncan Newlands anticipates some trickery and smuggles the candle and light into the barn, by virtue of his willingness to sleep in the barn anyway, Newlands' sleight is better read as insubordination. Following the previous examples examined above, Donaldson's contemporary Burker account is further evidence of the social reality that these narratives negotiate.

The Travellers' relationship with the settled community is what is at stake, and the relationship is far from one-sided. Consider Jock Stewart's escape from the turnip shed with his pocketknife, or Jess Smith's BEM grandmother hoodwinking the would-be child-snatcher, or Newlands smuggling a candle and card game into his captivity. What is consistently being undermined is the inequitable social relationship between the Travellers and the, ironically, unaccommodating settled population. The Travellers' Burker accounts often end with a new sense of equilibrium that challenges entrenched misunderstandings of the Travellers' deeds and intentions. Moreover, the use of intoxicants brings the Burker accounts to their most menacing zenith; the idea that your host will render you insensible, commit murder, then commodify your dead body is a universally unconscionable taboo. As McCracken-Flesher observes, many mainstream narrative re-imaginings intimated by the activities of Burke speak to deep human anxieties (2012: 19). The Travellers' Burker tradition is no exception. What *is* exceptional is the way that this national trauma continues to manifest itself in culturally significant ways among Scotland's Traveller communities. The binary antagonism between Travellers and the outside world certainly exists, both in reality and in the stories. However, by mapping the structure of these narratives, it has been demonstrated that these cultural expressions embody a more deeply felt imperative toward existential freedom and the ideological decision to favour a lifestyle that is at odds with mainstream sensibilities. Stanley Robertson's Burker warning – sung in Cant and the same as Donaldson's above – sums up this position more effectively:

Hah aa the hantle's habben,
[. . .]
But dinnae sloch the hantle's slab.[7]

(TAD 65216)

Both Donaldson's and Robertson's verses in Cant evoke a sentiment that goes a long way to encapsulate how the Travellers' oral traditions engage with mainstream discourses. The central sustenance is the same and palatable, but the nuances that wash it down can be none but their own. Or as Douglas concludes of the Burkean tradition, 'the function these stories have or had in the Traveller's life, can be summed up by saying they helped the Traveller to preserve his identity' (1985: 120). From these perspectives, the Travellers' Burker tradition functions as resistance to form of ideological contamination that reaches its monstrous apotheosis in the crimes of William Burke and his associates.

Notes

1. The adjective 'Burkean' could have other connotations, the main one being a connection to the eighteenth-century politician and author, Edmund Burke. For instance, one biographer observes of Burke that 'quite different positions have been supported by Burkean wisdom, and proponents of

new ones continue to find vindication in citing it' (Langford 2021: online). The term Burkean is used here and henceforth to refer specifically to the Traveller stories involving Burkers that are under analysis.
2. I do not dispute that Travellers in the past have suffered from criminal attacks and molestations by the medical establishment. It is beyond the remit of this study to test the veracity of any of the stories under analysis.
3. References beginning 'TAD ID' refer to the Person ID on *Tobar an Dualchais* which can be accessed via the website by searching the numerical Person ID – https://www.tobarandualchais.co.uk/
4. Bruford and MacDonald identify this tale as a version of AT 1281a ('AT' before Uther) – *The Wandering Piper* and note its adaptation to a Burker tale within the Traveller tradition (2003: 331).
5. 'Bing avree and feck awa' means 'go away and get away', whereas 'feek the neddies tae yer naggin' means 'take the tatties for yourself, or to your body'. Additional translations kindly provided by Shamus McPhee.
6. According to uí Ógáin, O'Connell is 'credited historically with encouraging the use of English', and his 'Parliamentary activity, career and life were quite far removed, both physically and psychologically, from the lives and experiences of the storytellers' (1995: 152, 154–155). From this perspective, 'O'Connell is an example, arguably an archetype, of someone who has an image in oral tradition which differs from the image presented in historical documentation' (ibid.: 1).
7. 'Eat all the non-Travellers' food / But do not drink the non-Travellers' tea'.

7

Storytelling and the Supernatural

WE HAVE SEEN HOW one function of the stories within Traveller storytelling traditions is to express and transmit complex Travellercentric themes between the people who share them. In this chapter, we consider narratives where supernatural elements appear within empirical reality and see how supernatural narratives serve a crucial social function within the Travellers' storytelling traditions. This chapter also reconceptualises the nomenclature in describing such stories, accounting for their status within the Travellers' traditions and advocates the term super-*empirical* to describe 'fantastical' story spaces. The ubiquity of the fantastic in international traditions speaks to its universal relevance to social life, while its local manifestations are ideal subjects for interrogations into the social experience of discrete communities.

The super-empirical world is an exemplary conduit for the sense of cultural continuity that we have encountered time and again throughout this book. This chapter gives a brief summary of historical attitudes toward the supernatural in Scotland and how these attitudes affected later folkloric scholarship. This summary illuminates previous conceptualisations of the supernatural in Scotland's folklore to place the Travellers' traditions within the context of the wider Scottish traditions. This summary is not intended to be comprehensive, but rather to invoke specific collectors of Scottish folklore, arguing that their contributions continue to shape the way we understand storytelling to this day. The chapter goes go on provide an overview of the fantastical in the Travellers' traditions using extant examples from the SSS Archives and related literature. Insights from critical analyses of the fantastic are then brought to bear on the super-empirical narratives of the Travellers. Our purpose here is to reinforce the conclusions of the preceding chapters with further detailed evidence. We find that the super-empirical story spaces of Traveller storytellers represent an antidote to perceptions of otherness whilst showcasing their distinctive ideological makeup.

As I have argued throughout this study, these types of stories are by no means unique to the Travellers' traditions; as Douglas points out, many of the stories are recognisably international tales recorded in the ATU catalogue (1985: 21). In the broader Scottish context, 'supernatural' narratives have been a staple concern during Scotland's cultural and intellectual development over the past few centuries. The Travellers' traditions have been party to that development in that they represent a distinctive idiom of such traditions and have been attracting the attention of folklorists since at least the publication of Campbell's *Popular Tales* (1860–62). The Travellers' traditions contain international tale variants, migratory legends and share motifs collated by Thompson in his *Motif-index of Folk Literature* (1955). For instance, the story of the magical pot we examine below is a variant of ATU 591 – *The Thieving Pot* (Uther 2004 Vol. I: 348). It is not our purpose here to evaluate the wider Scottish traditions in any great detail. However, it must be recognised that Travellers' stories form part of these wider traditions and that comparative exercises can be fruitful. As we have seen before, what makes the Travellers' versions of the stories idiosyncratic is the way that the plots, themes and characters reflect the distinctive worldviews of their narrators. Our own analyses therefore focus on stories that *use* the fantastic in different ways to negotiate the real social, cultural and ideological concerns faced by their narrators and Traveller communities more broadly.

SUPERNATURAL SCOTLAND

The association between folklore and the supernatural can be traced back to the earliest proponents of folkloric research. The publication of William Camden's *Britannia* in 1586 sparked an interest in 'antiquities', the study of the past which initially focused on physical remains but later recognised the value of folk memory when trying to understand the past. One such antiquarian, inspired by Camden's work, was John Aubrey (1626–97) who perceived that the lore of the folk was closely bound up with the supernatural (Dorson 1968: 9). In his survey of early folklore research in Britain, Dorson notes that Aubrey's *Miscellanies*, published in 1696, represents a record of conceptualisations of the supernatural that would not be out of place in the notebook of a modern folklorist (ibid.: 5). By conducting collections in the field during 'walking trips', early folklorists such as Aubrey realised that a central thread in the 'miscellanies' of the folk was supernatural in aspect. Aubrey also makes a penetrating insight into the behaviour of oral folklore when he remarks that 'the divine art of printing and gunpowder have frighted away Robingoodfellow [Puck, hobgoblin] and the fayries' (cited in Dorson 1968: 6). From the outset, then, those interested in the study of folklore realised that the supernatural played a central role in the material they encountered, but more significantly, that socio-cultural conditions impact the way that supernatural beliefs manifest themselves within folkloric expressions. These two characteristics of the supernatural in folklore feed directly into the purpose of the present study as we continue to examine how the Travellers' storytelling traditions condition and represent their distinctive worldviews. To situate and better understand Traveller expressions of fantastical happenings, a selection of pertinent discourses around the supernatural in Scotland's intellectual history are pertinent here.

As early as 1575 in Scotland, customs and rituals that exist outside of organised religion were already being condemned by the learned classes as 'fantastical imaginations' and 'abused science' (*Records of the Parliament of Scotland to 1707* 1575). Within the context of such fantastic imaginations – as perceived by the *Records of the Parliament of Scotland to 1707* – those specifically admonished were the 'idle people calling themselves Egyptians' and 'strong and idle beggars' (ibid.). As early in Scottish history as 1575, marginalised communities are viewed as particularly susceptible to such flights of fancy, ostracising them further through their association with irrational belief systems. Legislation followed throughout the sixteenth century in Scotland, specifically targeting those regarded as the custodians of folklore. By suppressing tradition-bearers, officialdom aimed to change the meaning and context of folk beliefs, a process that Max Weber termed the 'disenchantment of the world' (Henderson and Cowan 2001: 115–116). Outside of officially sanctioned belief systems then, the supernatural in Scotland is initially relegated to the very fringes of society in the early modern period. Henderson and Cowan put this down to the suppression of folk belief during the Scottish Reformation (c. 1530–60), where 'pagan' superstitions and supernatural events were reconceptualised under the auspices of Calvinistic Christianity (2001: 116).

The tide begins to turn around a hundred years later with Robert Kirk's *The Secret Commonwealth*, written around 1691 and distributed in manuscript form. Kirk was a church minister and accomplished scholar and his short book amounts to a defence of supernatural folk belief that aims to 'supress the impudent and growing atheism of this age' (1893: 3). Kirk fused first-hand accounts of supernatural experiences with biblical evidence, arguing that belief in fairies did not contradict Christian theology. Instead, supernatural beings, such as fairies and fauns, are merely a part of God's creation and ultimately must 'bow to the name of Jesus' (Kirk 1893: 69). Kirk's career as a minister in Highland parishes, along with his knowledge of Gaelic language and beliefs, resulted in what Michael Hunter calls 'a slightly strange book, which combines what is effectively reportage of folklore with erudite speculation and biblical exegesis' (2001: 12). *The Secret Commonwealth* is an unparalleled account of supernatural belief systems in Reformation Scotland and its legacy represents a milestone in our understanding of supernatural folk beliefs. In an edition of 1893, Andrew Lang introduces *The Secret Commonwealth* by commenting that 'as to the Fairy belief, we conceive it to be a complex matter, from which tradition, with its memory of earth-dwellers, is not wholly absent' (1893: lxv). Lang goes on to suggest that folk beliefs in the supernatural are in part due to the 'survival of the pre-Christian Hades, and to the belief in local spirits' (ibid.).

Kirk's book reconceptualises the supernatural in folklore because it highlights the fact that esoteric belief systems do not necessarily have to contradict dominant ontologies. Such beliefs are better understood as complex, localised negotiations of traditions that symbolically represent alternative worldviews. Another significant commentator writing at the beginning of the eighteenth century was Martin Martin. Born on Skye and a native Gaelic speaker, Martin was one of the first writers to capture the lives and culture of the Gaelic-speaking population in the Western Isles of Scotland (Cowan 2009: 20). Martin introduces his seminal work – *A Description of the Western Islands of Scotland* – by explaining that 'there are several instances of heathenism and pagan superstition among the inhabitants of the islands [but] only a few of the oldest and most ignorant of the vulgar are guilty' (1716: xiv). His introductory remarks are unsurprising, given the second edition which is quoted here is dedicated to the reigning protestant monarch, George I (ibid.: iii). 'These practices are only to be found where the reformed religion has not prevailed', Martin continues, 'for 'tis to the progress of that alone, that the banishment of evil spirits, as well as of evil customs, is owing, when all other methods proved ineffectual' (ibid.: xiv). Martin's book goes on to cover a range of topics from mackerel running ashore with the spring tide, to the longevity and charity of 'the natives', to his famous account of second sight. Here, despite his pious preface and dedication, Martin informs us that if 'everything for which the learned are not able to give a satisfying account be condemned as impossible, we may find many other things generally believed, that must be rejected as false by this rule' (ibid.: 308). Like Kirk, Martin's conceptualisations recognise that ostensibly 'impossible' phenomena do not necessarily have to contradict observable empirical reality. It is only that, from Martin's eighteenth-century perspective, we do not fully understand the phenomena and their role in human culture: 'if we know so little of natural causes, how much less can we pretend to things that are supernatural?' (ibid.: 309).

During the Scottish Enlightenment, the scepticism of David Hume highlighted the debate around the role of the supernatural; it was not only esoteric folk beliefs that were being challenged by rationalism and scepticism. In 'Of Miracles', Hume asks us to consider the miraculous incidents within 'a book [the Pentateuch], presented to us by a barbarous and ignorant people', concluding that the Christian religion 'cannot be believed by any reasonable person' (2007 [1748]: 94–95) without the person also believing in the miracles that Hume undermines. Hume's commentary gets to the core of the debate around the role of the supernatural in human societies by challenging the merits of one supernatural belief system over others. For Colin Kidd, such challenges to the Church's authority placed the supernatural at the 'forefront of public discourse in the age of Enlightenment', because 'church and state were inextricably intertwined' (2009: 91). One effect of Enlightenment debate around religious belief systems was that conceptualisations of the supernatural were fundamentally altered in the Scottish public's consciousness. 'Belief, or unbelief, in supernatural phenomena', says Lizanne Henderson, 'was just one of the realms of Scottish intellectual, social and political life' (2009: xx) affected by Enlightenment discourses. These effects are still being felt, as Kidd points out, 'the unofficial folkloric supernaturalism of the wider public is perceived as a quaint, but marginal, curiosity in a high technology-driven consumer society' (2009: 91). The forthcoming analyses showcase how supernaturalism manifests in the Travellers' storytelling traditions and how it functions to negotiate some of the central principles of consumer society, setting out challenges to dominant ideological constructs. Previous researchers have pointed out that supernaturalism is a pervasive element within the Travellers' traditions. In their study – having over twenty years' experience with Traveller storytellers – MacColl and Seeger point out that, 'the two most popular story types are those which deal with ghostly encounters and the ones commonly known as *Burkers*' (1986: 57, italics in original). Sheila Douglas also recognises the prevalence of supernaturalism within one Perthshire family's traditions; commenting on her voluminous source material, Douglas explains that 'a large proportion of the stories, both with and without AT [ATU] numbers, involve the supernatural' (1985: 21). Perhaps the most apposite insight comes from Niles; although elements of the supernatural appear in many of Scotland's cultural traditions,

Niles notes that 'the travellers' [sic] easy-going relationship with the numinous seems to have made them especially receptive to narratives that feature uncanny elements' (1999: 168).

WHAT IS 'SUPERNATURAL' IN FOLKLORE?

To get at such traditions, early students of folklore like Kirk relied on the collection of evidence from the folk, and it is to such discussion that we now turn. In Chapter 5 above – concurring with Zipes (1997: 42) – we saw that the Grimms' and others' versions of international tales were moulded by their authors to suit their own sensibilities and those of their elite readership. To a large extent in Scotland, James Macpherson's *Fragments of Ancient Poetry, Collected in the Highlands of Scotland and Translated from the Gaelic or Erse Language* (1760) represents a similar motivation by its author. Macpherson – an aspiring poet, schoolmaster and latterly MP for Camelford in Cornwall – claimed that his collection of prose-poems was the work of an ancient Scottish bard, 'Ossian' (Moore 2017: 2–5; West 2012: 48). The *Fragments* were indeed collected in the Highlands by Macpherson, and others, and based on Gaelic oral traditions. However, their antiquity and ascription to a single poet was a fabrication by Macpherson: the texts were composed from the twelfth century onwards by professional poets working in Classical Common Gaelic, then were absorbed into Gaelic tradition and adapted to vernacular Gaelic (Gunderloch 2013: 75–76). During his own lifetime, Macpherson was maligned over his editorial and marketing practices. William Shaw commented in 1781 that 'the whole machinery is nothing but the superstition of the Highlands, poetically embellished' (1781: 25). Modern scholarship is similarly aware of Macpherson's collection that was in fact 'based on oral and manuscript traditions, common to Scotland and Ireland, which were woven into a new and polished narrative to suit the modern tastes of the 18th century' (West 2012: 51). The supernatural aspects of Macpherson's *Fragments* – along with his subsequent Ossianic publications *Fingal* (1762) and *Temora* (1763) – were relegated during his 'translation'. Macpherson's Celtic world 'was one of noble warriors, not a quaint fairyland of giants and magicians', so 'the witches and monsters which feature in the popular Highland ballads had to be condemned as interpolations and stripped away' (Stafford 1988: 83). Although Macpherson's poetry cannot be viewed as folkloric, it worked to stimulate interest in Scotland's national folklore and had a tangible effect on the way folklore was perceived.

Writing in *The Edinburgh Review*, Walter Scott's admiration is clear when he remarks that 'Macpherson may have collected and used many original poems now lost', and that 'perhaps more than one half was authorised by an authentic original' (1805: 445, 461). Scott's own preoccupation with folk narrative appears throughout his published works and personal correspondence: *Minstrelsy of the Scottish Border* (1802–3), *Introductions and Notes and Illustrations to the Novels, Tales, and Romances of the Author of Waverley* (1833) and Scott's letters, to the likes of Jacob Grimm, are testament to his lifelong fascination with Scotland's oral traditions (Dorson 1968: 109; West 2012: 51–52). Scott's *Letters on Demonology and Witchcraft*, first published in 1830, was another landmark elucidation of supernatural narratives recorded in Scotland. Within the *Letters*, Scott recounts and reflects on a multitude of accounts of supernatural occurrences, some from persons of 'sense and estimation' (1830: 34). Scott's *Letters* can be read as a rational treatment of witches, fairies, ghosts and the generally uncanny as experienced by a broad range of individuals from various sectors of British society. Within his treatments of anecdotes and memorates, Scott anticipates the value that we now see in folkloric expressions because he does not dismiss them immediately as mere 'fantastical imaginations'. However, Scott laments that 'the present fashion of the world seems to be ill suited for studies of this fantastic nature', and that 'the most ordinary mechanic has learning sufficient to laugh at the figments which in former times were believed by persons far advanced in the deepest knowledge of the age' (ibid.: 401).

In the latter half of the nineteenth century, the concept that latent meanings exist within oral storytelling was recognised by John Francis Campbell while compiling his *Popular Tales of the West Highlands* (1860–62). In his introduction, Campbell observes that he became aware of many tales whose defining characteristics are sagacity and hidden meaning (1860–62 vol. I: xliii). Moreover, Campbell appreciated that not only do popular stories have specific meanings, but that the stories are conditioned by the cultural context in which they exist. Not only this, but the supernatural nature of many of the tales Campbell and his fieldworkers collected is clear. For example, the second volume of *Popular Tales* includes a selection of 'Twenty-nine Fairy Tales' (1860–62 vol. II: vi), on which Campbell comments, somewhat esoterically, 'I am quite sure that the fairy creed of the peasantry [. . .] is not a whit more unreasonable than the bodily appearance of the hand of Napoleon the First to Napoleon the Third in 1860' (ibid.: 72). Campbell understood that supernatural beliefs do not necessarily have to be taken literally and that fantastical stories can convey ideologically significant information using symbolism. As Campbell so eloquently expressed after first encountering the storytelling traditions of Scotland's Travellers, we too aspire to 'a train of thought, which leads at last to a wild weird story' (1860–62 vol. I: xvii).

Based on Campbell's commentary throughout *Popular Tales*, his understanding of the material he and his colleagues collected in Scotland is lucid and ground-breaking. That the 'mind of the class', and their 'own ideas', are intrinsic to the stories they tell is a penetrating insight into the nature of folklore (1860–62: xlvii). That these ideas are often cloaked in the fantastic, and not unreasonably, is further testament to the importance of Campbell's collection to our understanding of folklore and tradition. To put this in perspective, Campbell's contemporary Robert Chambers viewed the folkloric material that he collected differently. Chambers' preface to the third edition of *Popular Rhymes of Scotland* explains to his readers that the *Rhymes* constitute 'the production of rustic wits, in some the whimsies of mere children', and that we should not therefore 'expect here anything profound, or sublime, or elegant, or affecting' (1858 [1826]: vi). For Chambers, supernatural belief in Scotland was something that 'was universally acknowledged amongst the unenlightened' (ibid.: 110). Similarly, Hugh Miller's voluminous *Scenes and Legends of the North of Scotland* (1835) was motivated by the preservation of local 'histories', with little attention being paid to the substance of the material itself.

Of his *Scenes and Legends*, Miller remarks in his dedication that 'some of them seem to have sprung out of minds darkened by ignorance and superstition', while others 'may be considered as the fragments of codes of belief that have long since fallen into desuetude' (1835: ix). On the other hand, notes Dorson, John Francis Campbell broke new ground by 'focusing attention on the tellers and the way in which they manipulated their texts' (1968: 400). Mention must be made here of John Francis Campbell's contemporary and correspondent, John Gregorson Campbell. Gregorson Campbell's *Superstitions of the Highlands & Islands of Scotland*, published in 1900, is a collection of what Gregorson Campbell called 'Gaelic lore' that he hoped would 'prove of some scientific value' (cited in Black 2005 [1900]: lxxxiii). Gregorson Campbell's book captures a variety of narratives, collected from across Scotland, relating the attributes and activities of fairies, ghosts, second sight, witchcraft and the Devil. Like his contemporary John Francis Campbell, Gregorson Campbell understood that supernatural belief can provide insights into the social life of its proponents; 'the fairy creed', says Gregorson Campbell, 'is a polished and amusing satire on the vanity of human pleasures and the emptiness of what is commonly called "life"' (ibid.: xcii). By the beginning of the twentieth century then, the understanding that 'supernatural' phenomena within folklore reflect real social concerns had crystallised. Black states it plainly: the supernatural in folklore is 'a psychological and metaphorical construct designed to help ordinary people struggle through a difficult life from day to day [. . .] by the power of oral narrative' (2005: lxxviii).

The overarching point here is that so-called super-*natural* narratives allow narrators to resolve real anxieties and contradictions in imaginary story spaces (cf. Jameson 1981: 77), spaces that can therefore be regarded as super-*empirical* rather than super-*natural*. There is a subtle distinction between the two terms, supernatural and super-empirical, but it has significant implications when it comes to addressing ideological discourses within Traveller storytelling. This distinction and its relevance become apparent presently. What is crucial is the fact that fantastical narratives continue to be collected, scrutinised, collated and published in Scotland, and beyond. This fact is testament to their ongoing relevance to modern societies and cultures. When it comes to the symbolism inherent in 'supernatural' or fantastical narratives, Black suggests that when we use these symbols to inquire into the social significance of a given story, the answer can be startling (2005: lxxviii). For our purposes, the social aspect of super-empirical storytelling can be taken further to include ideological negotiations that get to the heart of how our societies are organised.

The term 'supernatural' itself is understood here not in theological terms that imply a hierarchical world where the divine transcends biological reality (Valk and Sävborg 2018: 16), but as a socio-cultural phenomenon, where the 'super-' prefix does not indicate something which is 'beyond natural'. Instead, stories that include a fantastical, miraculous or magical element are considered within a cognitive category. Thomas Raverty views such stories as cognitive spaces where 'human metaphorical and analogical capabilities, especially in imaginatively enlarging upon sense data and empirical reality, are given free rein' (2003: 118). Similarly, Barbara Walker remarks that 'aspects of the supernatural act as an integral part of belief constructions and behaviour patterns, and, in many instances, have significant cultural function and effect' (1995: 1). For Walker, these aspects are the pervasiveness of the supernatural in the everyday lives of a range of cultures, and the notion that the 'supernatural' is not necessarily synonymous with the 'miraculous' (ibid.). Konrad Talmont-Kaminski voices similar concerns when it comes to using the term 'supernatural' to describe apparently magical phenomena; the 'concept of the supernatural, understood as that which is beyond scientific investigation', says Talmont-Kaminski, 'does not provide us with an adequate description of either magic or religion' (2014: 52). Talmont-Kaminski puts this inadequacy down to common definitions of what supernatural phenomena *are*, that is, whatever science cannot investigate or explain (ibid.: 47). In other words, that which is deemed beyond our current scientific capabilities to comprehend is 'supernatural'; 'super-empirical' phenomena, on the other hand, are cognitive and cultural belief systems where empirical investigation is redundant because their contents do not require evidence in order to function (ibid.: 73).

In practice, the term super-empirical is useful to argue that narrative worlds are social realities in their own right because, despite their intangibility, they do the work of engendering social relationships and discourses. This is the key differentiator when defining the narratives under discussion here – the stories are not super-*natural* because the themes they engage with are based firmly on 'natural' social relations. Christian Smith agrees, citing an elementary sociological principle; with humans as narrating beings, super-empirical narratives function 'to make sense of the meaning of self, life, history, and the world', because 'one *has* to get outside of them, to "transcend" them, and interpret them within horizons and frameworks of perspective derived from beyond the object of interpretation' (2003: 120). Smith continues, arguing that individual humans cannot self-define without the ability to locate themselves 'within stories and cultural orders outside and beyond themselves' (ibid.). Narratives thereby allow us to 'inhabit orders that are not only moral but also super-empirical in their sources' (ibid.).

Fantastical episodes within traditional narratives can therefore function as metaphorical constructs and these constructs serve to communicate nuanced experiences of the world. The term super-*empirical* is deployed to describe a category of storytelling that reflexively *uses* 'supernatural' occurrences as rhetorical devices. For example, religious narratives can be termed super-empirical because their pro-social function does not rely on empirical evidence, but on faith. Or as Smith puts it, 'this approach intentionally emphasises the super-empirical rather than the more commonly referenced supernatural', this because the term 'supernatural implies that the unseen order is not a part of nature, and that nature consists only of physical matter' (ibid.: 95). The stories examined below and in the next chapter similarly rely on the awareness of their allegorical function. Moreover, the distinction between what is 'natural' and what is 'supernatural' can be conceptualised as a cultural one. Ní Fhloinn has pointed this out already, noting that the 'distinction between the natural world and the supernatural is often a subjective one, determined largely by culture' (1999: 223). In this sense, although the events and characters within the cultural expressions that the present study examines are outside of the consensus of 'reality', they are by no means beyond what is natural.

A SUPER-EMPIRICAL POT (OF MONEY)

In short, the 'reality' of the narratives might be outside of some empirically defined consensus, however the *culturally defined* narrative coheres and is consistent with the inner reality of the story space. Under these conditions a *truly* supernatural narrative is difficult to conceive of because all fictional narrative has a purpose, in one way or another. Herein lies the subtle distinction; the difference between supernatural and super-empirical narratives is that super-empiricist readings do not require evidence for the conclusions to be valid, whereas a supernaturalist reading implies that the narrative is somehow 'beyond' our ability to understand. The *function* of super-empirical story spaces is based on the argument that the 'construction of meaning is basic to humanity, and the cold rationalism of naturalistic philosophies can rarely be satisfactory in this endeavour' (Jindra 2003: 165). It is also important to point out that the stories under examination here are not fairy tales. This is because, although the narratives sometimes share characteristics with international (ATU) tales, they are not literary creations. Literary creations – such as D'Aulnoy's seventeenth-century *Contes des Fées* [Fairy Tales] seen in preceding chapters – are useful for comparative purposes because they imply hierarchical distinctions between literary versions of internationally common stories and their supposedly inferior, yet cognate, versions among 'the folk' (Teverson 2019: 11).

The stories discussed here are primarily oral and could arguably be described as legends. That is to say, the stories report the deeds of human actors and purport to have an historical basis – as opposed to myths, where the actors are often deities, and the narratives seek to account for the origin of human and/or natural phenomena. William Bascom sees legends as the 'counterpart in verbal tradition of written history' (1965: 5) that deal in hidden treasure and ghosts. Dégh goes further: 'the legend is a story about an extranormal (supernatural or its equivalent) experience', says Dégh, 'attested by situational facts' (1991: 30). Furthermore, the legend's narrative takes place within specific cultural realms, writes Dégh, and 'contradicts the accepted norms and values of society at large' (ibid.). The stories under analysis here satisfy Dégh's conceptualisation of legends: the 'situational facts' are the verisimilitudes with Travellers' lived experiences; fantastical experiences are had; and the stories challenge mainstream conventions. Dégh goes further still, proposing that legends are an 'ideology-sensitive genre par excellence', and that, even when not founded on reality, can 'create reality' (2001: 5). Linda Williamson – widow of the Traveller storyteller Duncan Williamson – points out that although some of Duncan's stories engender a fairy tale atmosphere, they are truthful in their portrayal of real life and how Traveller families lived (1983: 152). As becomes clear, the 'truth', in this sense, is yet another way that super-empirical story spaces function to negotiate social realities that are far from 'supernatural'. Instead, these stories negotiate a strong sense of socio-cultural otherness.

This sense of ideological otherness expands from the physiological, through the intellectual and eventually into the social. 'This deep-rooted ideology', says Fredric Jameson discussing 'magical narratives', 'has only too clearly the function of drawing the boundaries of a given social order' (1975: 140). Our perceptions of the other, the alien and the unfamiliar, then, are deeply entrenched in human experience. And when these perceptions interact with complex social structures, the resultant manifestations are equally complex. For Jameson, this means that the negotiation of difference that 'magical narratives' afford performs a crucial social function. The 'evil forces' of the supernatural realm are positional; they function as relational objects to the position of the 'good forces'. Like Olrik and his 'Law of Contrast' (1992: 50), Jameson recognises that magical narratives contain explicit dichotomies that function as mediators. From this perspective, the super-empirical, as a genre, facilitates the negotiation of otherness by allowing the narrator to interrogate their *own* ideologies. Considering the status of the communities under examination here – and their associated storytellers – this conceptualisation of the function of the super-empirical in storytelling is valuable. Consider the journey of Williamson's Hedgehurst explored in Chapter 5 above; the Hedgehurst's story expressed a self-awareness that transcends social hierarchies, allowing the protagonist to negotiate his own experience of the world. It is not that otherness – Traveller or otherwise – cannot be perceived, expressed or negotiated in other storytelling genres, only that the super-empirical represents a space where negotiations of otherness can be at their most precise.

Two related examples of this ideological negotiation come from Duncan Williamson – the strong tradition-bearer who we have encountered throughout our discussions – and storyteller and singer Betsy Whyte. Firstly, Williamson tells a story about a magic pot (TAD 33627). At the beginning of the narrative, we find the Traveller protagonists in precarious circumstances; Williamson frames his narrative by explaining that 'we [he and his family] wur nae very well off in these days and we nivir hud very much tae eat sometimes, like the family in the story [. . .] they had very little tae eat' (ibid.). Situations of dearth and/or precariousness often frame Traveller storytelling and here again we find Olrik's 'Law of Contrast' (1992: 50) at work, intimating a dichotomy that the story means to address. Hungry and struggling for a place to rest for the night, the family eventually manage to trade one of their artisanal baskets for some raw potatoes, eggs and milk. They then come across a ruined house, where they make camp for the night. Out collecting firewood from a dilapidated shed attached to the ruined house, the husband finds an old pot, meticulously cleans it and the family boil their potatoes for supper. After supper, the pot is 'clean as clean could be' (TAD 33627) and set outside the camp when the family bed down for the night. Williamson then explains that the house used to belong to a witch, and that the pot is enchanted; 'before the witch deid [died], she pit a spell on the pot', continues Williamson, adding, 'that whoever looked aftir the pot, wid always huv plenty luck' (ibid.).

As Williamson's narrative progresses, we discover that the true protagonist of the story is the enchanted pot. During the night, the pot springs to life and finds its way to the castle of a local laird. 'He was a big landowner, but he was a miser, he wis awfy mean', Williamson berates, '[he] taxed the folk on his land fir every penny they were worth and he saved all up his money' (ibid.). The laird was so miserly that he neglected even furnishing his cook with a pot to cook in. The laird's cook finds the enchanted pot and fills it with roast potatoes and beef. When the cook's back is turned, the filled pot escapes and makes its way back to the Travellers' camp; 'whaur did that come fi?', exclaims the husband, 'some kind creture [person] has takin it away durin the night an filled it [. . .] and feels sorry fir us' (ibid.). The spell that was cast on the pot means that it returns to the Travellers who took care of it, and therein lies the essence of the story. The pot returns once again to the castle of the laird, this time being discovered by the laird himself. The miserly laird covets money to the extent that he waits until his castle is asleep before he counts his money of an evening. This night, the laird discovers that there has 'been a moose [mouse] at the bags' (ibid.) and his money rattles to the floor as he lifts them to make account of his wealth. Espying the enchanted pot, the laird proceeds to decant his gold into it and hides the pot in his cupboard, before retiring. Of course, the pot flits during the night, returning to the Travellers' camp.

When the Travellers discover the pot – brimming with gold – in the morning, they realise that they will never want for anything again and vow never to speak of what happened. Fearful of accusations of theft, the husband empties the pot and buries the gold. The next day, the pot is nowhere to be found, and the Traveller family 'had plenty money that they could ask for [. . .] for the rest o' their days' (ibid.). Williamson concludes by adding that the Travellers 'growed up their family, and the man went, and he bought a wee property tae hissel and he pit his weans [children] tae school' (ibid.). What this story demonstrates is not the wholesale rejection of lifestyles associated with sedentarism or material wealth. Instead, Williamson's story is a negotiation of the associated values and what these mean to him as a Traveller. That these events take place in a supernatural story space enables the symbolic function of the pot. Within this space, fantastic events are taken for granted, allowing the meaning to be delivered. The agency given to the pot functions to highlight an ideological negotiation; central to this negotiation is the dichotomy between the Travellers' treatment of the pot – where the pot represents abundance and security – and the laird's. Where the Travellers took care of the pot and were rewarded, the greedy laird's actions meant that the pot abandoned him. As I have shown throughout my interpretations, value systems based on sagacity and moral rectitude are ingrained within the Travellers' storytelling traditions. In terms of the relationship with ATU 591 – *The Thieving Pot*, Williamson's story again demonstrates the Nackian folk idiom. The narrative trajectory of the Travellers' wealth-giving pot aligns with ATU 591: in Uther's description of this international tale, a poor man makes some sort of exchange for a magic pot that goes on to steal food and money from his neighbours (2004 Vol. I: 348). When the aggrieved parties attempt to catch the magic pot, it takes them back to the poor man and the thefts are forgiven (or the pot takes the poor man to hell). The plots are broadly the same, but the nuances and contextual information mean that Williamson's version is steeped in culturally significant meanings.

As a further example of the ideological negotiations under discussion here, a story from Betsy Whyte is useful. In the same vein as Williamson's story examined above, Whyte's story involves a supernatural source of wealth. 'A Traveller man', Whyte begins, 'wis gan awa intae the wuid [woodland] fir tae see a sloosh [urinate]' (TAD 76412). The Traveller comes across a ha'penny under a tree, picks it up, is thankful for his good fortune and returns to his camp without thinking of mentioning his find to his peers. The next day, the man goes out to the same tree 'and there wis a penny!' (ibid.). This pattern continues, with the amount doubling each day, until the Traveller finds a one-pound note under the tree. At this point, the Traveller tells someone at the camp about his good fortune, who exclaims '"awa!", he says, "I widnae believe ye' (ibid.). To prove the source of his pound note, the Traveller takes the sceptic to his money tree the following morning. Predictably, there is no money under the tree. Whyte explains: 'my mother says, "if he haudnae a telt naebody aboot this", that "it would a went on doublin itsel like that until he would'a haen a fortune"' (ibid.). Whyte concludes, 'the minute he telt, that wis the thing broken and he got nae mair aftir that' (ibid.).

Whyte's short narrative is further evidence of how Traveller storytellers negotiate attitudes towards conspicuous wealth. Again, the central theme of the story is the fortuitous acquisition of wealth by supernatural means. The surface meaning of the tale is plain; be thankful for what you have and/or resist boastful behaviour. However, the Travellers' stories have further, more complex, meanings that are negotiated below the surface. In Whyte's story, money is defined as an abstract concept in the way that the Traveller protagonist accumulates wealth. The 'doubling' pattern means that the growth of his wealth would be exponential. This means that after only sixty days, the Traveller would have £1.15 x 10^{18}, a truly astronomical number. Expressed in cardinal terms this amounts to over one *quintillion*, one hundred and fifty-two quadrillion, and so Whyte was quite right about the fortune. It is not the purpose here to enter into an in-depth economic debate on capital, only to recognise that the stories under examination confront pervasive issues about material wealth that affect us all. Where a system of direct barter is no longer possible – on account of the non-coincidence of interests in modern society (Harvey 2014: 25) – money as we know it functions as a relative measure of exchange value, simultaneously storing that value. If we proceed on the premise that, as a system, 'money' has no intrinsic value, it can be viewed as a social *process*, predicated on exchange.

In Whyte's story, the Traveller protagonist fluctuates between opposing ends of the money-spectrum: at one end, he has nothing and is simply answering the call of nature; on the other, the money tree represents the *potential* to acquire an unlimited source of exchange value. In both cases, there is an element of freedom because each state represents the subject no longer participating in any system of exchange in a meaningful way. Where the subject has no 'money', they have nothing to exchange and therefore cannot participate in the social process of exchange. Where the subject has unlimited 'money', any exchange is meaningless because the unlimited-money subject is effectively exchanging nothing for something. Another way of putting this would be as David Harvey does: 'endless compound growth [is] an extremely dangerous but largely unrecognised and unanalysed contradiction' (2014: 222). Compound interest is akin to exponential growth in that the cumulative effects of both begin modestly then accelerate rapidly after a certain point. The accumulation of wealth within the capitalist system is supposedly all fair and well, yet elements such as compound interest represent stark contradictions within the system. If a single economic entity was allowed to possess unlimited 'money', the exchange value system would be unable to function because the social process that is money would cease to be meaningful.[1] As a social process, Mary Douglas sees money as a singular form of ritual: 'money is only an extreme and specialised type of ritual', says Douglas, 'money can only perform its role of intensifying economic interaction if the public has faith in it. If faith in it is shaken, the currency is useless. So too with ritual' (2003: 70). Viewed as a ritualistic practice, the efficacy of money is scrutinised with a startling degree of insight in Whyte's story.

The contradiction perceived by Harvey is the very same contradiction that Whyte's narrative evokes when her Traveller protagonist is presented with the potential to possess unlimited wealth. Within the context of the Travellers' ideological imperatives, the focus of interpretation here, the distinction between these two states of 'wealth' acquires symbolism. As with the preceding chapters' findings, the rural and the urban are again juxtaposed: the rural identity of the Traveller protagonist is made clear by Whyte's jocose introduction involving his 'sloosh' in the woods; the urban can be viewed as the potential 'fortune' that the money tree represents. In his study of Traveller culture, Niles also perceived negative connotations associated with the accumulation of wealth. For Niles, the Travellers 'firmly believe that hoarding invites nemesis [. . .] in the view of the travelling people, life is as regular as the classic ballads in seeing that nemesis haunts greed' (1999: 167). The same can be perceived in Whyte's narrative, where the concept of material wealth is forced into abstraction and an inherent contradiction is laid bare. When the Traveller protagonist reveals the source of his wealth to his society, the spell is broken and the potential for unlimited wealth disappears. 'Money', then, is cast in Whyte's story as a *social* rather than an *economic* process, a process that relies on equitability for its very existence. Of course, our social reality is markedly different and we cannot suggest that the Traveller storytellers are somehow immune to the attractions of material wealth. This reality was also recognised by Niles when he pointed out that 'some people persist in the delusion that travellers [sic] live in rural isolation, uncorrupted by the dominant society and its industrial or postindustrial economy' (ibid.: 164). For instance, the renowned Traveller singer Jeannie Robertson's correspondence with Hamish Henderson in the 1950–60s is revealing. In one letter dated 25/11/1957, Robertson complains that the

Workers' Music Association have offered '22£s 9 shillings for my whole record, they must think I am a fool', levelling the claim of 'daylight robbery. I don't like to make records for sweetie [insignificant] money' (The University of Edinburgh, *Centre for Research Collections* E89.92). A further letter dated 24/02/1964, relating to a performance in London, sees Robertson exclaim that 'they have offered me £25 but I told them I would need £50, plus all expenses and a further £10 for Donald [her husband]' (ibid.).

To highlight the distinctiveness of the Traveller negotiations of magical wealth, a comparable narrative from elsewhere in Scotland is useful. John Elliot tells the story of a soldier who has an encounter with a mysterious old woman (TAD 14182). Elliot's story is a version of Hans Christian Andersen's *Fyrtøjet* [The Tinderbox] which Thompson aligns with *The Spirit in the Blue Light*, which in turn is linked to Aladdin and his magical lamp (1946: 71–72). Uther records the tale-type as ATU 562, where a discharged or deserter soldier acquires wealth, power and a princess using a magical tinderbox that he steals from an old woman (2004 Vol. I: 330). In Elliot's version, under the instructions of the old woman, an impoverished soldier acquires a fortune in gold from under a tree. The old woman stipulates that she wants a tinderbox, also under the tree, in return for telling the soldier about the gold. When the old woman refuses to tell the soldier why the tinderbox is so valuable, he murders her with his sword and heads into town to flaunt his wealth. After spending all his ill-gotten gold, the soldier realises that striking the tinderbox summons magical dogs that can bring him anything that he wants. In Andersen's version, the soldier, predictably, asks the dogs for more wealth and then commands them to kidnap a local princess whom he covets (1899: 365–366). The King discovers the kidnapping and sentences the soldier to hang, whereupon his last request for his tinderbox allows him to escape while he instructs the dogs to kill the King. Andersen's soldier then marries the now willing princess and becomes King himself. Elliot's version follows the same narrative trajectory, except that the soldier does not kill the King at the conclusion of the story; the King begs mercy, and the soldier is satisfied with a marriage to the princess (TAD 14182).

The fact that Andersen's literary fairy tale, first published in serial form in the 1830s, appears in an oral tradition is no surprise; in his metanarration, Elliot explains that he first heard the story during his days at school at the beginning of the twentieth century (ibid.). The characteristics of Elliot's story stand in stark contrast to the Traveller narratives examined above. Its appearance in a non-Traveller oral tradition illustrates my overarching point about the stories that we chose to tell. Writing about Scottish Travellers and folklore, Traveller Willie Reid captures this point succinctly; 'we need to consider how far', says Reid, 'selectively taking and rejecting cultural elements from others, the representation of European folklore was the legitimate assertion of their [Travellers'] own culture' (1997: 37). From the outset, the soldier's material wealth is blood-soaked, and his greed is plain and irrational. The fact that the soldier murders a presumably defenceless old woman over something as trivial as a tinderbox is striking. The motivation of the protagonist in Elliot's story goes beyond mere avarice when he, again, victimises a female character in his kidnapping of the princess. Furthermore, Elliot's soldier is not satisfied with wealth and a desirable female companion, he must also usurp the social order and become monarch. Zipes propounds that *The Tinderbox* has close ties to the 'peasant oral tradition and can be regarded ideologically and aesthetically as Andersen's challenge to the ruling notions of how such tales should be transformed' (2006: 227). That is, Andersen's literary version champions the downtrodden in society and functions to inspire compassion in its readers for the lowly soldier. The overall impetus of the narrative is again a desire for power; consider Williamson's Hedgehurst – in a version of ATU 441 – who undermined such desires and returned to his life in the forest. We see the same contradistinction when it comes to Elliot's story, where the ideological imperatives of the protagonist exist in fundamental opposition to the examples provided from the Travellers' traditions. The way that wealth is presented and *used* is what is being scrutinised in these story spaces, Traveller or otherwise.

Under close analysis, the above examples have revealed underlying ideological imperatives around material wealth and its implications. Material gain is not to be shunned wholesale, rather it should be predicated on equitable exchange and so retain its function as a social process. However, this somewhat facile interpretation of 'money' gathers significance when orientated within the context of the tradition to which it belongs. Considering what he terms the 'urbanisation of consciousness', Harvey points out that the city is both the high point of human achievement and 'the lightning rod of the profoundest discontents, and the arena of often savage social and political conflict' (1985: 250). The urban is defined here as a social landscape that is representative of capitalism's transformation of space relations (ibid.: xviii). The concept of an 'urban consciousness' is useful in the present context because it represents a set of ideas that want to dominate landscapes, usually in the form of built environments, as sources of social power. As Harvey points out, urban experience can provide untold opportunities, but it can also lead to alienation and violence. Scotland's Travellers have suffered persecution from the authorities over the preceding centuries from a multitude of perspectives, and, until recently, government policy around land use, education and welfare failed to accommodate itinerant lifestyles. Moreover, legislation such as the Trespass (Scotland) Act of 1865, the Caravan Sites Act (1968) and the Criminal Justice and Public Order Act (1994) effectively made it a criminal offence to be nomadic (Kenrick and Clark 1999: 57).

Traveller storytellers negotiate real world anxieties in imaginary story spaces and ideological negotiation is a central function of the narratives. In the case of Whyte's story about a money-producing tree, the rural and the urban are juxtaposed to create a striking profile of a social system that contradicts itself. 'Money', as proxy for 'the city/metropolis', is thereby interrogated in a super-empirical story space. The social process that should stand for equitable exchange of goods is portrayed as a system that produces inequality and suffering. This message is particularly relevant when viewed as the product of communities who have been persecuted for many centuries in Scotland. Moreover, a challenge is being made to the persecutors who demonstrably attempted the cultural assimilation of practitioners of divergent ideologies. Whyte's simple story therefore presents urban consciousness with a question, one that highlights the tension inherent to the dominant ideologies of capitalism. 'Money', viewed from this perspective, has the potential to undo social relationships, a scenario that is unnervingly close to home as the twenty-first century continues. The United Kingdom Parliament's *Economic Affairs Committee's* recent inquiry into the risks of 'quantitative easing' – a monetary policy tool where the Bank of England creates new money to purchase Government or corporate bonds – reported that 'while we recognise that quantitative easing has prevented economic crises from spiralling downwards, its effect on inflation and output is uncertain' (2021: 53). The *Committee's* report goes on to suggest that quantitative easing 'may also have increased wealth inequality by raising the price of certain assets, benefitting those who own them (ibid.). The *Committee* concludes that 'The Bank of England and HM Treasury must do more to acknowledge this uncertainty and to understand these effects' (ibid.).

The narratives presented here do not deliberately embody systematic critiques of monetary policy, rather they recognise that certain money systems have inherent flaws. The current system of *fiat* money – from the Latin 'let it be done' – is what John Maynard Keynes refers to as a form of representative money that is created and issued by the state, having no intrinsic value, like gold or silver (1930: 7). Critique of such systems has one modern economic commentator asking why 'public opinion accepts adherence to an economically and socially destructive fiat money regime', concluding that 'under a fiat money regime, people will be corrupted on the grandest scale' (Polleit 2011: 397). Elsewhere, Detley Schlichter envisions a 'paper money collapse' where addressing the 'terminal flaws inherent in the present elastic [*fiat*] money system [. . .] would require some profound ideological changes' (2014: 299–300). Both Polleit and Schlichter follow Ludwig von Mises' advocacy of a return to 'sound' money principles, where the units of exchange have intrinsic value. As Von Mises put it as early as the 1930s, 'the idea of sound money [. . .] was devised as an instrument for the protection of civil liberties against despotic inroads on the part of governments'; this means, for Von Mises, that 'ideologically it belongs in the same class with political constitutions and bills of rights' (1981: 454). The point here is that Traveller storytellers engage with issues that transcend their status as members of marginalised communities, tackling economic practices that affect our society more generally. Note the fact that in Whyte's story, the magical source of material wealth is *specifically* state sanctioned *fiat* currency, as opposed to a commodity with intrinsic value.

The comment here is that of a deep ideological tension between what someone tells you has value and what you yourself value. The supernatural source of wealth facilitates the agency of the protagonist in challenging power relations within a social system that is demonstrably flawed. Perhaps at an even deeper level, such stories contribute to the sense that a 'proliferation of magical stories [. . .] is correlated to a growing awareness of human separateness from the wild and the natural world' (Bernheimer 2010: xix), a sense that we have experienced repeatedly as this study continues to elucidate meaning within the Travellers' storytelling traditions. Super-empirical story spaces do not necessarily have to involve the familiar agents of 'supernatural' tales – fairies, dragons, ogres – to function as carriers of symbolic meaning. If the Burkers represent the quintessential existential threat to the Travellers' lifestyles, then the super-empiricism of the present chapter casts the net further. The stories and story spaces examined above encapsulate wider concerns about society itself. Super-empirical story spaces are ideal locations for Traveller storytellers to interrogate dominant ideologies and therein reconceptualise received modes of thought. The present chapter has shown how divergent ideological imperatives are contested within super-empirical story spaces to reveal worldviews that are underpinned by an optimistic social awareness and utopian outlook.

Note

1. Perhaps more realistically, such a scenario would undermine the power of whatever financial status quo existed at the time. Harvey provides the example of Peter Thelluson. On his death in 1797, Thelluson stipulated that a £600,000 trust fund – yielding 7.5% compound interest – could not be accessed until 100 years after his death. Given the compound interest, this would result in a fund of £19 million in 1897, approximately £2 billion in today's terms. This was unacceptable to the British State because it would mean immense financial power for Thelluson's heirs. Legislation was passed in 1800 limiting trusts to twenty-one years (2014: 225–226).

8

Magical Places, Magical Money

THIS CHAPTER EXPANDS ON the concept that the Travellers' storytelling traditions function as negotiations of their marginalisation. First, it takes a close look at stories about place, then by returning to the story of Geordie McPhee introduced in Chapter 3. It provides further detailed examples of how super-empirical story spaces function as quintessential ideological locations. Throughout this chapter, we retain the term 'supernatural' in keeping with the literature with which we engage and to describe certain characters. The term super-empirical is reserved for the definition of the story spaces as a genre. Citing Dégh, Braid notes that legends function to challenge listeners' understanding of the world and invite them to modify their beliefs and worldviews (2002: 74). This chapter expands upon such conceptualisations of legends – this expansion is necessary because although the examples provided conform to ideas around 'legends', they also display characteristics that set them apart. For instance, the stories have alignments with ATU magic tales, take place in liminal story spaces, or have direct relationships with place-names. From this perspective, the narratives under examination in this chapter inhabit a particular 'story space' that does not necessarily require a label for the stories to be investigable. It is not that these stories *defy* classification, only that the present study's questions can be sufficiently addressed without engaging in it. At the same time, as we have seen in previous chapters, this study continues to draw comparisons between the Travellers' stories and other cultural expressions to better understand the former.

FOLK ONOMASTICS

An underutilised resource when it comes to understanding the cultural characteristics of communities is the way they conceptualise the places they live in. Toponymy, the study of place names, can be expanded upon to uncover the social significance of place-name etymology. This section considers the theme of land/wealth relations and examines examples of place-naming within super-empirical story spaces. These examples confront the power relations associated with naming our landscapes and speak to the cultural differentiation highlighted throughout this study. The principles of socio-onomastics are invoked to argue that alternative etymologies for place-names within Traveller traditions function to meaningfully orientate the communities within landscapes. Specifically, we follow Terhi Ainiala's framework of 'folk onomastics' which considers people's beliefs and perceptions about the names of places (2016: 106). The way that the user of the name perceives its meaning can be thought of in terms of narrative; a story about the place-name can be invested with attributes that allow for interpretation. Consequentially, alternative conceptualisations of origins of place-names affirm distinctive cultural identity because in so naming, the narrator attaches meaning to a specific way of referring to the place. By reconceptualising the meaning of place-names, Traveller tradition-bearers situate themselves within their landscape in a way that stands in opposition to received etymologies.

When these conceptualisations occur within super-empirical story spaces, the etymological narratives engage with wider storytelling traditions. Donald Meek has already pointed out the close connection between folklore and place-naming. Using Gaelic ballads, Meek concludes that place-names can be symbolic, 'representing a point or event in time or place, within the mental and narratological "map" of the composer' (1998: 167). From this perspective, the intersection between folklore and onomastics is fertile ground, where further insights into Traveller worldview can be gleaned. Take, for example, the town of Rosehearty which on the Moray Firth coast, four miles to the west of Fraserburgh in Aberdeenshire. Several onomastic sources agree that the 'Rose' in the name is the Anglicised Gaelic *ros*, signifying a cape, headland, point or promontory (Blackie 1887: 168; Johnston 1892: 211; Milne 1912: 278; James and Taylor 2017: 197; Ainmean-Àite, 'Rosehearty Research Notes'). This corresponds to the physical appearance of Rosehearty, it being a slightly elevated settlement where the land juts out into the Moray Firth. However, these sources disagree on the significance of the 'Hearty' element: Blackie and Milne see a dwelling or sheiling (1887: 168; 1912: 278), whereas Milne translates *ros cheartach* as a guiding or directing promontory (1892: 211). Linguistic etymologies are useful in that they provide topographic information that has the potential to reveal historical land, or language, use. Wilhelm Nicolaisen gives the example of

Hawick in the Scottish Borders; the old English *haga wīc* [hedge farm] no longer has 'word meaning' because it is no longer an accurate description of the town (2001: 5). Armed with this linguistic knowledge, however, the onomastician considers what the name Hawick can tell them about historical farming practices, or early Anglian settlement in Scotland (ibid.: 6).

However, folk etymologies can go beyond pure description and language use to provide social insights and this approach can be taken even further in terms of folk onomastics. In the case of Rosehearty, James and Taylor align 'hearty', and the suffix *–averty*, with the Irish personal name *Ábhartach* (2017: 132), but the authors provide no clarification of its significance. *Ábhartach* is a figure associated with the Fenian Cycle – a medieval Irish literary work that revolves around the legendary character Finn mac Cumaill and his 'warrior-band' (Murray 2017: 19) – but who also appears elsewhere in Irish folklore and mythology. William Mackenzie agrees, noting that Rosehearty may represent a personal name, that of *Ábartach*, which in Irish is 'a name for a dwarf'. Mackenzie goes on to speculate that the dwarf appellation might have topographical significance, given the relative scale of Rosehearty as a promontory (1931: 151, 161). From the folk perspective, Patrick Joyce's fieldwork in the early twentieth century in Londonderry revealed that a certain *Ábhartach* – modern Irish for *Ábartach* – existed in local folklore as a powerful dwarf-magician, who had tyrannised the community with great cruelties (1910: 331).

In the Fenian Cycle *Ábhartach* first appears as *Giolla Deacair* [Hard Gilly] and his name is also applied to *Céadach* (MacKillop 1990: 1). *Céadach* is what Bruford refers to as an anomalous character, and the episode appears to be a retelling of an international folktale wherein the end of the story sees *Céadach* return from the dead (1969: 123, 126). Joyce alludes to a connection with the Fenian Cycle in his folkloric account when he records that *Ábhartach* 'was at last vanquished and slain by a neighbouring chieftain; some say by Finn Mac Cumhail' (1910: 331). Beforehand, however, using his powers, *Ábhartach* resurrected himself on two occasions, inflicting further cruelties on the community, before being finally contained in his grave with the help of a druid (ibid.: 331–332). At the time of publication in 1910, Joyce remarks that *Ábhartach's* sepulchre exists as a monument and that the legend is well known among the local population (ibid.: 332). Outside of the Fenian Cycle, the story of *Ábhartach* is recognisably a revenant legend, international examples of which abound; Thompson cites a multitude of examples involving various scenarios and circumstances, ubiquitous throughout the world (1946: 254–258). In folk onomastics, the area in modern County Derry named *Sleacht Ábhartaigh* [Eng. Slaghtaverty] translates to 'Ábhartach's Sepulchre'. The folk association with the revenant *Ábhartach* is thereby inscribed on the landscape, both symbolically in the place-name and tangibly through the cist grave that remains in the area. The place-name suffix 'Hearty' – or *–averty* in the case of Dunaverty on the southern tip of Scotland's Kintyre peninsula – is therefore the personal name of the revenant *Ábhartach*. This yields 'Ábhartach's Fort' for Dunaverty, and 'Ábhartach's Point' for Rosehearty.

Stanley Robertson tells a story that presents an alternative yet related explanation as to how Rosehearty got its name (TAD 64475). 'There wis this young Traveller man', begins Robertson, 'and he wis awfy tired and he was seeking lodgings' (ibid.). The Traveller is allowed to sleep in the barn of a friendly farmer and beds down for the night. During the night, the lad is woken by the presence of a young man asking for his help. '"Many, many years ago, I wis murdered here"', the young man explains, "and my body is buried under this barn and I can't get no rest"' (ibid.). The young man asks the Traveller to recover his bones and give him a proper Christian burial so that he can rest in peace. The Traveller takes this vision for a dream and goes back to sleep but tells the farmer of his experience in the morning. The farmer thinks nothing of it, but after the apparition appears to the Traveller a second time, the farmer, a religious man, tells him that they will seek the local minister on the apparition's third appearance.

When the apparition dutifully appears a third time, the trio 'dug up underneath the barn and they found the bones a the laddie' (ibid.) and gave the boy a proper burial. That night, when the Traveller went to sleep, the murdered boy's apparition reappears and says '"thank you, I can now get rest"' (ibid.). Robertson concludes his narrative with his folk etymology, 'in the morning, the young man [Traveller] "rose hearty", and that's how the name Rosehearty came' (ibid.). Note the parallel with the story of *Ábhartach*: Robertson's narrative also includes a revenant that requires three burials, and a religious figure is required to finally put them to rest. However, Robertson's narrative ultimately inverts the premise of the story. Instead of a cruel tyrant being removed from power, we find a young man murdered and hastily buried; in place of the disturbing folktale giving Slaghtaverty its name, we have an act of compassion and an emotional reward for the protagonist; and instead of a druid confining *Ábhartach* to his grave, Robertson's narrative employs a Christian minister to emancipate the murdered boy's soul. Moreover, because the Traveller protagonist arises 'heartily', Robertson's narrative evokes a sense of ebullience that is absent from the naming of Slaghtaverty. His story affirms the Travellers' awareness of their heritage and sense of belonging to the landscape, going so far as to ascribe the naming of places to the experience of a single Traveller. Furthermore, Robertson's metanarrative extends this cultural awareness to the settled population; 'that man Bob Strachan that telt me that story isnae a Traveller', Robertson says, 'but he wis broucht up wi Travellers [. . .] he kens aa the Travellers' weys [habits, characteristics]' (ibid.).

In this way, Robertson invites understanding from the settled community at the same time as affirming the long and distinguished heritage of the Travellers. The fact that his folk etymology challenges received topographical etymologies represents the underlying ideological imperatives of these divergent positions. Topographical place-names are motivated by the desire to exert control over the landscape; they are predicated on 'word meaning' that is underpinned by possession and stratification – *haga wīc* [hedge farm] and 'Ábhartach's Fort' being telling examples. On the other hand, Robertson's etymology transcends word meaning because it draws its meaning from the intangible cultural heritage of the Travellers. When delivered as a story, Robertson's folk etymology for Rosehearty embodies an ideology that is not based on power or control, but one that is based on compassion, understanding and positive connections with our landscapes. Or as Reith puts it, concealed etymologies such as the above mean that 'Stanley Robertson has found an illustrative way to tell the story of his people's unique knowledge and cultural contribution' (2008a: 82).

In an interview with the author, Nacken Shamus McPhee provides a further example of folk onomastics at work in his community. Using the same principles deployed above, analysis of Shamus' folk etymology provides a contemporary example of the way modern Travellers conceptualise their landscape. Shamus' explanation not only corresponds with modern toponomy but provides an alternative, culturally specific meaning for Balquhidder. The village of Balquhidder is situated in Stirlingshire, on the shores of Loch Voil, approximately 32 miles to the north-west of Stirling. The name Balquhidder is Gaelic in origin – *Both Chuidir* or *Both Phuidir* – although the full meaning is unclear. In Gaelic, *Both* translates to 'hut' or 'sheiling', but the *Chuidir / Phuidir* referent is obscure (Taylor 2003: 16). For example, writing for TSAS, Reverend Duncan Stewart has Balquhidder in 'the Celtic language' as a 'village in the centre of five Glens' (1793: 88), whereas the later account by Reverend McGregor has the Gaelic root '*baile-chul-tir*' signifying 'the town or territory at the back of the country' (TSAS 1845: 344). Later, Alexander MacGregor also suggests 'the land lying behind the country', 'land of the five glens' or 'town or land of joint occupancy', noting that 'none of these ways of accounting for the name Balquhidder is satisfactory' (1886: 11). It has also been suggested that the *Phuidir* element refers to a Neolithic standing stone called *Puidrac* that lies a few hundred metres to the east of Balquhidder (ibid.; Watson 2002: 36, 101). For Angus Watson, the 'stone's supposed great antiquity and its siting at an ancient pagan and, later, Christian centre indicate that it had considerable significance in the early ritual life of the district' (2002: 101). Residents of the area around Balquhidder have taken the appellation, often as a surname, *Puidireach* from as early as 1594 and the name endures in Gaelic into the twenty first century (ibid.). Watson contends that the *Puidrac* stone was somehow linked to the identity of the area and its people (2002: 101). The alternative onomastics examined below reveal a tangential perspective on the origin of the name Balquhidder, and one that is characteristically Traveller in aspect. Notably, this example from Shamus is couched in the same super-empirical story space used by Stanley Robertson in his folk onomastics for Rosehearty.

In Shamus' folk onomastics for Balquhidder, he begins with a story about when 'some of my mother's people, the old Johnstones, were comin back from huvin worked the ferms [farms]' (Interview 2021). The party stop at what Shamus describes as a sheiling, at Balquhidder, where they approach a nearby house to ask for victuals. 'They went an chapped the door and this old woman came to the door', Shamus continues, '"excuse me missus, would you mind givin us lodgings for the night?"' (ibid.). The Traveller party are refused entry to the house proper, instead being offered the use of the sheiling to spend the night. When the party are settled in the sheiling, the old woman arranges tea and sandwiches, after which the Travellers bed down for the night. 'It started rainin, didn't it, during the night', Shamus goes on, 'and they felt aw the rain drops comin in in the early mornin' (ibid.). When the party are woken by the dripping rain, they realise that the sheiling was 'just an old ruin and the rafters hud aw been razed, it was burnt to the ground' (ibid.). On venturing out, the Travellers find that the friendly house where they had been given sustenance the night before is similarly ruined. Perturbed, the Travellers ask at a nearby house, '"what's the crack wi that kain [Cant: 'house'] doon there, you know, that hoose?"' (ibid.). The inhabitants are surprised when they find out that the Travellers had received hospitality from the razed house; according to the inhabitants, the house '"burnt to the ground thirty years ago"', and the occupants were '"both burnt alive"' (ibid.).

Shamus concludes his story by adding that 'in a way it's a ghost story, but it's also linked to the name o the place and the fact that they went there for bread and sustenance' (ibid.). Shamus' folk onomastics for Balquhidder are, like Stanley Robertson's, couched in narrative. The super-empirical story spaces enable narrators to negotiate real–world concerns using narrative environments defined by symbolism. This practice is of course not unique to Scotland's Travellers, but the details within the stories yield insights into their distinctive ideological perspective. Shamus' explanation for Balquhidder shares the *Both* element with mainstream onomastics; the two explanations align the initial element *both* with a rudimentary individual dwelling, not a collection of the same, as in a town or village. Watson points out that earlier fifteenth-century forms of the name 'suggest that the 'P-Celtic *Puidir* was re-interpreted as if it were a Q-Celtic *Cuidir*', concluding that the 'first syllable *both* became assimilated to the more common *baile* [Gaelic: 'town/village']' (2002: 37). This etymological reanalysis of the place-name elements may account for the 'town/village' explanations given in TSAS (1793: 88; 1845: 344) and similarly by MacGregor (1886: 10), cited above.

In his metanarrative, Shamus explains that 'Balquhidder is a word we use in Cant for bread' (Interview 2021). Shamus clarifies this etymology, explaining that 'in Cant, "perram" or "perm" is bread, as are "brunston" and "balwhidder/balwhudder", since these lexemes form part of an oral and, concomitantly, evolutionary process' (Correspondence 2021a). At first glance, this etymology does not appear to correspond with the *–quhidder* element in Balquhidder. However, as Shamus points out, the reference forms part of a specific linguistic continuum where the meaning of the words is not dictated by their formal attributes. Nicolaisen realised the same, noting that 'semantic transparency is not required, indeed not expected, once a linguistic item has crossed the transforming threshold from lexicon to onomasticon' (1992: 2). Thus, for Shamus, Balquhidder as a place–name means 'shieling of the bread' and represents an *idea* rather than a description of the landscape. The cultural specificity is clear through Shamus' use of Cant and the narrative space where the symbolic etymology of Balquhidder crystallises. Shamus immediately links the place–name to his forebears, the Johnstones, signalling the cultural heritage revered by Traveller communities. When the Johnstones move through the landscape as part of their itinerant working lives, Shamus' story encompasses not only their chosen lifestyle but their relationship with the settled community. The fact that the Travellers are fed by revenants ironically positions their providers in a super-empirical space that negotiates their experience in the 'real world'. When the Travellers of the story are initially refused entry to the house proper, the revenant offers them the sheiling, 'where aa the cattle hud been, in among aa the coo shite' (Interview 2021). The Travellers are at once rejected and sustained by the settled homesteaders, speaking to an ambivalent relationship with society at large. The association between Balquhidder and its Cant etymology transforms its compound meaning into a culturally significant expression.

In telling this story, Shamus transmits a codified intergenerational meaning that encapsulates the lived experiences of Travellers. Again, deceptively simple narratives, when viewed in context, represent sophisticated cultural expressions that are infused with meaning. Shamus goes on to say that he thinks 'a lot o the place names huv become corrupted', pointing out that 'we huv here names that were imposed by people in wider society like *Baile nan Ceàrd* [Balnaguard] which is "Township of the Tinkers"' (ibid.). The example of Balnaguard is an explicit illustration of how place-names can be construed in different ways. *Ceàrdair* in Gaelic literally translates to craftsperson, or artisan (LearnGaelic), but the contextual meaning of the word is synonymous with Scottish Travellers, or the historic 'Tinkers'. *Baile nan Ceàrd*, then, could also mean 'Township of the Craftspeople'. However, the socio-cultural context in which Balnaguard exists means that its translation from the Gaelic signifies a place in the landscape that is explicitly associated with Travellers. This distinction captures Nicolaisen's observation around the uses of place-name analyses, where onomastics are 'able to throw considerable light on the concepts and frames of mind of their namers' (1992: 13). Shamus' folk onomastics bear this observation out; his explanation for Balquhidder – like Stanley Robertson's alternative naming of Rosehearty – challenges accepted toponymies from the mainstream and provides an insight into alternative conceptualisations of the landscape.

In its Anglicised form, Balnaguard's etymology might signify an historic military site on account of the Anglicisation of *Ceàrd* to – *guard*. Still, William Watson's authoritative place-name study, *The History of the Celtic Place-names of Scotland*, lists Balnaguard as the 'stead of the artificers' (1926: 242). However, as early as 1869 it was realised that the – *guard* element bears no relationship to the meaning of the place-name. In the 'county of Perth, there appears a hamlet, called in English "Balnaguard"', writes James Robertson, 'but the spelling in ancient writings is Balna*kaird*, which is nearly the pronunciation for the proper Gaelic for the name "Baile-nan-ceard", or "the tinker or smith's town"' (1869: 189). More modern etymologies agree, with Taylor giving Balnaguard as 'The Tinkers' Farm' (2003: 16). The corruption that Shamus refers to is clear because the Anglicisation of Balna*guard* effectively eliminates the – *ceàrd* element and transforms the cultural significance of the name. Elsewhere in Scotland, Anglicisation of Gaelic place-names associated with historic Travellers has not taken place. A few miles north of Balnaguard, for example, sits Creag nan Ceàrd, meaning 'Tinker's Rock or Hill'; at the mouth of the river Lussa in Argyll and Bute exists Bruach nan Ceàrd, 'Tinker's Brae'; and in Glen Urquhart, to the south-west of Inverness, lies Cnoc nan Ceàrd, 'Tinker's Knoll' – why not Cnocnaguard?

The fact that these place-names have *not* changed highlights the point here – in reclaiming the names that *have* changed, the cultural significance of those places within the landscape is recognised. A more tangible example of this reclamation is the case of the *Tinkers' Heart*, a scheduled monument overlooking the north-eastern tip of Loch Fyne, Argyll and Bute. The *Tinkers' Heart* is a pattern of quartz stones that marks a specific location in the landscape; it is a 'a space sacred to Scotland's Travelling people [. . .] where marriages were made, where children were named and where those Travelling men who lost their lives in wars were remembered' (*Heart of the Travellers* 'Home' 2020). After a petition to The Scottish Parliament in 2014, Historic Scotland agreed that the site should be recognised as such, noting that:

> the place clearly holds a high spiritual meaning for many Travellers and in this regard the significance the Heart holds for this community is in the intangible significance of the ceremonies and meetings conducted there. The stones serve, however, as a tangible symbol of the deep relationship of Travellers and their heritage with this location.
>
> (Historic Scotland 'Scheduling Recommendation' 2015: online)

This recognition of the cultural significance of the *Tinkers' Heart* site is a watershed in 'official' representations of the Travellers' relationship with the landscape. The fact that the site is now a State-mandated, and therefore protected, monument speaks to the importance of terminology when it comes to place-naming. The preceding examples of folk onomastics go further, amounting to critical toponymies that have their motivations in a distinctively Traveller worldview. This is because the retention of the original meanings exist outside of dominant ideological frameworks and have culturally specific meanings that do not necessarily correspond with mainstream etymologies. Doreen Massey makes an important point from this perspective: 'places do not have single, unique "identities"; they are full of internal conflicts' (1994: 155). Balquhidder has multiple identities and close examination of its naming reveals an intersection of social relations. On one hand, its name is literally possessed by those inhabitants who choose to take the appellation *Puidireach*; on the other, the naming of Balquhidder encompasses an experience that is infused with culturally specific meaning. The case of Balnaguard and the *Tinkers' Heart* demonstrates the wider implications of folk onomastics when it comes to recognising the cultural significance of the landscapes we share.

Laura Kostanski and Guy Puzey suggest that 'intricate analyses of the substantive power of naming practices are possible if researchers are bold enough to look deeper' (2016: xv–xvi). Consider the significance of Rosehearty, Balquhidder and Balnaguard: Alternative conceptualisations of these Scottish place-names speak to a unique experience of the landscape. Not only that, but the etymologies were distinctively Nackian, where the distinct Nackian idiom is driven by the Traveller characters who inhabit the world of the narratives. Kostanski and Puzey go on to point out that 'as names can represent identities, the silencing of a name or promotion of a preferred name can speak volumes for cultural politics' (ibid.: xx). This was demonstrably the case with the example of Balnaguard, where the Anglicisation of the placename divested it of its original meaning of 'Township of the Tinkers'. By reorientating the etymologies of named locations in the landscape, the storytellers challenge dominant conceptualisations of landscapes, reclaiming the cultural significance of the places and negotiating their own cultural identities in the process. The internal conflicts of our place-naming practices are clear when considered under the conditions presented here. What is at stake is the history and culture of marginalised communities being overwritten by arbitrary changes to meaningful places within our shared landscape. Seemingly inconsequential changes have the potential to undermine both the historical and contemporary contributions that such communities make to Scottish society. Davie Donaldson has pointed out how the Travellers' engagement with local communities has gone on for centuries, an engagement that is intimately connected to the landscape (Interview 2019). 'We know all of the local folklore, we know all of the local history', Davie reports, 'we have ingrained family histories within these pieces of land and within these communities' (ibid.). At the same time, Davie points out that 'often the local communities won't perceive us as being a local, with any connection to that piece of ground' (ibid.). 'How we see ourselves', Davie concludes, 'as a local of Scotland I think is quite an interesting and unique sort of thing for Travellers' (ibid.).

GEORDIE IN LIMINALITY

Another way that the social world of Traveller storytellers interacts with the super-empirical is when it comes to money. During the introductory chapter of the present work, a story from Andrew Stewart introduced us to a Traveller named Geordie MacPhee. MacPhee became wealthy after a ghostly helper told him of buried treasure, but MacPhee quickly squandered the money and was eventually ruined (TAD 13847). Returning to the story about Geordie, this section demonstrates how super-empirical stories can inhabit liminal environments that include elements that are both familiar and extraordinary. The following section takes a detailed look at an example of this in practice and thinks about what these story spaces can tell us about the narrators and communities who share them. The term liminality – from the Latin *limen* meaning 'threshold' – is deployed across a variety of disciplines in many different contexts. Most uses of the term agree that it refers to some sort of passage from one state of being to another or overcoming some threshold. The anthropologist Arnold van Gennep first used the term to refer to the 'rites of passage' that accompany changes of social state or position (cited in Turner et al 1969: 94). More recently, criticism of transnational literature uses the term to refer to the experiences of refugees and asylum seekers during border crossings (Tröger 2021: 45–67).

For our purposes, liminality is understood as both a period of transition and a particular space where this transition takes place. Liminal transitions do not necessarily have to include 'rites of passage' – such as the movement from childhood into adulthood – but can be transitions in understanding and experience. We shall see that super-empirical story spaces function within narratives as bridges between differing experiences of real social conditions. With money/material wealth as the central theme – and liminality as an interpretative frame – the remainder of this chapter scrutinises the Travellers' social realities through the lens of the super-empirical. The values and beliefs that underpin this study are negotiated within a storytelling genre that is not fettered by empirical reality. Within Traveller storytelling traditions, liminality can be used to facilitate entrance into carnivalesque spaces that challenge hierarchical discourses around the value of sedentarism and reveal trenchant mediations on the function of money. Given its central importance to capitalist society, money and/or material wealth as a theme has been latent during our discussions. However, as we shall see, super-empirical story spaces facilitate precise negotiations between binary conditions such as 'have' and 'have not' and so become more than just cautionary tales about the vicissitudes of wealth.

Our example comes from Andrew Stewart where his story begins with the protagonist, Geordie MacPhee, and his family on the road during a winter storm. The family's lack of material wealth is clear from the outset; with no permanent winter residence, the MacPhees take shelter in an abandoned blacksmith's forge. Stewart describes the scene: 'There were no windaes in the smiddy [smithy], just bits a bags' (TAD 13847) to keep the weather out, and Geordie complains, '"I've nae straw"' (ibid.) to make a bed. To warm some alms and heat the smithy, Geordie resorts to 'breakin bits o sticks off the rafters' (ibid.). As we have seen in preceding chapters, the framing of the narrative plays a key role during interpretations of the story. In this case, the frame functions to situate the protagonist in a state of dearth. However, as we will see, this frame functions on a separate level as the narrative concludes. According to Turner, the separation phase in liminality 'comprises symbolic behaviour signifying the detachment of the individual or group either from an earlier fixed point in the social structure, [or] from a set of cultural conditions' (1969: 94). Geordie's separation phase begins when an unusual character approaches the smithy and bids Geordie to follow him. The uncanniness of the character is engendered by his attire, given the freezing conditions outside; Stewart describes the uncanny visitor appearing in 'his stocking soles, no jacket on or nothing, and he's got galluses [braces], over his shoulders, hanging down at his side' (TAD 13847).

At first, Geordie refuses to follow, but when the stranger returns to the smithy the following night, Geordie acquiesces. The stranger promises Geordie a reward if he should follow him and the pair 'come doon to the seaside and rocks' (ibid.). Within a cave on the shoreline – a symbolically liminal space, the shore being between the land and the sea – is where Geordie receives his reward in the form of 'a heap of gold sovereigns [. . .] a fortune in gold there fir ye' (ibid.). It becomes clear that the stranger is a supernatural agent when Geordie refers to him as a 'spirit or whatever it was' and takes care only to visit the cave at night so as not to 'spoil the whole enchantment' (ibid.). The stranger promptly disappears as soon as Geordie discovers the hidden gold. Geordie fills his pockets with the gold and his separation from his fixed point in the social structure happens overnight. The next day, Geordie 'wisnae very well dressed, the toes were stickin oot his boots [and] his backside wis oot his troosers' (ibid.). We also discover that Geordie cannot read or write and is therefore unable to record the value of his new wealth. The intangibility of the wealth is an important point to note here, the significance of which becomes clear at the conclusion of Geordie's journey through liminality. Unperturbed, Geordie sees an estate for sale and engages the solicitor who is managing the sale. At first the solicitor is dismissive, but after Geordie produces his gold, the solicitor addresses Geordie as 'my lord' (ibid.) and immediately arranges a new suit of clothes for Geordie. By this point, Geordie's separation is complete; he is moneyed, landed and well-dressed, a far cry from the penury of the previous day in the smithy.

According to Turner's framework, the next stage in the transition through liminality is the 'margin', or *limen* proper. Geordie's margin phase consists of his experience with his wealth, an experience that stands in direct opposition to his previous state. The removal from a set of 'cultural conditions' alluded to above is a useful description of this section of Stewart's narrative. Geordie's newly purchased estate includes the use of several vehicles and Geordie now has members of staff. When Geordie asks the solicitor how he might retrieve his family from the smithy, the solicitor replies, '"well," he says, "the only thing we can do is go up and get the chauffeur to take you out in the Rolls [Royce]"' (ibid.). The cultural conditions in which we found Geordie and his family have been removed. The family's itinerancy, Geordie 'begging pennies' (ibid.) as a travelling piper, and the material dearth of their smithy dwelling, have all been replaced by the norms of the opposite end of the social hierarchy. Geordie's transition from one social state to another is, for him, another state of being.

The symbols of success that Geordie has acquired – facilitated by the 'spirit' – engender a carnivalesque episode within the narrative. For Mikhail Bakhtin, carnival festivities within communities in the past 'built a second world and a second life outside officialdom' (1984: 6). Within the carnival world, Bakhtin observes that hierarchical relationships are put to one side and that the carnival spirit encouraged 'purely human relations' (ibid.: 10). Discussing Bakhtin's conceptualisation of carnival, Simon Dentith perceives 'an attitude in which the high, the elevated, the official, even the sacred, is degraded and debased, but as a condition of popular renewal and regeneration' (1995: 66). As we will see, it is no accident that the pivotal episode in Stewart's narrative takes place during market day and in a carnivalesque environment. But first, Geordie heads to the local public house where he 'wis in haein a drink and enjoying a drink wi the men, he's got half o the pub [. . .] he's got the pub man [publican] drunk an everything, with his gold sovereigns' (TAD 13847). Even the chauffeur is ordered a drink; when his chauffeured car arrives, Geordie 'shoves a bottle ay beer in his hand, "take a slug [drink] ootay that", Geordie says' (ibid.).

By the time Geordie and his family – who are also now clad in fine clothes – arrive at their new estate, Geordie is singing drunk and decides to double all his staff's wages. The carnival atmosphere of Geordie's liminal experience continues the next day when he and his family head into town to attend the market. 'He went and got himsel drunk at the market day', explains Stewart, 'and he has all the men drunk, an they're dealin in horses' (ibid.). The normal run of horse dealing is subverted at the market because, before Geordie was finished, 'they were handing the horses to each other for nothing, they were a' drunk. They had plenty a money, ye see, Geordie wis gien them plenty a money and gien thum a good treat' (ibid.). The festivities continue until the local police become involved and attempt to arrest some revellers. However, Geordie, with his new status, intervenes; '"where are you takin these men, these Tinker men?"' (ibid.), demands Geordie, at which point the police sergeant explains that the men are being arrested for disturbing the peace. '"Ye'll dae nothing of the kind", says Geordie, "jist leave them away"' (ibid.). '"Alright m'lord"', responds the sergeant, 'so the police jist left them away' (ibid.). Stewart explains that Geordie was in fact 'Laird o this village tae, he bought the village too, it was an estate this village, ye see' (ibid.). The story world where Geordie's experiences in liminality take place is entire. Geordie's new social status makes him lord of all he surveys and allows him to behave as he sees fit. As the market day ends, the Travellers from the market are given camping equipment and invited by Geordie to camp on his estate. But Geordie's carnival generosity soon takes its toll, and his solicitor tells him, '"You've no more money left and you've nothing in the bank, m'lord"' (ibid.). The narrator, Stewart, tells us that 'with him [Geordie] goin back and forward to the cave, the gold's beginning a sink [. . .] Geordie's gettin some money in but he's spending more [. . .] he's ruinin hisself' (ibid.).

As the carnival atmosphere subsides and Geordie's fortune dwindles, the narrative shifts into Turner's third phase of liminality, aggregation. Geordie's aggregation is intimated by an arrival that signals a return to 'reality'. One day, 'a big car comes up to the door, and here wis the man fae London and this other lady' (ibid.). The arrival of the couple from London marks the conclusion of Geordie's experience in liminality when they refuse the hospitality of his house. '"Are ye fir a cup o tea, wuman?"', enquires Geordie's wife, 'but the lady shrugs her shoodirs [shoulders] and she's lookin at her, an she says, "my word, this terrible woman" (ibid.). Geordie has a similar experience when he offers the London man a drink of low-quality whisky; '"oh no", he says, "this is disgraceful, I'm going away"' (ibid.). During Geordie's liminal experience, he has managed not only to squander his wealth, but also to physically ruin his house and the surrounding landscape. Stewart's narrative concludes when he resituates Geordie MacPhee outside of his experience of liminality, 'still campin in a barricade [Traveller tent] to this day, way up the other side o Dunkeld there' (ibid.). Geordie's aggregation, using Turner's term cited above, comes when he returns to his previous way of life. For Turner, aggregation involves the return to a relatively stable state, where the subject of the liminal experience has 'rights and obligations' and is expected to adhere to 'customary norms and ethical standards binding on incumbents of social position in a system of such positions' (1969: 95). Aggregation, from this perspective, is somewhat deterministic and Geordie's experience in liminality is testament to this determinism when his social position is restored at the conclusion of the story. Turner's framework is useful in interpreting Geordie's journey since it reaffirms a perceptible class division that is based to a large extent on material wealth.

Yet, Geordie's journey through liminality can be interpreted in other ways. Considering Geordie's experience in liminality in terms of Jameson's binary conceptualisation of magical narratives, invoked above, the dichotomy of 'good' and 'evil' can be mapped onto Geordie's behaviour in each of his social positions. As we have seen, Geordie's humble existence in penury before his encounter with the supernatural agent is juxtaposed with his debauchery and neglect during his liminal experience. From this perspective, Geordie's journey through the three phases of liminality described above encompasses a cautionary tale: easy come, easy go. However, Jameson's proposition also asks us to consider the inherent otherness that is engendered by such stories. This otherness is embodied within Stewart's story by the social position of the protagonist. Geordie's social position – an illiterate, itinerant piper, with no fixed abode – is contrasted with solicitors, police officers and landed gentry, who exist at the opposite end of the social spectrum. Geordie's self-awareness of his position is clear throughout the narrative; "'whit are ye saying *m'lord* for?'", Geordie asks the solicitor, "'they cry [call] me Geordie MacPhee'", he says, "no *m'lord* they cry me, it's Geordie MacPhee they cry me'" (TAD 13847). Later, Geordie informs his subservient chauffeur, "'don't cry me m'lord, cry me Geordie MacPhee, I'm Geordie MacPhee the Tinkerman'" (ibid.). This is an important distinction, considering Turner's framework of liminality; Geordie is *not* aggregated into the world of the landed gentry, where he would be bound by the incumbents of his social position. For instance, the morning after the purchase of his estate, Geordie refuses to be driven into town, telling his chauffeur: "'naw,'" says Geordie, "me an the wife's gonnae walk doon'" (ibid.). And where he wore a suit of tailored clothes the day before, Stewart tells us that Geordie 'was in rags the next day' (ibid.).

Jameson contends that because otherness is a constitutive element of magical narratives, any analysis of such a genre must come to terms with the boundaries that it sets (1975: 140). The function of otherness in the context of the supernatural, says Jameson, is to set up these boundaries between social orders – within a fictive environment – to act as a deterrent against subversion (ibid.: 141). For Geordie MacPhee, what is at stake are the values and beliefs that he recognises in himself as he occupies the status of the 'Tinkerman'. By super-empirical means, Geordie transgresses a social boundary by occupying a position in the social hierarchy to which he does not belong. The impetus for Geordie's subversion is the courage that he displays when confronted with the uncanny visitor at the beginning of the narrative; the narrator, Stewart, describes Geordie as 'a big wild man [. . .] he wisnae feared a nothing like that' (TAD 13847). The supernatural agent himself tells Geordie, '"you're the only man that [has] risen and followed me, none of the rest would follow me, for years," so he says, "you're a brave man"' (ibid.). Geordie's movement into liminality, viewed from this perspective, is volitional, rather than something which just happens to him or is forced upon him during some 'rite of passage'. To confront his own desires and impulses, Geordie willingly enters the liminal space, as if he is somehow aware that this altered reality will provide him with an experience not to be had elsewhere. By *becoming* the 'other', Geordie can scrutinise his own ideological constitution and imperatives. Within the liminal space that Geordie experiences, the 'other' is a relational concept, a concept that is available for scrutiny in a consequence-free story space.

As Geordie enters the liminal space, the atmosphere of the narrative changes and Geordie's daily piping activities are replaced by frivolity. The first thing that Geordie does after filling his pockets with gold is to go for a drink. Although this seems something of an obvious reaction to newfound wealth after penury, its function within the narrative is to fundamentally suspend the everyday reality in which the story began. The subversion engendered by Geordie's entry into the liminal space is operating on more than one level, then; a cautionary tale about the vicissitudes of wealth is plain, but this reading is augmented when we reconsider Geordie's experience as carnivalesque. The carnival atmosphere of the narrative amounts to a series of symbolic inversions: consider Geordie's dismissal of the police officers who attempt to subdue the drunken revellers; or the authority that Geordie wields, despite his appearance in rags; and then there is the gold that flows freely during the horse trading, upending the very nature of the trade itself; and finally, the 'big hoose' is converted into a Traveller camp as the festivities come to a close, juxtaposing the distinction between the prestige of immovable property and the precarity of an itinerant lifestyle. These spaces, liminal and otherwise, thereby function to allow the narrators the freedom to symbolically negotiate sometimes dichotomous ideological imperatives. Within Geordie's experience, the 'Other', from his perspective, is lampooned in a carnivalesque liminality. Braid draws similar conclusions when discussing Traveller storytelling, seeing the narratives expressing 'the absurdity of settled worldview' while 'vindicating Traveller worldview' (1997: 116). Geordie's own values and beliefs were interrogated during the narrative and Andrew Stewart's story is therefore more sophisticated; Stewart gives us an ironically naïve protagonist who challenges deeply-entrenched social hierarchies by flouting conventions and sedentarist attitudes towards conspicuous wealth.

GEORDIE'S IDEOLOGY

When Geordie takes his values with him into the carnivalesque environment – recall his return to his familiar rags and his refusal of his chauffeur – his experience of inhabiting the status of the 'other' sheds light on these very values. Part of this attitude functions to enact inversions of hierarchical discourses; Bakhtin saw such inversions as a sort of mask, where the wearer enacts a 'gay relativity' (1984: 40) and violates natural boundaries during a period of transition. In Geordie's case, the concept of carnival, as an arena for inversions of this sort, is thereby linked to the relativity of 'good' and 'evil', explicated above. Good and evil, viewed as positional notions, are representations of absolute otherness that function to present mirror images of opposing ideological characteristics (Jameson 1975: 161). In Stewart's narrative, the mirror is erected by super-empirical means when Geordie encounters the uncanny man and becomes the opposing image of his initial status as a poor, itinerant piper with no property or expendable means. 'Magical narrative' or super-empirical story spaces, when viewed as a genre, makes Geordie's experience possible because the genre sets up a set of social antagonisms that would be problematic in more realist genres. If Geordie had won a lottery or robbed a bank, his transformation into an unquestioningly influential landowner would be less plausible. This is because such *empirical* sources of wealth would engender different narrative trajectories: a lottery win may very well result in the protagonist squandering their fortune, but their *experience* would be wholly different because their contrition would be felt in the *real world*. The robbing a bank scenario would condemn the protagonist to illicit spending and the perpetual fear of prosecution by the authorities.

Instead, Geordie's experience in liminality is necessarily predicated on the super-empirical and his experience of lordship is enacted within the carnivalesque. It is here again that we witness the sophistication of the narratives within the Travellers' storytelling traditions. Geordie's own carnival mask is embodied by his magical wealth and status within the defined carnival space of 'his estate', which includes the village and therefore its market. However, Geordie's mask is not physical; he rejects the trappings of a gentleman-of-means and enters the market in his familiar rags. It is in this way that Geordie's experience is a symbolic negotiation of the ideological imperatives that underpin his Traveller identity. By assuming the status, but not the appearance, of his ultimate ideological other, Geordie's experience within Stewart's narrative is a reaction to the sedentarism that underpins *the other's* ideological imperatives. Bear in mind the premise of the narrative as a whole: Geordie MacPhee represents the archetypal travelling 'Tinkerman', playing his bagpipes door-to-door to make his living, propertyless, gaining shelter through his knowledge of his environment. During his liminal experience, Geordie encapsulates the opposite of this lifestyle, acquiring immovable property, motor vehicles, land and staff. By the conclusion of Stewart's story, Geordie returns to his original status. Commenting on the same story, Sheila Douglas explains that Geordie 'goes back to the road without bitterness, for basically he is not a materialist, and regards wealth as something to share [. . .] not something to give him status' (1987: 11).

Given the analysis furnished above and considering the purpose of this study – which examines how Travellers' values and beliefs, or ideologies, are embedded within their storytelling traditions – Stewart's narrative is further evidence of how such ideologies manifest themselves. To elucidate the contention that Stewart's narrative engages with sedentarism as an ideological position, it is useful to consider the way that this term is being deployed. MacLaughlin has pointed out that, beginning with Enlightenment theorists such as John Locke, and Hugo Grotius before him, sedentarism came to be viewed as the abandonment of 'primitive' lifestyles associated with nomadism (1995: 23–24). Respect for private property and the rights of the individual, prioritising industry and expansionism over pastoralism, were all viewed as hallmarks of a superior civilisation. As these ideas percolated into nineteenth century nationalist ideologies, MacLaughlin asserts that 'there was literally no room for Travellers and Gypsies in nation-building Europe' (ibid.: 26). This discourse contributed to the racialisation of Gypsies and Travellers throughout twentieth-century Europe and persists largely to the present day. The contextual chapters of the present book provided an abundance of evidence supporting the marginalisation of Scotland's Travellers in this respect.

We have seen in preceding chapters – as have others elsewhere (Douglas 1985; Braid 2002; Marcus 2019) – that Traveller storytelling is sensitive to continually changing socio-economic landscapes and cultural conditions. Moreover, it is clear that a central function of the stories under examination is to negotiate these changes using expressions of distinctive ideological imperatives. For Geordie, the fact that this ideological negotiation takes place within a carnivalesque, super-empirical space is telling. Geordie's generosity and flippant attitude within this space follows Bakhtin's conceptualisation of a violation of 'natural' boundaries, with Geordie transgressing the rigid, inequitable social hierarchy and proceeding to flout all conventions therein. Jameson's binary of 'good and evil', evoked here as an expression of innate otherness, takes on significant meaning from this perspective. Stewart's story places sedent and nomad in a carnival atmosphere where the former is parodied by the latter. These lifestyle choices represent deep-seated, oppositional ideologies where the dominant institutions regard sedentarism as the developmental zenith of Western society. Sedentary values and beliefs are predicated on the appropriation and utilisation of territory and natural resources. MacLaughlin also argues that the prioritisation of sedentarism throughout the Enlightenment period in Europe meant that lifestyles associated with nomadism were delegitimised (1995: 24). For Europe's Travellers and Gypsies – who MacLaughlin observes 'made no claims on property and did not "accumulate" wealth' (ibid.) – this meant that their lifestyle choices denied them social and political agency. Not only were peripatetic lifestyles delegitimised during the Enlightenment period, and beyond, they were also demonised to a demonstrable extent. Consider the evidence presented from TSAS and elsewhere in earlier chapters; Scotland's Travellers were regarded as parasitical, even 'criminal by nature', on account of their favouring alternative or informal economic strategies.

Throughout this book, we have seen how the Travellers' lifestyle choices and cultural identities manifest themselves and are negotiated within their storytelling traditions. A further example of how this happens is Geordie's negotiation of his extraordinary experience. Geordie at once inhabits and rejects the trappings of a sedentary lifestyle in a non-confrontational story space, a space that is accommodated by the super-empirical genre. In Williamson's story *The Hedgehurst* (TAD 36536), the protagonist refused to forsake his identity, preferring instead to return to his life in his native forest after his transformative experience. The same can be said of Geordie, when at the end of the story he returns to his piping and an itinerant lifestyle. Geordie's renewal is embodied by his return to his life on the road; his experience in carnivalesque liminality represents a resistance to sedentarist ideologies that prioritise the domination of landscapes and people. From this perspective, Geordie does not foolishly squander the gift of wealth and security, rather his story rejects the very premise on which such ideologies are based. By viewing Geordie's story from certain critical perspectives – notably Bakhtin's insights into carnival spaces – Traveller storytelling embodies a negotiation of social relationships. Within Andrew Stewart's narrative, the society that Geordie keeps is brought face-to-face with its contrasting 'Other' in the form of the landed gentry. 'Otherness', in this sense, is projected not on to the marginalised Travellers, but on to the sectors of society that view sedentarism as the apex of human society. Thomas McKean recognises similar sentiments in the Travellers' balladry when he notes that 'Travellers use tradition to mediate their relationship with mainstream society' (2015: 208). Under these conditions, the stories being examined here represent a dialogue between the Traveller storytellers' ideologies and that of the settled population. The storytellers do this by placing their protagonists within the social world of mainstream society, thereby incorporating mainstream values into the narrated events. In this way, the Traveller protagonists vicariously experience mainstream social conditions and impose their own value systems upon them. McKean concludes that contextualising stories in this way creates 'meaning and a richer depth of understanding, a more complete picture of human frailty and nobility' (ibid.: 222).

Consider Geordie's story from the perspective of the arrivals from London; '"my word", says the lady', when she sees the Travellers ensconced in the mansion house, '"what a terrible mess"' (TAD 13847). The arrivals from London go on to eschew Geordie and his wife's offers of hospitality and beat a hasty retreat. The Londoners' revulsion at what they find is indicative of their own ideological imperatives. Rather than squander such fortuitous wealth, listeners to the story imagine the Londoners making tidy investments and consciously advancing their material position. In this way, the Othering that takes place in Stewart's narrative is a dialogical critique of ideologies that stand in opposition to 'Travelling', or nomadic, lifestyles. It is not that purely capitalist, sedentarist social systems are being rejected wholesale. Instead, storytelling genres such as the super-empirical are used as arenas in which these value systems can be interrogated. Geordie's 'rags-to-riches (to rags)' story is yet another example of how Traveller storytellers engage with familiar tale-types to create specialised narrative expressions of worldview. Consider the contrast between Geordie's miraculous wealth and motivations of the blood-thirsty soldier in *The Tinderbox* (cf. TAD 14182) from the previous chapter; yes, Geordie flaunts his wealth, but his motivation is beneficent and carnivalesque when he shares his good fortune with his peers. These close examinations of Traveller storytelling continue to reveal that the storytellers' distinctive cultural identities are expressed within their narratives. As this study draws to its conclusion, it is clear that the 'cultural identities' of the Traveller storytellers are linked to underlying ideological imperatives. What makes the narratives 'Traveller', or Nackian, are the values and beliefs that underpin the stories as necessities. The impulse behind these stories must not be viewed as anti-capitalist, or the stories themselves as 'vessels of peasant wisdom' (Warner 2014: 133). Instead, the worldview being extolled by the Traveller storytellers is utopian in the sense that the messages the stories transmit are those of self-awareness and social responsibility. From this perspective, the challenges being levelled at material wealth are not antagonistic, they are representative of a society where the folk can confidently express their own points of view. Zipes sees this impulse as the utopian purpose of folklore, which seeks to 'enable people to give voice and form to their needs and dreams in a free manner', thereby enabling 'communities to be established on a non-antagonistic basis, to expose and overcome social antagonisms' (1984: 335).

Conclusion: Storytelling as Cultural Continuity

As we move towards the second quarter of the twenty first century, close attention to the intangible cultural heritage of Scotland's diverse Traveller communities is puzzlingly sparse. In a 1989 newspaper article, Hamish Henderson famously quipped that collecting the songs and stories of Scotland's Traveller communities at the annual berry harvest in Blairgowrie was akin to 'holding a tin can under the Niagara Falls' (2004: 2). Yet the abundance of material that was collected from Scotland's Traveller communities during the twentieth century – now housed in the SSS Archives, a sizable proportion of which has been made available digitally through TAD – is often underutilised. The central purpose of this book has been to address this scarcity and offer the reader a glimpse of the cultural abundance recognised by Henderson. Along with our archives, the living tradition-bearers from the Traveller communities represent robust and vibrant Scottish cultural identities. A dramatic change in working lifestyles – lamented by Duncan Campbell at the beginning of this study (1910: 24–25) – and a mainstream shift toward sedentary ideals should not mean the obliteration of marginalised cultural identities. One commentator recently put it as strongly as this: 'Gypsies, Roma and Travellers are Britain's internal refugees – shunned and abandoned by their country of birth [. . .] perceptions need changing. Biases need questioning. Discrimination needs challenging' (Henry 2022: 3).

This book has shown how we can begin to address such concerns by looking closely at the cultural heritage that the communities hold dear. Despite the Rehfisches bemoaning the gallons of ink and effort that have been spent developing theories around the origins of Scotland's Travellers (1975: 272), this book gives us better understandings of how the most recent generations of the communities express their culture. The wasted gallons and sustained fascination with these communities speaks to an inherent curiosity in their perceived 'otherness'. However, this otherness need not be reviled and belittled, rather it should be better understood and celebrated. Scotland's diverse Traveller communities are the bearers of a set of traditions that simply should not be lost through mistrust and misunderstanding. I have therefore presented new ways to critically engage with storytelling as an antidote to the cultural 'otherness' often associated with Traveller communities in mainstream discourses. The earlier texts and the many subsequent reports commissioned by the state – the 1895 report being the most notorious – seek to measure this 'otherness' as means to subjugate its presence in Scotland. At the heart of such endeavours is a fundamental ideological differentiation that took root in a rapidly industrialising landscape. A generous appraisal of efforts to allay this differentiation might be misguided paternalism and misunderstanding; another way would be to understand that the changing sociopolitical landscape in Scotland meant that the ideological constitution and lifestyle choices of Scotland's 'other' simply did not gel with the increasingly sedentary ideals of the ruling elite. The Rehfisches might also have pointed out that much of the discourse refers to 'Traveller culture' without explaining what this culture represents. Previous scholarship in this area – along with governmental grey literature and aside from a handful of attentive authors – often alludes to Traveller 'culture', without articulating what this culture resembles and then critically engaging with it.

These important cultural traditions have been attracting the attention of collectors and folklorists for many generations and the sophistication of the Traveller tradition-bearers' verbal art did not go unnoticed. This book has reanimated this attention by thinking about the stories, oral histories, memorates and songs from new perspectives. Expanding on Braid's (2002) observation that Travellers' stories are vehicles for identity negotiation, we have seen that there are definable threads of meaning within Traveller culture that amount to sets of coherent ideological commitments. Along with the contextual evidence from TAD and elsewhere, the examples presented in this study show that these commitments amount to the affirmation of the Travellers' cultural legitimacy. Geertz's concept of 'patterns of feeling' (2000: 95), invoked in the Introduction above, is a useful way to understand cultural systems at work in given communities, and we return to Geertz here: 'Whatever else ideologies may be', says Geertz, 'they are, most distinctively, maps of problematic social reality' (1994: 288). The social problems faced by generations of Travellers are an observable theme throughout the narratives we have encountered. The problematic realities are negotiated in such a way as to make sense of them and to reaffirm cultural identities.

The central threads of the arguments put forward here, then, are the underlying ideological commitments that manifest within Travellers' cultural expressions. Our discussions are based on the premise that the storytellers place great cultural value in the folkloric traditions that they continue to share. The semantic promiscuity of the term 'ideology', recognised by Gerring (1997: 957), was carefully addressed throughout this study as a useful way to encompass the values and beliefs of a distinct set of minority communities. As Eagleton reminds us, common usage of the term often has pejorative connotations, where an 'ideological' person or group has a distorted view of the world based on inflexible assumptions (1994: 1). For our purposes, the term, although not divested of unproblematic connotations, simply refers to a coherent cultural identity that stands in contradistinction to the mainstream Scottish population. This cultural identity is neither belligerent nor imposing at its core; it is rather a set of sophisticated social and cultural priorities that perhaps lie dormant within more mainstream communities whose own interests and values are coherent in different ways. During his expansive 'definitional analysis', Gerring notes that most empirical investigations agree that coherence is the key attribute within meaningful conceptualisations of ideology (1997: 984). The coherence of the Traveller ideology examined in the present study is based on environmental awareness, acute moral sensitivity, a sagacious appreciation of the pitfalls of material wealth and, most importantly, a keen sense of cultural identity and legitimacy. Not only were cultural realities on display, but also the view that folk narratives can be viewed as 'ideological battle grounds'. The Travellers' folkloric expressions critically engage with cultural authority and discourse, concurring with Teverson's contention that folktales have the 'capacity to be resistant to, or critical of, dominant ideological interests' (Teverson 2013: 127, 134).

The narratives examined in this book not only engage with perennial themes around personal growth and transformation, but they do so in a way that typifies the 'Nackian' folkloric idiom. For instance, the versions of the Cinderella masterplot, or cycle, from Duncan Williamson represent culturally significant variations. In the 'Notes on the Narrations' of *A Thorn in the King's Foot*, Williamson explains that he had 'never saw any versions of the story wrote down in any book or any way. But I've heard it told in different ways fra many travellers [sic]' (1987: 275). Williamson's individual creativity engages with the wider Traveller community of storytellers so that the story of Mary Rashiecoats is invested with meaning at both levels. This is an example of an ecotype *par excellence*, with Williamson's version of the story artfully conceived so that the protagonists' journeys reflect the meaning that he sees in the ubiquitous Cinderella masterplot. As David Campbell so eloquently puts it in his biography of Williamson, 'Duncan's legacy was not just the stories, but the spirit that infused them and the way there were carried and transmitted' (2012: 162).

In Duncan Williamson's *The Hedgehurst*, the critical approach taken by this study was used in tandem with more orthodox comparative techniques to provide fresh insights into traditional narratives. Like the authors of the literary fairy tales that were used for comparison, Williamson's version of ATU 441 – *Hans my Hedgehog* reconfigures this international tale to suit the ideological commitments of the narrator and the traditional resource on which he draws. The concept of ecotypes (Von Sydow 1934: 349) was again invoked to provide further evidence of the distinctive characteristics of the Nackian idiom that this book showcases. The journey of Williamson's Hedgehurst was shown to be a narrative not about a social climber who undergoes a physical transformation, like the literary versions. Instead, the protagonist in the Nackian version of the story embodied a close affinity with the natural environment, resisting the temptations of wealth and power, choosing instead to remain in his self-made abode in the forest. This sense of harmony and balance with nature is a sentiment expressed by Traveller Janet Robertson:

> Everybody in time of stress looks for a haven, a harbour, their own private piece of velvet. This is what Travellers call "Blue Velvet". You know some people when they think of other things often say a taste of honey, if they're speaking about something that applies to them. But I think with Travellers it really was their Blue Velvet, it was a haven if you like, it was a place where they go for refuge, and they could find companionship. They could identify themselves, but they could also identify themselves as children of nature, for they were children of nature, and they live close to nature.
>
> (TAD 49824)

Robertson's points here go a long way to capturing the essence of the Hedgehurst's journey; he at once becomes comfortable and confident in his skin, while figuring out that his identity draws him back to a place in nature. Given what we know about the Travellers' chosen lifestyles, it is not surprising that Williamson situates his story in a setting that his audiences could identify with. In his memoirs, Williamson himself tells us that his early years were spent around a forest, explaining that 'in Furnace wood, my father raised thirteen children' (1994: 3). Perhaps a laudable relationship with the Scottish landscape and the natural environment – one that is not based on control or possession – is a more meaningful way to conceptualise nomadic 'ways of thinking'.

It is important not to romanticise the communities into some idyllic, prelapsarian landscape where lifestyle conflicts do not exist. Instead, this book has suggested that close attention be paid to the cultural expressions of the communities to better understand their ideological motivations and celebrate their culture. When it comes to the ideological differentiation between Travellers and mainstream society, parallels with attitudes towards Gaelic can be drawn. Chapter 1 above traced the hostility towards Travellers and their chosen lifestyles from the eighteenth century onwards through a variety of documentary sources. The many examples from TSAS are evidence for the developing contempt for a previously valued sector of pre-industrial Scottish society. The numerous governmental reports cited represent harrowing incitements to cultural obliteration, with William Mitchell, for example, calling for Traveller children to be 'looked after and sent to school, and the whole tinker clan thus gradually brought into association with the other labourer' (*Minutes of Evidence*, in Cameron et al 1895: 9).[1] For Wilson McLeod, the value of Gaelic was similarly maligned when 'from the eighteenth century onwards, a discourse of modernisation, improvement and progress became dominant in relation to Gaelic' (2020: 44). McLeod goes on: 'Gaelic monolingualism was said to hold Gaelic speakers back, preventing them from accessing opportunities and from participating fully in civic and cultural life' (ibid.: 44–45). The present study extends this insight further to mobilise debates around the role of marginalised communities in Scottish culture. McLeod concludes that in parts of Scotland, 'deeply rooted language ideologies that devalued Gaelic remained in play, often reinforced by people's direct personal experience that Gaelic had brought them no benefit in life' (ibid.: 333). Traveller culture in contemporary Scotland suffers similarly, with the present generation often hiding their ethnicity for fear of discriminatory reprisals. As an antidote, a more celebratory examination of a unique folk idiom has been presented here. One that, although underrepresented at present, undoubtedly merits further detailed investigation.

The most precise example of the Nackian idiom at work is found in the Travellers' narratives about Burkers. Writing in *The Scotsman* in 1829, an anonymous columnist predicted that Burke's name 'will stand conspicuous – it will mark an era in the black record of human delinquency, and future ages will shudder at his horrid deeds, and fling back their curses on the name' (1829: 62). That it did, and the way that William Burke and his associates perpetrated the murders seeped into the Travellers' storytelling traditions in a unique way. The examinations presented showed how mainstream representations of the crimes are often biographical, sometimes comical, but that the Nackian manifestations are of an altogether different sort. Here, the ideological negotiation is elevated from the symbolic to the visceral. According to Braid, the Burkean narratives may also 'be used to instil a healthy fear of outsiders in Traveller children. These stories therefore reinforce the desire for isolation and strengthen the sense of shared identity in Traveller communities' (2002: 83). Although Braid has a point, the examples presented in the present study enhance his summation about Burkers because the narratives examined are more redolent of the original crimes. The 'unresolvable social trauma' recognised by McCracken-Flesher (2012: 23) was shown to manifest itself in specific ways in the Travellers' tradition. The fear instilled during our examples transcends the bodily threat of the Burkers to represent an existential threat of a higher order. What is at stake during the 'Burking' episodes – understood as deliberate intoxication and smothering – is the confrontation between the ideological commitments of the protagonists and their would-be annihilators.

The lifestyle choices of the Traveller protagonists are undisguised during the Burker tales, where the protagonists find themselves on the road and in peril. Their peril is not only symbolic of the precarious lifestyles they choose, but also of the problematic relationship they have with mainstream society. At the same time, the Burker accounts are instilled with a recognisable sense of hope and self-affirmation that challenges the passive persecution highlighted by Henderson and others. In the Burker stories, the worldviews and beliefs being expressed are the fundamental human right to making your own lifestyle choices and peacefully resisting contamination by values with which you do not agree. This conceptualisation is a further countermeasure to what Zoë James sees as the negation of Traveller cultures and a failure to acknowledge the communities' experience of racism and prejudice (2020: 101). James goes on to suggest that 'the hierarchies of legitimacy between Gypsy and Traveller communities, as well as between Gypsies and Travellers and wider white sedentarist society, have been augmented' (ibid.). This is especially true in the contemporary Burker examples, where an overt challenge to the lifestyles of the would-be Burkers is a quintessential Nackian narrative. James points out that 'Gypsies and Travellers struggle to subjectively console their cultural norms and expectations with the norms and expectations of neoliberal capitalism' (ibid.). However, as Nacken author and artist Shamus McPhee puts it, the function of Nackian narratives is to represent 'an inherent contradistinction to the sedentarist prototype that society has drafted for us' (Personal Correspondence 2021).

This book comes at a time when a recent study reported harrowing insights into the mental health of Gypsies, Roma and Travellers across the

United Kingdom. The report, entitled *Hate: "As Regular as Rain"*, set out to analyse 'anecdotal evidence that highlights the "ripple effect" of experiencing hate crime on mental health' (Greenfields and Rogers 2020: 10). The authors found that eighty percent of Scottish Traveller respondents reported having relatives who had attempted suicide in the previous five years, linking these statistics to experiences of hate crime and discriminatory practices (ibid.: 14). One Scottish Traveller reported that 'in some cases I have seen community members even go as far as to internalise the false beliefs outsiders make about our culture' (ibid.: 112). Throughout this book, the argument has been that discrimination is nothing new for Scotland's Traveller communities and our analyses show that 'false beliefs' can be undermined by positive representation and by fostering better understandings between Scotland's diverse communities.

This study, along with fieldwork activities and communications with contemporary members of the communities, therefore, began with a commitment to a better understanding of Travellers' experiences and cultural expressions. In the Introduction above, I included a quote from Traveller John Stewart that is worth repeating here; 'our way of thinking, our deep concern inside', says Stewart, 'our jealousies and oor hatreds, our loves and our likes are far different from yours' (TAD 56424). Stewart's poignant evocation of 'deep concern inside' and 'ways of thinking' encompasses the point of this book precisely. It has not been the intention to describe a new 'unified field' of Traveller identity, worldview and ideology. Rather, the analyses have shown that through close attention to the *narrative* voices that come from the communities, much safer conclusions can be drawn about the nature of the Nackian tradition. Shared understandings around history, folklore, placenames, ancestry and local knowledge are key identity markers within the communities. 'Nackens set great store in any art form', explains Shamus McPhee, 'musicians, craftspeople, artists and, by extension, storytellers, occupy an exalted status within our culture. It is an arts-driven culture; that is what matters most to us, in a nutshell' (Personal Correspondence 2021). This nutshell amounts to a vigorous sense of cultural continuity and self-determination. The attributes of the Nackian narratives thereby function as a challenge to group identities that are based on external naming conventions and the misunderstandings that Traveller communities continue to face. Both personal and cultural autonomy are at the heart of the Nackian folk idiom; cultural identity, folklore and ideology are ultimately linked in the Travellers' storytelling traditions through the affirmation of the communities' cultural legitimacy. Like the storytellers and tradition-bearers we have met throughout this book, we must not delegitimise certain of Scotland's cultural identities based on misunderstandings. Recognising our differing cultural identities, we must challenge ourselves and negotiate alternative ideological commitments without simply discounting them, forging more meaningful intellectual and cultural connections.

Note

1. It is worth noting here, as Becky Taylor reminds us: 'It is clear that reformers and state officials saw Travellers as an anomaly and their continued presence in modern Britain an aberration. Yet it is equally clear that Travellers sat alongside other groups like vagrants and habitual offenders, who were similarly seen as a blot on society' (2023: 659).

Bibliography

All references beginning 'TAD' refer to the track ID on *Tobar an Dualchais* (TAD), a digital archive which contains material from the School of Scottish Studies, The Canna Collection and BBC Radio nan Gàidheal. The recorded material can be accessed via the TAD website by searching the numerical track ID using the 'Search' function – https://www.tobarandualchais.co.uk/. The associated alpha-numeric references beginning 'SA' refer to the original tape and track ID, held in the School of Scottish Studies Archives.

Abbot, H. Porter. 2008. *The Cambridge Introduction to Narrative*, 2nd edn (Cambridge: Cambridge University Press).

Acts of Parliament. 1908. 'Children Act (1908)' https://www.legislation.gov.uk/ukpga/1908/67/pdfs/ukpga_19080067_en.pdf [accessed 18 March 2024].

Ainiala, Terhi. 2016. 'Attitudes to Street Names in Helsinki', in *Names and Naming: People, Places, Perceptions and Power*, ed. Guy Puzey and Laura Kostanski (Bristol: Multilingual Matters), pp. 106–119.

Ainmean-Àite. 'Rosehearty Research Notes' https://www.ainmean-aite.scot/placename/rosehearty/ [accessed 18 March 2024].

Amnesty International. 2012. *Caught in the Headlines*. Online https://www.amnesty.org.uk/files/amnesty_international_caught_in_the_headlines_2012.pdf [accessed 18 March 2024].

Andersen, Hans Christian. 1899. *Fairy Tales from Hans Christian Andersen*, trans. E. Lucas (London: J. M. Dent & Sons.).

Anonymous. 1829. 'Life of William Burke', in *The Scotsman*, 28 January, p. 62.

Anonymous. 1836. 'The Tinkers of Scotland', *Penny Magazine of the Society for the Diffusion of Useful Knowledge* (1832-1845), Vol. 5, Issue 303, pp. 502–503.

Anonymous. 1838. 'State of Crime in Scotland', in *The Scotsman*, 21 April, p. 2.

Anonymous. 1869. 'Savages in Scotland', *The Friend; A Religious and Literary Journal* (1827–1906), Vol. 43, No. 13, pp. 102–103.

Anonymous. 1893. 'Editorial Article 5 – No Title', in *The Scotsman*, 13 January, p. 4.

Anonymous. 1918. 'The Wandering Tribes', in *The Scotsman*, 17 May, p. 4.
Aristotle. 2010. From 'Poetics', in *The Norton Anthology of Theory and Criticism*, eds. Vincent B. Leitch et al, 2nd edn (New York and London: Norton), pp. 88–115.
Article 12 in Scotland. 2018. 'I Witness: The Concluding Observations' https://www.article12.org/wp-content/uploads/2020/09/I-Witness_the-Concluding-Observation_2018_web.pdf [accessed 18 March 2024].
A. W. T, and M. C. B. 1890. 'English and Scotch Fairy Tales', *Folklore*, Vol. 1, No. 3, pp. 289–312.
Baird, John. 1845. 'Account of Yetholm, County of Roxburgh', in *The Statistical Accounts of Scotland*, Vol. III, p. 166.
Baird, William. 1869 [1763–73]. *Genealogical Memoirs of the Duffs* (Aberdeen: D. Wyllie & Son).
Bakhtin, Mikhail. 1984. *Rabelais and His World*, trans. Helene Iswolsky (Bloomington: Indiana University Press).
Bal, Mieke. 2009. *Narratology: Introduction to the Theory of Narrative*, 3rd edn (Toronto: Toronto University Press).
Bancroft, Angus. 2005. *Roma and Gypsy-Travellers in Europe: Modernity, Race, Space and Exclusion* (Aldershot: Ashgate Publishing).
Bancroft, Angus, M. Lloyd, and R. Morran. 1996. *The Right to Roam: Travellers in Scotland 1995/6* (Dunfermline: Save the Children Fund).
Barthes, R. 1975. 'An Introduction to the Structural Analysis of Narrative', *New Literary History*, Vol. 6, No. 2, pp. 237–272.
Bascom, William. 1954. 'Four Functions of Folklore', *The Journal of American Folklore*, Vol. 67, No. 266, pp. 333–349.
——. 1965. 'The Forms of Folklore: Prose Narratives', *The Journal of American Folklore*, Vol. 78, No. 307, pp. 3–20.
Baum, Paull F. 1922. 'Judas's Red Hair', *The Journal of English and Germanic Philology*, Vol. 21, No. 3, pp. 520–529.
Bauman, Richard. 1971. 'Differential Identity and the Social Base of Folklore', *The Journal of American Folklore*, Vol. 84, No. 331, pp. 31–41.
——. 1986. *Story, Performance and Event: Contextual Studies of Oral Narrative* (Cambridge: Cambridge University Press).
Belfiore, Elizabeth. 2009. 'The Elements of Tragedy', in *A Companion to Aristotle*, ed. Georgios Anagnostopoulos (Chichester: Wiley-Blackwell), pp. 628–642.
Ben-Amos, Dan. 1984. 'The Seven Strands of Tradition: Varieties in Its Meaning in American Folklore Studies', *Journal of Folklore Research*, Vol. 21, No. 2/3, pp. 97–131.
Bernheimer, Kate. 2010. 'Introduction', in *My Mother She Killed Me, My Father He Ate Me: Forty New Fairy Tales* (New York: Penguin).
Bhreatnach, Aoife. 2007. 'Confusing Origins and Histories: The Case of Irish Travellers', *Irish Journal of Anthropology*, Vol. 10, No. 1, pp. 30–35.
Black, Ronald. 2005. 'Introduction', in *The Gaelic Otherworld*, ed. Ronald Black (Edinburgh: Birlinn), pp. xix–lxxxii.

Blackie, Christina. 1887. *A Dictionary of Place-Names, Giving Their Derivations*, 3rd ed. (London: John Murray).
Boswell, John. 1988. *The Kindness of Strangers: The Abandonment of Children in Western Europe from Late Antiquity to the Renaissance* (New York: Pantheon).
Bottigheimer, Ruth B. 2002. *Fairy Godfather: Straparola, Venice, and the Fairy Tale Tradition* (Philadelphia: University of Pennsylvania Press).
Braid, Donald. 1997. 'The Construction of Identity Through Narrative: Folklore and the Travelling People of Scotland', in *Romani Culture and Gypsy Identity*, eds. Thomas Acton and Gary Mundy (Hatfield: University of Hertfordshire Press), pp. 40–68
———. 1999. '"Our Stories are not just for Entertainment": Lives and Stories Among the Travelling People of Scotland', in *Traditional Storytelling Today: An International Sourcebook*, ed. Margaret Read MacDonald (Chicago: Fitzroy Dearborn Publishers), pp. 301–309.
———. 2002. *Scottish Traveller Tales: Lives Shaped Through Stories* (Mississippi: Mississippi University Press).
Bronner, Simon J. 1998. *Following Tradition: Folklore in the Discourse of American Culture* (Logan: Utah State University Press).
———. 2000. 'The Meaning of Tradition: An Introduction', *Western Folklore*, Vol. 59, No. 2, pp. 87–104.
———. 2012. *Explaining Traditions: Folk Behaviour in Modern Culture* (Lexington: University Press of Kentucky.
———. 2017. *Folklore: The Basics* (Oxon: Routledge).
Bruford, Alan. 1969. *Gaelic Folk-Tales and Medieval Romances: A Study of the Early Modern Irish 'Romantic Tales' and Their Oral Derivatives* (Dublin: The Folklore of Ireland Society).
Bruford, Alan, and Donald A. MacDonald. 2003. 'Notes', in *Scottish Traditional Tales*, eds. Alan Bruford and Donald A. MacDonald (Edinburgh: Birlinn), pp. 439–486.
Burke, Mary. 2009. *'Tinkers': Synge and the Cultural History of the Irish Traveller* (Oxford: Oxford University Press).
Cameron, Charles et al. 1895. *The Report of the Departmental Committee on Habitual Offenders, Vagrants, Beggars, Inebriates and Juvenile Delinquents* (Edinburgh: Neill & Co.).
Campbell, David. 2012. *A Traveller in Two Worlds Volume Two: The Tinker and the Student*, 2 vols., II (Edinburgh: Luath Press).
Campbell, Duncan. 1910. *Reminiscences and Reflections of an Octogenarian Highlander* (Inverness: The Northern Counties Newspaper and Print. and Pub. Co.).
Campbell, John Francis. 1860–62. *Popular Tales of the West Highlands: Orally Collected*, 4 vols., I and II (Edinburgh: Edmonston and Douglas).
Campbell, John Gregorson. 2005 [1900]. 'Preface', in *The Gaelic Otherworld*, ed. Ronald Black (Edinburgh: Birlinn), pp. lxxxiii–lxxxiv.
———. 2005 [1900]. 'The Origin of the Fairy Creed', in *The Gaelic Otherworld*, ed. Ronald Black (Edinburgh: Birlinn), pp. lxxxv–xciii.

Cashman, Ray. 2011. 'The Role of Tradition in the Individual: At Work in Donegal with Packy Jim McGrath', in *The Individual and Tradition: Folkloristic Perspectives*, eds. Ray Cashman et al (Bloomingdale: Indiana University Press), pp. 303–322.

Cashman, Ray, Tom Mould and Pravina Shukla. 2011. 'Introduction: The Individual and Tradition', in *The Individual and Tradition: Folkloristic Perspectives*, eds. Ray Cashman et al (Bloomingdale: Indiana University Press), pp. 1–26.

Cemlyn, Sarah, and Colin Clark. 2005. 'The Social Exclusion of Gypsy and Traveller Children', in *At Greatest Risk: The Children Most Likely to be Poor*, ed. Gabrielle Preston (London: Child Poverty Action Group), pp. 146–162.

Cemlyn, Sarah, et al. 2009. *Inequality Experienced by Gypsy and Traveller Communities: A Review* (Manchester: Equality and Human Rights Commission).

Chambers, Robert. 1858 [1826]. *Popular Rhymes of Scotland*, 3rd edn (Edinburgh: W. & R. Chambers).

Cheape, Hugh. 2007. 'Foreword', in *The Making of Am Fasgadh: An Account of the Origins of the Highland Folk Museum by its Founder*, ed. Alexander Fenton (Edinburgh: NMS Enterprises).

Clark, Colin. 2006. 'Defining Ethnicity in a Cultural and Socio-Legal Context: The Case of Scottish Gypsy/Travellers', *Scottish Affairs*, Vol. 54, No. 1, pp. 39–67

——. 2006a. 'Who are the Gypsies and Travellers of Britain?', in *Here to Stay: The Gypsies and Travellers of Britain* (Hatfield: University of Hertfordshire Press), pp. 10–27.

——. 2018. 'Sites, Welfare and 'Barefoot Begging': Roma, and Gypsy/Traveller Experiences of Racism in Scotland', in *No Problem Here: Understanding Racism in Scotland*, eds. Neil Davidson et al (Edinburgh: Luath Press), pp. 107–118.

Clark, Colin and Margaret Greenfields. 2006. *Here to Stay: The Gypsies and Travellers of Britain* (Hatfield: University of Hertfordshire Press).

Council of Europe. 2023. 'Advisory Committee on the Framework Convention for the Protection of National Minorities' https://rm.coe.int/0900001680ab55b4 [accessed 18 March 2024].

Cowan, Edward J. 2009. 'The Discovery of the Future: Prophesy and Second Sight in Scottish History', in *Fantastical Imaginations: The Supernatural in Scottish History and Culture*, ed. Lizanne Henderson (Edinburgh: John Donald), pp. 1–28.

Cox, Marian R. 1893. *Cinderella: Three Hundred and Forty-Five Variants* (London: David Nutt).

Cramond, William. 1902. *The Records of Elgin: 1234–1800*, ed. William Cramond, 2 vols., I (Aberdeen: New Spalding Club).

Crearie, Robin S. 1958. 'Integration of the Tinker in Society', in *The Scotsman*, 11 October, p. 12.

Danandjaja, James. 1982. 'A Javanese Cinderella Tale and its Pedagogical Value', in *Cinderella: A Folklore Casebook*, ed. Alan Dundes (New York: Garland Publishing), pp. 169–179.

D'Aulnoy, Marie-Catherine. 1892 [1697]. *The Fairy Tales of Madame D'Aulnoy*, trans. A. MacDonnell (London: Lawrence and Bullen).

Dawkins, R. M. 1951. 'The Meaning of Folktales', *Folklore*, Vol. 62, No. 4, pp. 417–429.

Dégh, Linda. 1991. 'What is the legend after all?', *Contemporary Legend*, Vol. 1, pp. 11–38.

——. 1995. *Narratives in Society: A Performer-Centered Study of Narration*, FF Communications No. 255 (Helsinki: Suomalainen Tiedeakatemia).

——. 2001. *Legend and Belief: Dialectics of a Folklore Genre* (Bloomington: Indiana University Press).

Dentith, Simon. 1995. *Bakhtinian Thought: An Introductory Reader* (London: Routledge).

Devine, T. M. 1994. *Clanship to Crofters' War: The Social Transformation of the Scottish Highlands* (Manchester: Manchester University Press).

Dictionary of the Scots Language. 'Tynklar/tincler/tinker/tinkard, etc.' http://www.dsl.ac.uk/entry/dost/tynklar [accessed 11 June 2024].

Dobie, Alexander. 1792. 'Account of Eaglesham, County of Renfrew', in *The Statistical Accounts of Scotland*, Vol. II, p. 124.

Donaldson, Davie. 2017. 'The government is at "war with our lifestyle", claim Scotland's Travellers', *The Ferret* https://theferret.scot/government-war-lifestyle-claim-scotlands-travellers/ [accessed 18 March 2024].

——. 2019. Interview with the Author.

——. Online. 'Home' http://www.nawken.com/ [accessed 11 June 2024]

Dorson, Richard M. 1968. *The British Folklorists: A History* (London: Routledge & Kegan Paul).

Douglas, Mary. 2003. *Purity and Danger: An Analysis of Concepts of Pollution and Taboo* (Abingdon: Routledge).

Douglas, Robert. 1792. 'Account of Bunkle and Preston, County Berwick', in *The Statistical Accounts of Scotland*, Vol. III, p. 157.

Douglas, Sheila. 1985. *The King o' the Black Art: A Study of the Tales of a Group of Perthshire Travellers in their Social Context* (Unpublished PhD thesis, University of Stirling).

——. 1987. *The King o' the Black Art: and Other Folk Tales*, eds. Sheila Douglas et al (Aberdeen: Aberdeen University Press).

Duff, William. 1845. 'Account of Grange, County of Banff', in *The Statistical Accounts of Scotland*, Vol. XIII, p. 219.

Dundes, Alan. 1964. *The Morphology of North American Indian Folktales*, FF Communications No. 195 (Helsinki: Suomalainen Tiedeakatemia).

——. 1980. *Interpreting Folklore* (Bloomington: Indiana University Press).

——. 1982. 'Introduction', in *Cinderella: A Folklore Casebook*, ed. Alan Dundes (New York: Garland Publishing), pp. xiii–xvii.

——. 2002. 'Projective Inversion in the Ancient Egyptian "Tale of Two Brothers"', *The Journal of American Folklore*, Vol. 115, No. 457/458, pp. 378–394.

——. 2007. 'The Study of Folklore in Literature and Culture: Identification and Interpretation', in *The Meaning of Folklore: The Analytical Essays of Alan Dundes*, ed. Simon J. Bronner (Logan: Utah State University Press), pp. 67–76.

——. 2007a. 'Folk Ideas as Units of Worldview', in *The Meaning of Folklore: The Analytical Essays of Alan Dundes*, ed. Simon J. Bronner (Logan: Utah State University Press), pp. 179–195.

Eagleton, Terry. 1994. 'Introduction', in *Ideology*, ed. Terry Eagleton (Harlow: Longman), pp. 1–20.

——. 2016. *Culture* (New Haven: Yale University Press).

Elliot, John. 1956. 'A soldier got possession of a magic tinder-box and gained wealth and a princess', Francis Collinson, Calum Iain Maclean (fieldworkers), SA1956.144.1 (TAD 42990).

Equality and Human Rights Commission Scotland. 2013. 'Gypsy Travellers in Scotland: A Resource for the Media' https://www.equalityhumanrights.com/sites/default/files/gt_media_guide_final.pdf [accessed 18 March 2024].

Falck, Colin. 1994. *Myth, Truth and Literature: Towards a True Post-Modernism*, 2nd edn (Cambridge: Cambridge University Press).

Fenton, Steve. 2010. *Ethnicity*, 2nd edn (Cambridge: Polity Press).

Ferney, David. 1793. 'Account of Kinnettles, County of Forfar', in *The Statistical Accounts of Scotland*, Vol. IX, p. 201.

Foley, John Miles. 1992. 'Word-power, Performance, and Tradition', *The Journal of American Folklore*, Vol. 105, No. 417, pp. 275–301.

Fountainhall, John L. 1848. *Historical Notices of Scottish Affairs: Selected from the Manuscripts*, ed. David Laing, 2 vols., II (Edinburgh: [s.n.]).

Frank, Arthur W. 2010. *Letting Stories Breathe: A Socio-narratology* (Chicago: The University of Chicago Press).

Fraser, Lord of Tullybelton. 1983. 'Mandla, Sewa Singh; Mandla, Gurinder Singh (an infant suing through Sewa Singh Mandla, his father and next friend) v Lee, A. G. Dowell; Park Grove Private School Limited' (UK Parliamentary Archives: HL/PO/JU/18/243).

Geertz, Clifford. 1973. *The Interpretation of Cultures: Selected Essays* (New York: Basic Books).

——. 2000. *Local Knowledge: Further Essays in Interpretative Anthropology*, 3rd edn (New York: Basic Books).

Geills, John and James Fraser. 1846. 'Process Against the Egyptians at Banff', *Miscellany of the Spalding Club*, Vol. 3, pp. 175–191.

Gentleman, Hugh. 1993. *Counting Travellers in Scotland: The 1992 Picture* (Edinburgh: The Scottish Office Central Research Unit).

George, Gordon. 1845. 'Account of Knockando, County of Elgin', in *The Statistical Accounts of Scotland*, Vol. XIII, p. 81.

Gerring, John. 1963. 'Ideology: A Definitional Analysis', *Political Research Quarterly*, Vol. 50, No. 4, pp. 957–994.

Glassie, Henry. 1995. 'Common Ground: Keywords for the Study of Expressive Culture', *The Journal of American Folklore*, Vol. 108, No. 430, pp. 395–412.

Grant, Isabel F. 2007. *The Making of Am Fasgadh: An Account of the Origins of the Highland Folk Museum by its Founder*, ed. Alexander Fenton (Edinburgh: NMS Enterprises).

Gray, Alexander. 1845. 'Account of Monteith, County of Perth', in *The Statistical Accounts of Scotland*, Vol. X, p. 1281.

Greenfields, Margaret and Carol Rogers. 2020. *Hate: "As regular as rain": A Pilot Research Project into the Psychological Effects of Hate Crime on Gypsy, Traveller and Roma (GTR) Communities* (Buckinghamshire New University) http://bucks.ac.uk/__data/assets/pdf_file/0028/54649/Hate-As-regular-as-rain-report.pdf [accessed 18 March 2024].

Grellmann, Heinrich. 1787. *Dissertation on the Gipsies*, trans. M. Raper (London: [s.n.]).

Gunderloch, Anja. 2013. 'The Heroic Ballads of Gaelic Scotland', in *The Edinburgh Companion to Scottish Traditional Literatures*, eds. Sarah Dunnigan and Suzanne Gilbert (Edinburgh: Edinburgh University Press), pp. 74–84.

Gypsy, Roma, Traveller History Month (GRTHM). 2017– . 'About' https://www.grthm.scot/about [accessed 1 May 2024]

——. 2020. 'No Less a Traveller: My Gypsy/Traveller Identity' https://www.grthm.scot/our-events/2020/week-2/my-gypsy-traveller-identity [accessed 1 May 2024]

——. 2021. 'Maggie McPhee: Our History is all Around' https://www.grthm.scot/our-events/2021/week-1/our-history-is-all-around [accessed 1 May 2024]

——. 2021. 'Heartbreak Through Her Eyes' https://www.grthm.scot/our-events/2021/week-4/heartbreak-through-her-eyes-by-maggie-mcphee [accessed 1 May 2024]

Haldane, A. R .B. 1952. *The Drove Roads of Scotland* (London: Thomas Nelson).

Hallowell, A. Irving. 1947. 'Myth, Culture and Personality', *American Anthropologist*, Vol. 49, No. 4, pp. 544–556.

Hartland, Edwin S. 1891. *The Science of Fairy Tales: An Inquiry into Fairy Mythology* (London: Walter Scott).

Harvey, David. 1985. *Consciousness and the Urban Experience* (Oxford: Basil Blackwell).

——. 2014. *Seventeen Contradictions and the End of Capitalism* (London: Profile Books).

Hasse, Donald. 2010. 'Decolonizing Fairy-Tale Studies', *Marvels & Tales*, Vol. 24, Issue 1, pp. 17–38.

Henderson, Hamish. 1981. 'The Tinker', in *A Companion to Scottish Culture*, ed. David Daiches (London: Edward Arnold), pp. 377–378.

——. 1987. 'Introduction', in *A Thorn in the King's Foot: Folktales of the Scottish Travelling People* (Harmondsworth: Penguin), pp. 13–29.

——. 1995. 'Tinkers', in *Man, Myth and Magic*, ed. Richard Cavendish, 21 vols., XV (New York: Marshall Cavendish), pp. 2635–2637.

——. 2004. *Alias MacAlias: Writings on Songs, Folk and Literature*, ed. Alec Finlay, 2nd edn (Edinburgh: Birlinn).

Henderson, Lizanne, and Edward J. Cowan. 2001. *Scottish Fairy Belief: A History* (East Linton: Tuckwell Press).

Henry, Declan. 2022. *Gypsies, Roma and Travellers: A Contemporary Analysis* (St Albans: Critical Publishing).

Higgins, Lizzie. 1974. 'Unlucky people to meet or mention; taboo names; lucky and unlucky omens', Hamish Henderson, Ailie Edmunds Munro (fieldworkers), SA1974.287.A6: SA1974.287.B2 (TAD 38906).
Hobsbawm, Eric. 1983. 'Introduction: Inventing Traditions', in *The Invention of Tradition*, eds. Eric Hobsbawm and Terence Ranger (Cambridge: Cambridge University Press), pp. 1–14.
Holbek, Bengt. 1987. *Interpretation of Fairy Tales: Danish Folklore in a European Perspective*, FF Communications No. 239 (Helsinki: Suomalainen Tiedeakatemia).
Honko, Lauri. 1988. 'Studies on Tradition and Cultural Identity: An Introduction', in *Tradition and Cultural Identity*, ed. Lauri Honko (Turku: The Nordic Institute of Folklore), pp. 7–26.
Hoyland, John. 1816. *A Historical Survey of the Customs, Habits Present State of the Gypsies* (York: [s.n.]).
Hunter, Michael. 2001. 'Introduction', in *The Occult Laboratory: Magic, Science and Second Sight in Late Seventeenth-Century Scotland*, ed. Michael Hunter (Woodbridge: The Boydell Press), pp. 1–32.
Hume, David. 2007 [1748]. *An Enquiry Concerning Human Understanding*, ed. Peter Millican (Oxford: Oxford University Press).
Hutchison, Davy. 1955. 'A woman hawker taken by burkers; body snatchers given a fright', Hamish Henderson (fieldworker), SA1955.155.A6; SA1955.155.B1 (TAD 74614).
Ireland, Thomas. 1829. *West Port Murders: or an Authentic Account of the Atrocious Murders Committed by Burke and his Associates* (Edinburgh: Thomas Ireland).
Jacobs, Joseph. 1893. 'The Folk', *Folklore*, Vol. 4, No. 2, 233–238.
Jacobson-Widding, Anita. 1983. 'Introduction', in *Identity: Personal and Socio-Cultural*, ed. Anita Jacobson-Widding (Stockholm: Almqvist & Wiksell), pp. 13–32.
James, A. G. and Simon Taylor. 2017. *Index of Celtic and Other Elements in W. J. Watson's 'The History of the Celtic Place-names of Scotland'* (Scottish Place-Name Society: https://spns.org.uk/resources/index-celtic-elements) [accessed 20 March 2024].
James, Zoë. 2020. *The Harms of Hate for Gypsies and Travellers: A Critical Hate Studies Perspective* (Cham: Palgrave Macmillan).
———. 2023. 'Criminalizing Gypsies, Roma, and Travellers in the UK', in *The Routledge International Handbook on Decolonizing Justice*, eds. Chris Cunneen et al (Abingdon: Routledge), pp. 103–112.
Jameson, Fredric. 1975. 'Magical Narratives: Romance as Genre', *New Literary History*, Vol. 7, No. 1, pp. 135–163.
———. 1981. *The Political Unconscious: Narrative as a Socially Symbolic Act* (Ithaca: Cornell University Press).
Jindra, Michael. 2003. 'Natural/supernatural Conceptions in Western Cultural Contexts', *Anthropological Forum*, Vol. 13, Issue. 2, pp. 159–166.

Joyce, Patrick Weston. 1910. *The Origin and History of Irish Names of Places*, 3 vols., I (London: Longmans, Green & Co.).
Johnston, James B. 1892. *Place-Names of Scotland* (Edinburgh: David Douglas).
Kamenetsky, Christa. 1992. *The Brothers Grimm and their Critics: Folktales and the Quest for Meaning* (Athens: Ohio University Press).
Kenrick, Donald, and Colin Clark. 1999. *Moving On: The Gypsies and Travellers of Britain* (Hatfield: University of Hertfordshire Press).
Keynes, John Maynard. 1930. *A Treatise on Money*, 2 vols., I (London: Macmillan & Co.).
Kidd, Colin. 2009. 'The Scottish Enlightenment and the Supernatural', in *Fantastical Imaginations: The Supernatural in Scottish History and Culture*, ed. Lizanne Henderson (Edinburgh: John Donald), pp. 91–109.
Kirk, Robert. 1893 [1691]. *The Secret Commonwealth of Elves, Fauns and Fairies: A Study in Folklore and Psychical Research*, ed. Andrew Lang (London: David Nutt).
Kockel, Ullrich. 2008. 'Putting the Folk in Their Place: Tradition, Ecology, and the Public Role of Ethnology', *Anthropological Journal of European Cultures*, Vol. 17, No. 1, pp. 5–23.
Kockel, Ullrich and Mairi McFadyen. 2019. 'On the Carrying Stream into the European Mountain: Roots and Routes of Creative (Scottish) Ethnology', *Anuac*, Vol. 8, No. 2, pp. 189–211.
Kostanski, Laura and Guy Puzey. 2016. 'Trends in Onomastics: An Introduction', in *Names and Naming: People, Places, Perceptions and Power*, eds. Guy Puzey and Laura Kostanski (Bristol: Multilingual Matters), pp. xiii–xxiv.
Lamb, William. 2012. 'The Storyteller, the Scribe, and a Missing Man: Hidden Influences from Printed Sources in the Gaelic Tales of Duncan and Neil MacDonald', *Oral Tradition*, Vol. 27, No. 1, pp. 109–160.
Lang, Andrew. 1885. *Custom and Myth* (New York: Harper & Brothers).
——. 1893. 'Kirk's Secret Commonwealth: Introduction', in *The Secret Commonwealth of Elves, Fauns and Fairies: A Study in Folklore and Psychical Research*, ed. Andrew Lang (London: David Nutt), pp. ix–lxv.
LearnGaelic – 'Ceàrdair' https://learngaelic.scot/dictionary/index.jsp?abairt=ce%C3%A0rdair&slang=both&wholeword=false [accessed 18 March 2024].
Leighton, Alexander. 1861. *The Court of Cacus; or, the Story of Burke and Hare* (London: Houlston and Wright).
Leitch, Roger. 1988. 'Introduction', in *The Book of Sandy Stewart*, ed. Roger Leitch (Edinburgh: Scottish Academic Press), pp. xi–xxxiii.
Lüthi, Max. 1982. *The European Folktale: Form and Nature*, trans. J. Niles (Philadelphia: Institute for the Study of Human Issues).
MacColl, Ewan and Peggy Seeger. 1986. *Till Doomsday in the Afternoon: The Folklore of a Family of Scots Travellers, the Stewarts of Blairgowrie* (Manchester: Manchester University Press).
MacDonald, Norman. 1953. 'Origin of the saying: Thoir bò gu ruige taigh mòr is iarraidh i don bhàthaich', Calum Iain Maclean (fieldworker), SA1953.23. B1 (TAD 8571).

MacGregor, Alexander M. 1886. *Gaelic Topography of Balquhidder Parish as Given in The Ordnance Survey Maps* (Edinburgh: [s.n.]).
Mackay, G. A. 1917. 'The Tinker Problem', in *The Scotsman*, 4 April, p. 10.
Mackenzie, Alexander. 1878. *Historical Tales and Legends of the Highlands* (Inverness: A & W Mackenzie).
Mackenzie, William Cook. 1931. *Scottish Place-Names* (London: Kegan Paul, Trench, Trubner & Co.).
MacKillop, James. 1990. *Dictionary of Celtic Mythology* (Oxford: Oxford University Press).
MacLaughlin, Jim. 1995. *Travellers and Ireland: Whose Country, Whose History?* (Cork: Cork University Press).
Macritchie, David. 1894. *Scottish Gypsies Under the Stewarts* (Edinburgh: David Douglas).
M'Ara, Duncan. 1792. 'Account of Fortingal, County of Perth', in *The Statistical Accounts of Scotland*, Vol. II, p. 455.
Marcus, Geetha. 2015. 'Marginalisation and the Voices of Gypsy/Traveller Girls', *Cambridge Open-Review Educational Research e-Journal*, Vol. 2, pp. 55–77.
——. 2019. *Gypsy and Traveller Girls: Silence, Agency and Power* (Cham: Palgrave Macmillan).
——. 2023. 'Talking of Silence: Young Scottish Gypsy/Traveller Women in Scotland', in *Living Legacies of Social Injustice: Power, Time and Social Change*, eds. Chis Beasley and Pam Papadelos (Abingdon: Routledge), pp. 93–115.
Martin, Martin. 1716. *A Description of the Western Islands of Scotland*, 2nd edn (London: A. Bell).
Martin, Neill. 2013. 'Custom, Belief and Folk Drama', in *An Introduction to Scottish Ethnology: A Compendium of Scottish Ethnology*, eds. Alexander Fenton and Margaret A. Mackay, 14 vols., I (Edinburgh: Birlinn), pp. 614–688.
Masoni, Licia. 2013. 'Folk Narrative', in *An Introduction to Scottish Ethnology: A Compendium of Scottish Ethnology*, eds. Alexander Fenton and Margaret A. Mackay, 14 vols., I (Edinburgh: Birlinn), pp. 430–483.
Massey, Doreen. 1994. *Space, Place, and Gender* (Minneapolis: University of Minnesota Press).
Matthews, Jodie. 2012. *Romanies/Gypsies, Roma & Irish and Scottish Travellers Histories, Perceptions and Representations* (Connected Communities) https://ahrc.ukri.org/documents/project-reports-and-reviews/connected-communities/romanies-gypsies-roma-irish-and-scottish-travellers/ [accessed 18 March 2024].
McCormick, Andrew. 1907. *The Tinkler-Gypsies* (Edinburgh: John Menzies & Co.).
McDermitt, Barbara. 1980. 'Duncan Williamson', *Tocher*, No. 33, pp. 141–148.
McCracken-Flesher, Caroline. 2012. *The Doctor Dissected: A Cultural Autopsy of the Burke and Hare Murders* (Oxford: Oxford University Press).
McGregor, [forename unavailable]. 1845. Account of Balquhidder, County of Perth, in *The Statistical Accounts of Scotland*, Vol. X, p. 344.
McKean, Thomas A. 2015. 'Stories Beyond the Text: Contextualizing Narratives and "The Jolly Beggar"', *Narrative Culture*, Vol. 2, No. 2, pp. 208–226.

McKinney, Rebecca. 2003. 'Views from the Margins: Gypsy/Travellers and the Ethnicity Debate in the New Scotland', *Scottish Affairs*, No. 42, pp. 13–31.
McLeod, Wilson. 2020. *Gaelic in Scotland: Policies, Movements, Ideologies* (Edinburgh: Edinburgh University Press).
McPhee, Shamus. 2008. *The Forgotten Experiment*, dir. Philippa Brady et al https://youtu.be/yF8z1zV8USo [accessed 18 March 2024].
——. 2021. 'Interview with the Author'.
——. 2021a. 'Correspondence with the Author'.
——. 2021b. 'The Uglier Side of Bonnie Scotland: The Tinker Housing Experiments', *International Journal of Roma Studies*, Vol. 3, No. 2, pp. 180–208.
McGuire, Michael. 1990. 'The Rhetoric of Narrative: A Hermeneutic, Critical Theory', in *Narrative Thought and Narrative Language*, eds. Bruce K. Britton and A.D. Pellegrini, (New Jersey: Lawrence Erlbaum), pp. 219–236.
McKean, Thomas A. 2015. 'Stories Beyond the Text: Contextualizing Narratives and "The Jolly Beggar"', *Narrative Culture*, Vol. 2, No. 2, pp. 208–226.
Mechling, Jay. 2006. 'Solo Folklore', *Western Folklore*, Vol. 65, No. 4, pp. 435–453.
Meek, Donald E. 1998. 'Place-names and Literature: Evidence from the Gaelic Ballads', in *The Uses of Place-Names*, ed. Simon Taylor (Edinburgh: Scottish Cultural Press), pp. 147–168.
Meek, Ronald L. 1976. *Social Science and the Ignoble Savage* (Cambridge: Cambridge University Press).
Miller, Hugh. 1835. *Scenes and Legends of the North of Scotland, or The Traditional History of Cromarty* (Edinburgh: Adam & Charles Black).
Milne, John. 1912. *Celtic Place-Names in Aberdeenshire* (Edinburgh: David Douglas).
Mises, Ludwig von. 1981 [1934]. *The Theory of Money and Credit*, trans. H. E. Baston (Indianapolis: Liberty Fund).
Mitchell, William. 1885. *Rescue the Children, or Twelve Years' Dealing with Neglected Girls and Boys* (London: Wm. Ibister).
Moore, Dafydd. 2017. 'Introduction', in *The International Companion to James Macpherson and the Poems of Ossian*, ed. Dafydd Moore (Glasgow: Scottish Literature International), pp. 1–13.
Morris, Michael W. et al. 1999. 'Views from Inside and Outside: Integrating Emic and Etic Insights about Culture and Justice Judgement', *Academy of Management Review*, Vol. 24, No. 4, pp. 781–796.
Murray, Andrew. 1791. 'Account of Auchterderran, County of Fife', in *The Statistical Accounts of Scotland*, Vol. I, p. 458.
Murray, Kevin. 2017. *The Early Finn Cycle* (Dublin: Four Courts Press).
National Records of Scotland. 2014. 'Statistical Bulletin: 2011 Census: Key Results from Releases 2A to 2D' https://www.scotlandscensus.gov.uk/media/p4ac0tiv/statsbulletin2.pdf [accessed 12 June 2024].
Neat, Timothy. 1996. *The Summer Walkers: Travelling People and Pearl-Fishers in the Highlands of Scotland* (Edinburgh: Birlinn).
——. 2007. *Hamish Henderson: A Biography*, 2 vols., I (Edinburgh: Birlinn).

Nicolaisen, Wilhelm F. H. 1992. 'The Onomastic Legacy of Gaelic in Scotland', *Proceedings of the Harvard Celtic Colloquium*, Vol. 12, pp. 1–15.

——. 2001. *Scottish Place-Names* (Edinburgh: John Donald).

Nicolson, Alexander. 1882. *A Collection of Gaelic Proverbs and Familiar Phrases*, ed. Alexander Nicolson, 2nd edn (Edinburgh: MacLachlan and Stewart).

Ní Fhloinn, Bairbre. 1999. 'Tadhg, Donncha and Some of their Relations: Seals in Irish Oral Tradition', in *Islanders and Water-Dwellers: Proceedings of the Celtic-Nordic-Baltic Folklore Symposium held at University College Dublin, 16-19 June 1996*, eds. Patricia Lysaght et al (Dublin: DBA Publications Ltd.), pp. 223–245.

——. 2015. 'On the Edge: Portrayals of Travellers and Others in Irish Popular Tradition', *Béaloideas*, Vol. 83, pp. 128–157.

Niles, John D. 1999. *Homo Narrans: The Poetics and Anthropology of Oral Literature* (Philadelphia: University of Pennsylvania Press).

——. 2022. *Webspinner: Songs, Stories, and Reflections of Duncan Williamson, Scottish Traveller* (Jackson: University Press of Mississippi).

Ó hAodha, Mícheál. 2011. *'Insubordinate Irish': Travellers in the Text* (Manchester: Manchester University Press).

Okely, Judith. 1983. *The Traveller-Gypsies* (Cambridge: Cambridge University Press).

——. 2014. 'Recycled (mis)representations: Gypsies, Travellers or Roma Treated as Objects, Rarely Subjects', *People, Place and Policy*, Vol. 8, No. 1, pp. 65–85.

Olrik, Axel. 1992. *Principles for Oral Narrative Research*, trans. K. Wolf and J. Jensen (Bloomington: Indiana University Press).

Onega, Susana and José Ángel García Landa. 1996. 'Introduction', in *Narratology: An Introduction*, eds. Susana Onega and José Ángel Garcia Landa (London: Longman Group), pp. 1–35.

Oxford English Dictionary, 'Tinker', Entry No. 202260.

Palmer, Philip M. and Robert Pattison More. 1936. *The Sources of the Faust Tradition: From Simon Magus to Lessing* (Philadelphia: University of Pennsylvania Press).

Perrault, Charles. 1791 [1697]. *Histories or Tales of Past Times, told by Mother Goose*, trans. G. M. Gent (Salisbury: B. C. Collins).

Polleit, Thorsten. 2011. 'Fiat Money and Collective Corruption', *The Quarterly Journal of Austrian Economics*, Vol. 14, No. 4, pp. 397–415.

Ramanujan, A.K. 1982. 'Hanchi: A Kannada Cinderella', in *Cinderella: A Folklore Casebook*, ed. Alan Dundes (New York: Garland Publishing), pp. 259–275.

Raverty, Thomas. 2003. 'Starting with the supernatural: Implications for method, comparison, and communication in religious anthropology and inter-religious dialogue', *Anthropological Forum*, Vol. 13, No. 2, pp. 187–194.

Records of the Parliament of Scotland to 1707. 1575. A1575/3/5 http://www.rps.ac.uk/trans/A1575/3/5 [accessed 12 June 2024].

Rehfisch, A. and F. Rehfisch. 1975. 'Scottish Travellers or Tinkers', in *Gypsies, Tinkers and other Travellers*, ed. Farnham Rehfisch (London: Academic Press.), pp. 271–283.

Reid, Willie. 1997. 'Scottish Gypsies/Travellers and the Folklorists', in *Romani Culture and Gypsy Identity*, eds. Thomas Acton and Gary Mundy (Hatfield: University of Hertfordshire Press), pp. 31–39.

Reith, Sara. 2008. 'Representing Traveller Identity from Within: Negotiating Diversity and Belonging in Scotland', *The International Journal of Diversity in Organisations, Communities and Nations*, Vol. 7, No. 6, pp. 99–110.

——. 2008a. 'Through the "Eye of the Skull": Memory and Tradition in a Travelling Landscape', *Cultural Analysis*, No. 7, 77–106.

Richards, Eric. 1993. 'Margins of the Industrial Revolution', in *The Industrial Revolution and British Society*, eds. Patrick O'Brien and Ronald Quinault (Cambridge: Cambridge University Press), pp. 203–228.

Richardson, Ruth. 1987. *Death, Dissection and the Destitute* (London: Routledge & Kegan Paul).

Robertson, James A. 1869. *The Gaelic Topography of Scotland, and What it Proves, Explained; with Historical, Antiquarian and Descriptive Information* (Edinburgh: William P. Nimmo).

Robertson, Janet. 1981. 'Travellers' love of nature, expressed in poems and spirituality; family solidarity', Barbara McDermitt (fieldworker), SA1981.85 (TAD 49824).

Robertson, Jeannie. 1954. 'Cant words for groups of people', Hamish Henderson (fieldworker), SA1954.94.B13 (TAD 10285).

——. 1954a. 'Names and reputations of Traveller families', Hamish Henderson (fieldworker), SA1954.94.B5-B7 (TAD 10279).

——. 1957. *Personal Correspondence* (Edinburgh: Edinburgh University Centre for Research Collections E89.92).

——. 1964. *Personal Correspondence* (Edinburgh: Edinburgh University Centre for Research Collections E89.92).

Robertson, Stanley. 1978. 'A man makes a pact with the Devil to surrender his soul', Alan J. Bruford (fieldworker), SA1978.12.A1-A4 (TAD 44606).

——. 1978a. 'Stanley Robertson on descriptive detail in storytelling', Alan J. Bruford (fieldworker), SA1978.12.A8-A10 (TAD 44613).

——. 1978b. 'A dead warlock possesses the body of a Traveller', Alan J. Bruford (fieldworker), SA1978.13.B2 (TAD 44812).

——. 1979. 'Storytelling as a family activity', Barbara McDermitt (fieldworker), SA1979.29.B3 (TAD 65165).

——. 1979a. 'Stanley Robertson's experience of prejudice against Travellers, summer travelling and storytelling', Alan J. Bruford (fieldworker), SA1988.006 (TAD 85439).

——. 1979b. 'The decline of Traveller traditions through intermarriage; Stanley Robertson's passing on of tradition', Barbara McDermitt (fieldworker), SA1979.133.A2 (TAD 67492).

——. 1979c. 'Reading cards; the Tarot; Traveller and Mormon beliefs', Barbara McDermitt (fieldworker), SA1979.31.A4 (TAD 65426).

——. 1979d. 'Stanley Robertson's experiences of guardian angels', Barbara McDermitt (fieldworker), SA1979.31.A3b (TAD 65425).

——. 1979e. 'Stanley Robertson's Traveller traditions in conflict with his Mormon beliefs', Barbara McDermitt, David Clement (fieldworkers), SA1979.22.B5 (TAD 64651).
——. 1979f. 'Fortune-telling; the black arts; Mormon beliefs about spirit', Barbara McDermitt (fieldworker), SA1979.23.B4 (TAD 64940).
——.1979g. 'A man sold his soul to the Devil', Barbara McDermitt (fieldworker), SA1979.20.A3 (TAD 64353).
——. 1979h. 'A song in Cant warns a Traveller not to drink drugged tea given by people in league with Burkers', Barbara McDermitt (fieldworker), SA1979.30.A2 (TAD 65216).
——. 1979i. 'How Rosehearty got its name: a lad rose hearty after helping a ghost to find rest', Barbara McDermitt (fieldworker), SA1979.21.B5 (TAD 64475).
——. 1980. 'A man is given a protective parchment but can never find out what is written there; comments on inventive storytelling', Barbara McDermitt (fieldworker), SA1980.56.3 (TAD 38319).
——. 1980a. 'The Devil, who lives inside Bennachie, makes a wager with a young man and the young man wins', Barbara McDermitt (fieldworker), SA1980.52.1 (TAD 38124).
——. 1980b. 'A Traveller couple's abandoned child grows up to be a judge', Barbara McDermitt (fieldworker), SA1980.52.4 (TAD 38131).
——. 1981. 'William Robertson liked hawking, travelling was in his blood, and he never mixed with townspeople', Barbara McDermitt (fieldworker), SA1981.25.6 (TAD 42990).
——. 1982. 'The place of stories in Stanley Robertson's upbringing', Barbara McDermitt (fieldworker), SA1982.28.1a (TAD 50189).
——. 1988. 'Travellers' fear of burkers; stories of escapes from burkers and other kidnappers', Alan J. Bruford (fieldworker), SA1988.011 (TAD 85577).
——. 1989. *Nyakim's Windows* (Nairn: Balnain Books).
——. 2009. *Reek Roon a Camp Fire: A Collection of Ancient Tales* (Edinburgh: Birlinn).
Röhrich, Lutz. 1991. 'The Quest of Meaning in Folk Narrative Research', in *The Brothers Grimm and Folktale*, ed. James M. McGlathery et al (Urbana: University of Illinois Press), pp. 1–15.
Rooth, Anna B. 1951. *The Cinderella Cycle* (Lund: Gleerup).
Roughneen, Dualta. 2010. *The Right to Roam: Travellers and Human Rights in the Modern Nation-State* (Newcastle upon Tyne: Cambridge Scholars Publishing).
Rosner, Lisa. 2010. *The Anatomy Murders: Being the True and Spectacular History of Edinburgh's Notorious Burke and Hare, and of the Man of Science who Abetted Them in the Commission of Their Most Heinous Crimes* (Philadelphia: University of Pennsylvania Press).
Schacker, Jennifer. 2011. 'Fluid Identities: Madame d'Aulnoy, Mother Bunch, and Fairy-Tale History', in *The Individual and Tradition: Folkloristic Perspectives*, ed. Ray Cashman et al (Bloomington: Indiana University Press), pp. 249–263.
Schlichter, Detlev S. 2014. *Paper Money Collapse: The Folly of Elastic Money*, 2nd edn (New Jersey: John Wiley & Sons).

Schmiesing, Ann. 2014. *Disability, Deformity, and Disease in the Grimms' Fairy Tales* (Detroit: Wayne State University Press).

Scott, Walter. 1805. 'Report of the Highland Society Upon Ossian', *The Edinburgh Review*, Vol. 6, pp. 429–462.

———. 1830. *Letters on Demonology and Witchcraft, Addressed to J.G Lockhart, Esq.* (London: John Murray).

Scottish Executive. 2001. 'Inquiry into Gypsy Travellers and Public Sector Policies', *Equal Opportunities Committee* http://archive.scottish.parliament.uk/business/committees/historic/equal/reports-01/eor01-01-vol01-02.htm [accessed 12 June 2024].

———. 2017. '30th Meeting, 2017 (Session 5)', *Equalities and Human Rights Committee Meeting* http://www.parliament.scot/S5_Equal_Opps/Meeting%20Papers/20171207papers.pdf [accessed 12 June 2024].

Scottish Government. 2000. 'The Information Base', *Advisory Committee on Scotland's Travelling People: Final Report* https://webarchive.nrscotland.gov.uk/20190118092154/http://www2.gov.scot/Publications/2007/05/22093426/0 [accessed 20 March 2024].

———. 2015. 'Gypsy/Travellers in Scotland: A Comprehensive Analysis of the 2011 Census' https://www.gov.scot/publications/gypsy-travellers-scotland-comprehensive-analysis-2011-census/ [accessed 18 March 2024].

———. 2018–2023. *Ministerial Working Group on Gypsy/Travellers* https://www.gov.scot/groups/ministerial-working-group-on-gypsy-travellers/ [accessed 12 June 2024].

Seifert, Lewis C. 2011. 'Animal-Human Hybridity in d'Aulnoy's "Babiole" and "Prince Wild Boar"', *Marvels & Tales*, Vol. 25, No. 2, pp. 244–260.

Shaw, Martin. 2006. *Narrating Gypsies, Telling Travellers: A Study of the Relational Self in Four Life Stories* (Unpublished PhD thesis, Umeå Universitet).

Shaw, William. 1781. *An Enquiry into the Authenticity of the Poems Ascribed to Ossian* (London: J. Murray).

Shils, Edward. 1971. 'Tradition', *Comparative Studies in Society and History*, Vol. 13, No. 2, 122–159.

Smith, Christian. 2003. *Moral, Believing Animals: Human Personhood and Culture* (Oxford: Oxford University Press).

Smith, Donald. 2001. *Storytelling Scotland: A Nation in Narrative* (Edinburgh: Polygon).

Smith, Jess. 2002. *Jessie's Journey: Autobiography of a Traveller Girl* (Edinburgh: Mercat Press).

Smith, Joseph. 1981. *The Book of Mormon: An Account Written by the Hand of Mormon upon Plates Taken from the Plates of Nephi*, trans. Joseph Smith (Salt Lake City: Church of Jesus Christ of Latter-day Saints).

Smout, Thomas C. 1998. *A History of the Scottish People: 1560–1830* (London: Fontana).

Simson, James. 1865. 'Editor's Introduction', in *A History of the Gipsies: With Specimens of the Gipsy Language*, ed. James Simson (London: Samson Low, Marston & Co.).

Simson, Walter. 1865. *A History of the Gipsies: With Specimens of the Gipsy Language*, ed. James Simson (London: Samson Low, Marston & Co.).
Smith, Laurajane. 2006. *Uses of Heritage* (London: Routledge).
Spicer, Edward H. 1971. 'Persistent Cultural Systems: A Comparative Study of Identity Systems That Can Adapt to Contrasting Environments', *Science: New Series*, Vol. 174, No. 4011, pp. 795–800.
Stafford, Fiona J. 1988. *The Sublime Savage: A Study of James Macpherson and the Poems of Ossian* (Edinburgh: Edinburgh University Press).
Stewart, Alec. 1957. 'Discussion about Traveller family origins', Hamish Henderson (fieldworker), SA1957.49.B5 (TAD 35360).
Stewart, Andrew. 1955. 'Story of Geordie MacPhee's treasure: found and quickly spent', Hamish Henderson (fieldworker), SA1955.149.B2 (TAD 13847).
———. 1955a. 'A baker accepts three pieces of good advice instead of pay and is rewarded with riches', Hamish Henderson (fieldworker), SA1955.150.B5 (TAD 31634).
Stewart, Belle. 1972. 'Traveller handicrafts', James Porter (fieldworker), SA1972.234. B4 (TAD 100320).
———. 1978. 'The start of a Burker story and discussion of Burkers', Sheila Douglas (fieldworker), SA1978.160 (TAD 55956).
Stewart, Charles. 2016. 'Historicity and Anthropology', *Annual Review of Anthropology*, Vol. 45, pp. 79–94.
Stewart, Duncan. 1793. Account of Balquhidder, County of Perth, in *The Statistical Accounts of Scotland*, Vol. VI, p.88.
Stewart, Geordie. 1954. 'A boy sings a song to warn Travellers', Hamish Henderson (fieldworker), SA1954.101 (TAD 3817).
———. 1983. 'Discussion on storytelling', Hamish Henderson (fieldworker), SA1983.157 (TAD 81408).
Stewart, John (Jock). 1955. 'Travellers have a narrow escape from Burkers', Maurice Fleming (fieldworker), SA1955.17.A2 (TAD 11474).
Stewart, John. 1978. 'The Scottish Traveller outlook on life; some terms and idioms', Sheila Douglas (fieldworker), SA1978.167 (TAD 56424).
———. 1978a. 'Travellers' ways of affirming the truth; the distinctiveness and envi-ableness of Scottish Travellers', Barbara McDermitt (fieldworker), SA1978.131 (TAD 65889).
———. 1979. 'Storytelling around Travellers' campfires; the travelling way of life', Peter Cooke, Barbara McDermitt (fieldworkers), SA1979.33 (TAD 65775).
———. 1979a. 'Two family accounts of Travellers being attacked by burkers', Sheila Douglas (fieldworker), SA1979.167 (TAD 75777).
Stewart, Maggie. 1954. 'A fellow Traveller on a lonely road mistaken for a burker', Hamish Henderson (fieldworker), SA1954.93.B7 (TAD 10224).
Stewart, Sheila. 2002. 'Cant: A Scottish Traveller's Perspective', in *Travellers and Their Language*, eds. John M. Kirk and Dónall P. Ó Baoill (Belfast: Cló Ollscoil na Banríona), pp. 188–191.
———. 2008. *Pilgrims of the Mist: The Stories of Scotland's Travelling People* (Edinburgh: Birlinn).

Stone-Mediatore, Shari. 2003. *Reading across Borders: Storytelling and Knowledges of Resistance* (New York: Palgrave MacMillan).

Straparola, Giovanni Francesco. 1894 [1551–1553]. *The Nights of Straparola*, trans. W. G. Waters, 2 vols., I (London: Lawrence and Bullen).

Talmont-Kaminski, Konrad. 2014. *Religion as Magical Ideology: How the Supernatural Reflects Rationality* (Abingdon: Routledge).

Taylor, Becky. 2008. *A Minority and the State: Travellers in Britain in the Twentieth Century* (Manchester: Manchester University Press).

——. 2014. *Another Darkness, Another Dawn: A History of Gypsies, Roma and Travellers* (London: Reaktion Books).

——. 2023. 'Intermittent Citizens: Scotland's Travellers, Welfare, and the Shifting Boundary of State and Voluntary Action in the Early Twentieth Century', *Journal of British Studies*, Vol. 62, No. 3, pp. 640–661.

Taylor, Becky and Jim Hinks. 2021. 'What field? Where? Bringing Gypsy, Roma and Traveller History into View', *Cultural and Social History*, Vol.18, No. 5, pp. 629–650.

Taylor, Iain. 2003. *Gaelic Place-names A-B: A'Chleit (Argyll), A' Chleit* (Edinburgh: The Scottish Parliament https://archive2021.parliament.scot/Gaelic/placenamesA-B.pdf [accessed 20 March 2024].

Tammi, Lynne. 2020. 'Across the Great Divide: The Impact of Digital Inequality on Scotland's Gypsy/Traveller Children and Young People during the COVID-19 Emergency', *International Journal of Roma Studies*, Vol. 2, No. 2, pp. 52–65.

Telegraph. 2009. 'Stanley Robertson' https://www.telegraph.co.uk/news/obituaries/culture-obituaries/music-obituaries/6068547/Stanley-Robertson.html [accessed 18 March 2024].

Teverson, Andrew. 2013. *Fairy Tale* (Abingdon: Routledge).

——. 2019. 'Introduction', in *The Fairy Tale World*, ed. Andrew Teverson (London: Routledge), pp. 1–14.

Thompson, Stith. 1946. *The Folktale* (Berkeley: University of California Press).

——. 1955. *Motif-index of Folk-literature: A Classification of Narrative Elements in Folktales, Ballads, Myths, Fables, Mediaeval Romances, Exempla, Fabliaux, Jest-books and Local Legends*, 6 vols., IV (Copenhagen: Rosenkilde and Bagger).

Thoms, William J. 1846. 'Folk-Lore', *The Athenaeum*, Vol. 2, No. 982, pp. 862–863.

Thomson, James. 1719. *The Last Speech and Dying Words of James Thomson Tincklar* (National Library of Scotland: Project Reference 15771).

Todorov, Tzvetan. 1969. 'Structural Analysis of Narrative', trans. A. Weinstein, *NOVEL: A Forum on Fiction*, Vol. 3, No. 1, pp. 70–76.

Tröger, Anja. 2021. *Affective Spaces: Migration in Scandinavian and German Transnational Narratives* (Cambridge: Legenda).

Turner, Victor, et al. 1969. *The Ritual Process: Structure and Anti-Structure* (New York: Routledge).

Tylor, Edward B. 1881. 'Kamilaroi and Kurnai', *The Academy*, Vol. 19, No. 466, pp. 264–266.
uí Ógáin, Ríonach. 1995. *Immortal Dan: Daniel O'Connell in Irish folk Tradition* (Dublin: Geography Publications).
United Kingdom Parliament *Economic Affairs Committee*. 2021. 'Quantitative easing: A Dangerous Addiction?' https://committees.parliament.uk/publications/6725/documents/71894/default/ [accessed 8 May 2024]
United Nations Educational, Scientific and Cultural Organisation. 2011. *List of Intangible Cultural Heritage in Need of Urgent Safeguarding*, 'Hezhen Yimakan storytelling', 6.COM 8.6 https://ich.unesco.org/en/USL/hezhen-yimakan-storytelling-00530 [accessed 8 May 2024]
———. 2022. *Basic Texts of the 2003 Convention for the Safeguarding of the Intangible Cultural Heritage* https://ich.unesco.org/doc/src/2003_Convention_Basic_Texts-_2022_version-EN_.pdf [accessed 8 May 2024]
Uther, Hans-Jörg. 2004. *The Types of International Folktales: A Classification and Bibliography*, 3 vols., I and II (Helsinki: Suomalainen Tiedeakatemia).
Valk, Ülo and Daniel Sävborg. 2018. 'Place-Lore, Liminal Storyworld and Ontology of the Supernatural: An Introduction', in *Storied and Supernatural Places: Studies in Spatial and Social Dimensions of Folklore and Sagas*, eds. Ülo Valk and Daniel Sävborg (Helsinki: Finnish Literature Society), pp. 7–24.
Walker, Barbara. 1995. 'Introduction', in *Out of the Ordinary: Folklore and the Supernatural*, ed. Barbara Walker (Logan: Utah University Press), pp. 1–7.
Warner, Marina. 2014. *Once Upon a Time: A Short History of Fairy Tale* (Oxford: Oxford University Press).
Watson, Angus. 2002. *Place-names, Land and Lordship in the Medieval Earldom of Strathearn* (Unpublished PhD Thesis: University of St Andrews).
Watson, William J. 1926. *The History of the Celtic Place-names of Scotland* (Edinburgh: William Blackwood & Sons).
West, Gary. 2012. *Voicing Scotland: Culture and Tradition in a Modern Nation* (Edinburgh: Luath Press).
Weitz, Morris. 1965. *Hamlet and the Philosophy of Literary Criticism* (London: Faber).
Whyte, Betsy. 1973. 'Travellers used cant words when people in authority were about', Peter Cooke, Linda Williamson (fieldworkers), SA1973.161 (TAD 76578).
———. 1975. 'The Traveller way of life has changed, but they still don't like to work for a boss', Peter Cooke, Linda Williamson (fieldworkers), SA1975.10 (TAD 76669).
———. 1975a. 'The lingering fear of Burkers amongst Travellers and horror of doctors', Rosalind McAskill, Linda Williamson, Alison McMorland (fieldworkers), SA1975.150 (TAD 77229).
———. 1976. 'The contributor's schooldays and the persecution she experienced as a Traveller child', Linda Williamson (fieldworker), SA1976.150.A4; SA1976.150.B1 (TAD 39610).

―――. 1976a. 'Discussion of role of henwives in Traveller stories; Traveller superstitions and beliefs about red hair and Jesus', Linda Williamson (fieldworker), SA1976.81.B2 (TAD 36470).

―――. 1976b. 'A tree produced money, but only until the secret was told', Linda Williamson (fieldworker), SA1976.109.B4 (TAD 76412).

―――. 1976c. 'A girl who was ill-treated by her stepmother and ugly stepsisters married a prince in the end', Linda Williamson (fieldworker), SA1976.80.A2; SA1976.80.B1 (TAD 36559).

―――. 1978. 'The impact on Betsy Whyte of her relationship with the SSS', Peter Cooke (fieldworker), SA1978.122 (TAD 64239).

―――. 1978a. 'Betsy Whyte talks about storytelling, story transmission, and the need to be relaxed with the audience', Alan J. Bruford, Peter Cooke (fieldworkers), SA1978.126 (TAD 67341).

―――. 1979. 'A Traveller girl saw a farm's broonie', Barbara McDermitt, SA1979.1 (TAD 63443).

―――. 1979a. *The Yellow on the Broom: The Early Days of a Traveller Woman* (Edinburgh: W. & R. Chambers).

―――. 1985. 'Betsy Whyte answers questions about the Traveller lifestyle and traditional cures', Alan J. Bruford (fieldworker), SA1985.120 (TAD 82053).

―――. 1986. 'The role of stories and storytelling in the Traveller community' (TAD 82457).

Whyte, Bryce. 1975. 'The Traveller way of life has changed, but they still don't like to work for a boss', Peter Cooke, Linda Williamson (fieldworkers), SA1975.10 (TAD 76669).

Whyte, Ian D. 2013. *Scotland Before the Industrial Revolution: An Economic and Social History c.1050 – c.1750* (Oxon: Routledge).

Williamson, Duncan. 1976. 'A rich American brings Travellers as his guests to a hotel that turned them away', Linda Williamson (fieldworker), SA1976.40.A3 (TAD 36850).

―――. 1976a. 'Duncan Williamson heard many stories from Johnnie MacDonald, a Traveller who walked with crutches, and was a great storyteller', Linda Williamson (fieldworker), SA1976.71.A2 (TAD 30610).

―――. 1976b. 'A wicked fairy made a baby into a hedgehurst (half human, half hedgehog)', Linda Williamson (fieldworker), SA1976.83.A2 and B1 (TAD 36536).

―――. 1976c. 'Henwives often feature in Travellers' stories', Linda Williamson (fieldworker), SA1976.71.B2 (TAD 30617).

―――. 1976d. 'Discussion of role of henwives in Traveller stories; Traveller superstitions and beliefs about red hair and Jesus', Linda Williamson (fieldworker), SA1976.81.B2 (TAD 36470).

―――. 1977. 'A poor Traveller family found a lucky magic pot, which brought them dinner and enough money to keep them in comfort', Linda Williamson (fieldworker), SA1977.203.A5; SA1977.203.B1 (TAD 33627).

―――. 1979. 'Duncan Williamson can trace his ancestors back two hundred and fifty years, though Traveller births were not registered', Barbara McDermitt (fieldworker), SA1979.14 (TAD 65494).

——. 1979a. 'The Hawker's Lament', Peter Cooke (fieldworker), SA1979.19.8 (TAD 68649).
——. 1980. 'Duncan Williamson', *Tocher*, No. 33, pp. 141–148.
——. 1983. *Fireside Tales of the Traveller Children* (Edinburgh: Canongate).
——. 1985. *The Broonie, Silkies and Fairies: Travellers' Tales* (Edinburgh: Canongate).
——. 1987. 'Mary Rashiecoats an the Wee Black Bull', in *A Thorn in the King's Foot: Folktales of the Scottish Travelling People* (Harmondsworth: Penguin), pp. 62–77.
——. 1987. 'Notes on the Narrations', in *A Thorn in the King's Foot: Folktales of the Scottish Travelling People* (Harmondsworth: Penguin), pp. 148–153.
——. 1989. 'The Travellers' Cinderella', in *The Cinderella Story*, ed. Neil Philip (London: Penguin), pp. 161–174.
——. 1994. *The Horsieman: Memories of a Traveller 1928–58* (Edinburgh: Canongate).
Williamson, Linda. 1983. 'Notes on the Narrations', in *Fireside Tales of the Traveller Children* (Edinburgh: Canongate), pp. 148–153.
Wright, Thomas. 1845. 'Account of Borthwick, County of Edinburgh', in *The Statistical Accounts of Scotland*, Vol. I, p. 185.
Yamasaki, Ryo. 2020. 'Nomadic Storytellers: Scottish Traveller Self-Representation in Stanley Robertson's *Exodus to Alford*', *Bulletin of the National Museum of Ethnology*, Vol. 44, No. 3, pp. 535–556.
Ziolkowski, Jan M. 2009. *Fairy Tales from Before Fairy Tales: The Medieval Latin Past of Wonderful Lies* (Ann Arbor: University of Michigan Press).
——. 2010. 'Straparola and the Fairy Tale: Between Literary and Oral Traditions', *The Journal of American Folklore*, Vol. 123, No. 490, pp. 377–397.
Zipes, Jack. 1975. 'Breaking the Magic Spell: Politics and the Fairy Tale', *New German Critique*, No. 6, pp. 116–135.
——. 1984. 'Folklore Research and Western Marxism: A Critical Replay', *The Journal of American Folklore*, Vol. 97, No. 385, pp. 329–337.
——. 1991. 'Dreams of a Better Bourgeois Life: The Psychosocial Origins of the Grimms' Tales', in *The Brothers Grimm and Folktale*, ed. James M. McGlathery et al (Urbana: University of Illinois Press), pp. 205–219.
——. 1997. *Happily Ever After: Fairy Tales, Children, and the Culture Industry* (New York: Routledge).
——. 2002. *The Brothers Grimm: From Enchanted Forests to the Modern World* (New York: Palgrave MacMillan).
——. 2006. 'Critical Reflections about Hans Christian Andersen, the Failed Revolutionary', *Marvels & Tales*, Vol. 20, No. 2, pp. 224–237.
——. 2014. *Grimm Legacies: The Magic Spell of the Grimms' Folk and Fairy Tales* (Princeton: Princeton University Press).

Index

Aarne-Thompson-Uther (ATU) tale-type taxonomy, 30, 48, 86, 99, 100, 107, 120n, 147, 167
ATU 313 – *The Magic Flight*, 89
ATU 327A – *Hansel and Gretel*, 100–1, 106
ATU 441 – *Hans My Hedgehog*, 107–14, 115–17, 118, 163, 191
ATU 510A – *Cinderella*, 86, 88, 92
ATU 510B – *Peau d' Asne*, 86, 88, 89, 92
ATU 511 – *One-Eye, Two-Eyes, Three-Eyes*, 86–7, 88–9, 92, 98n
ATU 591 – *The Thieving Pot*, 49, 147, 159
ATU 850 – *The Birthmarks of the Princess*, 100, 106
ATU 1187 – *Meleager*, 97
ATU 1419H – *Woman Warns Lover of Husband by Singing Song*, 141
Andersen, Hans Christian, 162–3
Aubrey, John, 147
authorised heritage discourse (AHD), 29

Bakhtin, Mikhail, 179, 183, 185, 186
Balquhidder (Stirlingshire), 171–4, 175–6

Bauman, Richard, 33, 38–9
Beurla Reagaird, 14n
Boccaccio, Giovanni (*Decameron*), 130
Braid, Donald, 9, 11–12, 32, 52–5, 62, 77, 80, 89–90, 92, 119, 123, 167, 183, 189, 193
Bronner, Simon, 31, 32, 47, 51, 56n, 64
Bruford, Alan, 41, 92, 145n, 169
Burke and Hare, 4, 125, 127
Burke, Edmund, 144n
Burke, Mary, 18, 19
Burke, William, 121–2, 124, 125, 126, 127, 133, 137–8, 144, 192; *see also* Burke and Hare
Burkers, 49, 121–4, 125–9, 131–144, 150, 165, 192–3; *see also* 'Burking'
'Burking' (method of murder), 122, 124, 139, 193

Campbell, Duncan, 21, 83, 188
Campbell, John Francis, 8, 85–6, 98n, 147, 152–3
Campbell, John Gregorson, 153
Cant (language), 2, 140–2, 144, 172–4
capitalism, 62, 161, 163–4, 177, 186–7, 193
Chambers, Robert (*Popular Rhymes of Scotland*), 153

INDEX

Cinderella, 84–93
  Cinderella Cycle, 85–6, 88–9, 98n
  masterplot, 84–5, 86, 88, 89–90, 190–1
  see also ATU 510A
Clark, Colin, 2, 8, 23, 24, 40, 45, 58
Cox, Marian Roalfe, 84–5
Christ, Jesus, 132, 134
Christianity, 42, 95–7, 148, 150

D'Aulnoy, Marie-Catherine (*Les Contes des Fées*), 109–11, 112–13, 114, 115, 117, 119, 156
Dégh, Linda, 9, 48, 50, 156, 167
Dictionary of the Scots Language, 18, 36n
Donaldson, Davie, 2, 8, 24, 36n, 56n, 139–42, 143–4, 176
Dundes, Alan, 29, 43, 44–5, 50, 88, 89, 98n, 128

ecotypes (traditional narrative), 85, 86, 92, 95, 99, 108, 109, 190–1
ethnicity, 1–4, 6, 23–4, 29, 40, 70–1, 142, 192
equilibrium (storytelling), 57, 130–2, 135, 144

fairies, 118–19, 153
fairy tales, 38, 42, 105, 113, 152, 156, 191
Faust, 95–7
Fenian Cycle, 169
folklore, 4, 6–7, 13, 28, 32–3, 37n, 42, 44–8, 51, 63, 64, 85, 102, 104, 105, 142, 163, 176, 187, 194
  folk ideas, 50
  folk narrative, 30–1, 32–3, 34–5, 44, 48, 64, 114, 152, 190
  functions, 11–12, 30, 33, 46–8, 52, 54–5, 60, 74, 150
  onomastics, 168
  supernatural, 146–9, 151–4
  see also folk onomastics; intangible cultural heritage (ICH)

Frank, Arthur, 13–14, 27, 30, 34, 48, 107

Gaelic (language), 21, 140, 142, 149, 192
  narratives, 41–2, 58–9, 98n, 141, 151, 153, 168
  place-names, 168, 171–2, 173–5
Geertz, Clifford, 10–11, 12, 189
Glassie, Henry, 31, 37n
Grellmann, Heinrich, 17–19
Grimm, Hermann, 112
Grimm, Jacob, 45–6, 152
Grimms (*Kinder- und Hausmärchen*), 112, 151
'Hansel and Gretel', 102, 104–6, 120n
'Hans My Hedgehog', 110, 111–12, 114–15, 117–18
see also ATU 327A; ATU 441
Gypsy (Gypsies), 1–2, 4, 7, 17–19, 20, 21, 36n, 70–1, 73, 78–9, 98n, 184, 185, 188, 193
Gypsy/Traveller(s), 1–2, 4, 8, 17, 27, 36n, 69–72
'The Gypsy Laddie' (ballad), 117
Gypsy, Roma, Traveller History Month (GRTHM), 62, 72

Henderson, Hamish, 6, 8–9, 21, 45, 81, 86, 122–3, 125, 126, 128, 161–2, 188
Higgins, Lizzie, 60
historicity, 131
Historic Scotland, 175
Holbek, Bengt, 42–4, 51–2, 102, 104–5
Horners (Travellers), 19, 83
Hosie, Judge, 4
Hoyland, John, 17–18, 19
Hume, David, 150
Hutchison, Davie, 132
'A woman hawker taken by Burkers' (story), 132–3, 134–6

ideology, 4, 10, 36, 107, 157, 190
  storytelling, 11–13, 171
  Traveller, 21, 72, 108, 171, 183–7, 190, 194
identity strategies, 57–8, 63, 74, 121, 126
industrialisation, 22–3, 79, 132, 161, 189, 192
industrial schools, 66–7
Iscariot, Judas, 134
intangible cultural heritage (ICH), 28–30, 37n, 45, 60, 171, 188
itinerancy, 4, 6, 17–18, 19, 21, 26, 36n, 71, 78, 164, 173, 179, 182

Jameson, Fredric, 95, 157, 181–2, 185

Kirk, Robert (*The Secret Commonwealth*), 148–9

Lang, Andrew, 44, 149
Lowenthal, David, 37n
liminality, 167, 176–83, 186
  'Geordie MacPhee's Treasure' (story), 182–4, 186–7

Macpherson, James, 72–3, 78, 123
Macpherson, James (*Fragments of Ancient Poetry*), 151–2
Macritchie, David, 17, 19, 83
Mandla vs. Dowell Lee, 3
Martin, Martin (*A Description of the Western Isles of Scotland*), 149
McCormick, Andrew, 8, 19
McPhee, Shamus, 2, 56n, 68, 145n, 171–4, 193, 194
Miller, Hugh (*Scenes and Legends of the North of Scotland*), 153
Mormon (Book of), 94–5
Muggers (Travellers), 19, 36n

Nachin, 2; *see also* Nacken; Nawken; Nyakim
Nacken, 2, 5, 71, 171, 193, 194, 202; *see also* Nachin; Nawken; Nyakim

Nackian (folk idiom), 5–7, 60, 141, 159, 176, 187, 190–3, 194
narratology, 13; *see also* socio-narratology
National Records of Scotland (NRS), 1–2, 70
Nawken, 2, 5, 8, 14n, 18, 24, 71, 139; *see also* Nachin, Nacken, Nyakim
Neat, Timothy, 6, 9, 79, 104, 115
Niles, John D., 7, 11–12, 24, 33–5, 36n, 38, 52–3, 57, 60, 83, 150–1, 161
Nyakim, 2; *see also* Nacken; Nawken

O'Connell, Daniel ('Immortal Dan'), 142–3, 145n
Olrik, Axel, 40, 42, 79, 101–2, 126, 157–8
onomastics, 167–9, 174
  folk onomastics, 49, 168, 169–71, 171–4, 175, 176
  socio-onomastics, 168
orality, 6, 38, 99
oral literature, 38–9

Perrault, Charles, 85, 90, 109–11, 114, 115, 117

Robertson, Jeannie, 2, 58, 98n, 117, 161–2
Robertson, Stanley, 2, 11, 24, 25, 36, 58, 98n, 114, 118
  Burkers, 140, 141, 143, 144
  Exodus to Alford (1998), 71–2
  Mormon, 93–5
  obituary, 93
  'Rosehearty' (story), 170–1, 172
  storytelling, 11–12, 29–30, 35, 50, 60–1, 74, 78, 93, 99, 173, 174
  'The Candle' (story), 96–8, 98n
  'The Story o' Robbie Ha'' (story), 93–5
  'The Traveller-Judge' (story), 78–82, 84, 100–2, 104–7, 108, 135
Traveller culture, 12, 24, 58, 93

Roma, 1, 7, 19, 21, 25, 36n, 72, 140, 188, 193
Rosehearty (Moray Firth), 168–70, 171, 172, 174, 176

Scotsman (newspaper), 20–1, 25, 39, 68, 103, 192
Scott, Walter, 151–2
Scottish Government, 1, 36n, 64, 69, 70, 71, 72
School of Scottish Studies (SSS) Archives, 8, 11, 23, 24, 25, 36n, 39, 127, 146, 188
sedentarism, 21, 23, 40, 67, 105, 131, 159, 177, 183–6, 188–9, 193
Simson, Walter, 17–18
Smith, Donald, 117
Smith, Jess, 56n, 62, 136–7, 143
Smith, Joesph (*The Book of Mormon*), 94
socio-narratology, 13, 30, 48; *see also* Frank, Arthur
Statistical Accounts of Scotland (TSAS), 19–20, 22, 36n, 39, 64, 65, 67, 83, 98n, 122, 123, 127, 171, 173, 185, 192
Stewart, Andrew, 59, 73
　'A baker accepts three pieces of good advice instead of pay' (story), 134
　'Geordie MacPhee's Treasure' (story), 59, 177–87
Stewart, Belle, 83, 124
Stewart, Geordie, 61, 138
　'A boy sings a song to warn Travellers' (story), 138–9
Stewart, John (Jock), 129, 143
　'Travellers have a narrow escape from Burkers' (story), 129–30, 131–2, 135–6, 137
Stewart, John, 23, 61–2, 98n, 194
Stewart, Maggie, 122, 124
Stewart, Sheila, 70, 80–1
　Pilgrims of the Mist (2008), 80

Straparola, Giovanni Francesco (*Le Piacevoli Notti*), 109–11, 112, 114, 115, 117
structuralism, 35, 55, 101, 128, 129, 136, 143–4
super-empiricism, 146, 154–5, 167, 184
　stories, 156–7, 164–5, 168, 172–3, 176–7, 183, 185–6
supernaturalism, 9, 41, 146, 147–51, 156–7, 167
　folklore, 151–5
　stories, 41, 59, 79, 118, 159–60, 165, 178–82

'The Man in the Cassock (TMC)' (story), 41–2
Thoms, William, 45–46
Thompson, Stith, 12, 30, 48, 49, 85, 86, 88, 89, 95, 97, 102, 112, 147, 162, 169
Tincklar, 21; *see also* Tinker(s); Tinkler(s)
Tinker(s), 8, 17–20, 21–2, 78, 83, 103, 132
　official reports, 65–7, 70, 192
　place-names, 174–6
　stories, 39–40, 59, 80, 124, 126, 137, 138, 180–2, 184
　see also Tincklar; Tinkler(s)
Tinkler(s), 18–19, *see also* Tincklar; Tinker(s)
Tobar an Dualchais (TAD), 11, 14n, 145n
Todorov, Tzvetan, 130–1
tradition, 3, 5, 7, 8, 10–12, 27–36, 63, 146
　filiation, 31–2, 53, 54, 63, 93
　tradition-as-resource, 11, 27, 31, 33–4, 37n, 50, 53, 56, 107
　tradition-bearer(s), 3, 27, 29–30, 33–4, 35–6, 50, 52, 87, 99, 101, 121
　see also intangible cultural heritage (ICH); folklore
Travellers (Irish), 6–7, 22, 26

Travellers (Scottish), 1–5, 6–8, 17, 18–23, 36n, 55–6, 57–8, 64–70, 115, 120, 157, 164, 193–4
  Burkers, 122–7, 134, 137–8, 142, 144, 145n, 192
  Children Act (1908), 67, 102–3
  cultural identity, 3, 7, 24, 45, 57–9, 77–8, 84, 90, 117, 141–2, 144, 163, 188–90, 194
  education, 23, 25–6, 52, 60–1, 65, 68, 103, 164
  ethnicity, 1–4, 6, 8, 23, 24, 40, 70–1, 142, 192
  folk idiom (Nackian narrative), 5–6, 7, 56, 60, 86, 88, 89, 95, 101–2, 107, 141, 147, 159, 176, 187, 190–1, 192, 193, 194
  prejudice, 7–8, 20–1, 24–6, 36n, 68–9, 71, 72–3, 78, 81, 122–3, 127, 164, 184, 193, 195n
  Race Relations Act (1976, amended 2000), 4, 70
  storytelling, 5, 7, 8–14, 39, 43–4, 47–51, 52–3, 58–9, 60–2, 71–2, 74, 99, 113, 121, 146, 153–4, 159, 165, 167, 177, 183–4, 187, 194
  'The Report of the Departmental Committee on Habitual Offenders, Vagrants, Beggars, Inebriates and Juvenile Delinquents' (1895), 64, 65–7, 189
  'Tinker Experiment', 67–8
  'Tinkers' Heart', 175–6
  work, 26, 79, 172
  worldview, 3, 10, 48, 52–5, 62, 71, 74, 81–2, 90, 93, 108, 121, 126, 131, 147, 165, 168, 175, 183, 187, 193–4
Tullybelton, Lord Fraser, 3–4

United Nations Educational, Scientific and Cultural Organisation (UNESCO), 28, 37n
Uther, Hans-Jörg, 49, 86, 88, 89, 97, 108, 109, 117, 120n, 159, 162

Von Sydow, Carl, 85, 99, 191

Williamson, Duncan, 32, 35, 36, 58–9, 100, 101, 104, 120, 135, 190
  'A Lovely Spoon' (story), 82–4
  'A Rich American' (story), 39–41, 101
  A Thorn in the King's Foot: Folktales of the Scottish Travelling People (1987), 86, 190
  Burkers, 123, 134
  Fireside Tales of the Traveller Children (1983), 120n, 134
  'Mary Rashiecoats an the Wee Black Bull (story)', 86, 87–93, 190
  storytelling, 32, 54, 62, 74, 77, 101, 113
  'The Hawker's Lament' (verse), 120
  'The Hedgehurst' (story), 107–19, 120n, 157, 185, 191
  'The Magic Pot' (story), 157–9
  'The Traveller and the Hare' (story), 54–5
  'The Traveller-Fox' (story), 32
  'The Travellers' Cinderella', 90–1
  see also ATU 441; ATU 511; ATU 591
Williamson, Jimmy, 32, 56n
Williamson, Linda, 86, 157
Whyte, Betsy, 23, 25–6, 35, 51, 61, 86–7, 98n, 103–4
  Burkers, 122, 123–4, 127, 132, 134
  'The Money Tree' (story), 159–61, 164–5
  The Yellow on the Broom (1979), 23
  worldview, 8–10, 12, 13, 29, 36, 50–1, 63, 149, 167

Zipes, Jack, 105, 111–12, 116, 151, 163, 187

Printed and bound by CPI Group (UK) Ltd, Croydon, CR0 4YY
20/01/2025
01822670-0003